REBEL SOULS

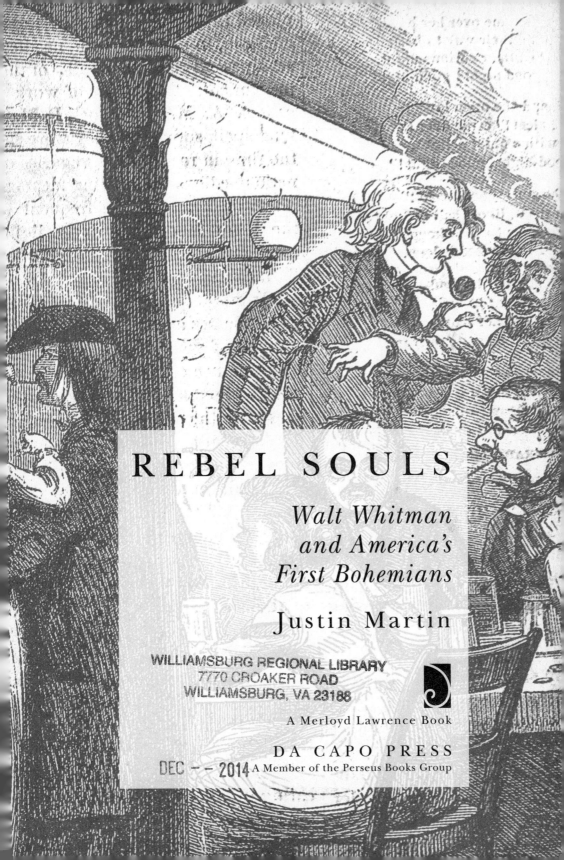

REBEL SOULS

*Walt Whitman
and America's
First Bohemians*

Justin Martin

A Merloyd Lawrence Book

DA CAPO PRESS
A Member of the Perseus Books Group

Cover design by Jonathan Sainsbury
Book design by Brent Wilcox and Cynthia Young

Library of Congress Cataloging-in-Publication Data
Martin, Justin.
    Rebel Souls : Walt Whitman and America's First Bohemians / Justin Martin.
        pages cm. — (A Merloyd Lawrence book)
    Includes bibliographical references and index.
    ISBN 978-0-306-82226-1 (hardback) — ISBN 978-0-306-82227-8 (e-book)
1. Whitman, Walt, 1819–1892—Friends and associates.   2. Bohemianism—New York (State)—New York—History—19th century.   3. New York (N.Y.) Intellectual life—19th century.   4. Ward, Artemus, 1834–1867.   5. Booth, Edwin, 1833–1893. 6. Ludlow, Fitz Hugh, 1836–1870.   7. Menken, Adah Isaacs, 1835-1868.   8. Bars (Drinking establishments)—New York (State)—New York—History—19th century. I. Title.
    PS3231.M19 2014
    811'.3—dc20
    [B]

                            2014008822

Published as a Merloyd Lawrence Book by Da Capo Press
A Member of the Perseus Books Group
www.dacapopress.com

Da Capo Press books are available at special discounts for bulk purchases in the U.S. by corporations, institutions, and other organizations. For more information, please contact the Special Markets Department at the Perseus Books Group, 2300 Chestnut Street, Suite 200, Philadelphia, PA 19103, or call (800) 810-4145, ext. 5000, or e-mail special.markets@perseusbooks.com.

10 9 8 7 6 5 4 3 2 1

To Rex and Donna Martin, my parents,
who have always managed to embrace
the best of Bohemia

"Bohemia" comes but once in one's life.
Let's treasure even its memory.

— WALT WHITMAN

At Pfaff's! At Pfaff's! At Pfaff's!

—Toast the Bohemians would make
at their legendary saloon

CONTENTS

PHOTO CREDITS

Photos following page 180

Broadway in the 1860s (Courtesy of New-York Historical Society)

Henry Clapp Jr. (Courtesy of special collections, Fine Arts Library, Harvard University)

Ada Clare (Courtesy of the Bancroft Library, University of California, Berkeley)

Whitman, 1854 (Courtesy of the Library of Congress)

Whitman frontispiece from *Leaves of Grass* 1860 edition (Courtesy of New York Public Library)

Leaves of Grass title page (Courtesy of New York Public Library)

Whitman at Pfaff's (Courtesy of *Harper's Magazine*)

Menken reclining (Courtesy of collection of Houghton Library, Harvard University)

Menken in *Mazeppa* (Courtesy of Victoria and Albert Museum)

Fitz Hugh Ludlow (Courtesy of special collections, Schaffer Library, Union College)

Artemus Ward (Courtesy of special collections, Fine Arts Library, Harvard University)

Abraham Lincoln (Courtesy of the Library of Congress)

Mark Twain (Courtesy of the Library of Congress)

Harper's meteor cover (Courtesy of Texas State University)

Armory Square Hospital (Courtesy of the Library of Congress)

Whitman and Doyle (Courtesy of the Library of Congress)

Edwin Booth (Courtesy of the Library of Congress)

Booth brothers (Courtesy of Brown University archives)

Julius Caesar playbill (Courtesy of New York Public Library for the Performing Arts/Billy Rose Theatre Division)

Whitman as good gray poet (Courtesy of the Library of Congress)

All other photos are in the public domain.

INTRODUCTION

A Visit to Pfaff's

TAKE A WALK ALONG Broadway in Manhattan. As you make your way—amid the rushing taxis, pedestrians lost in their smartphones, and other scenes of modern bustle—you might just catch some hints of the distant past. Pause for a moment at 647 Broadway, a few doors north of Bleecker Street. A women's shoe store is here, assorted boots, sandals, and stiletto heels displayed in the window. It appears to be just another shop along Broadway. But once upon a time, this was the location of the famous Pfaff's saloon.

To be precise, Pfaff's (pronounced *fafs*) was beneath where the shoe store is now. It was an underground saloon in every sense of the word. There's still a hatchway in the Broadway sidewalk, just as there was in the nineteenth century. It provides entry into the store's basement, a long, narrow space, lit by electric bulbs and piled high with boxes of shoes. During the 1850s, it was dim, gaslit, and packed with artists. Pfaff's saloon was the site of an incredibly important cultural movement, the meeting place of America's first Bohemians.

Their leader, Henry Clapp Jr., was editor of the hugely influential *Saturday Press*. Clapp deserves credit as the person who brought Bohemianism to America, both the word and the way of life. He was joined by a struggling experimental poet, well into middle age, yet still living at home in Brooklyn with his mother, Walt Whitman.

Around these two figures, a circle formed that included journalists, playwrights, sculptors, and painters. Among the mainstays were Artemus Ward, America's first stand-up comedian, and the elegant writer Ada Clare (libertine Pfaff's was the rare saloon that welcomed women

1

in those days). There was also Fitz Hugh Ludlow, psychedelic pioneer and author of *The Hasheesh Eater;* Fitz-James O'Brien, a talented but dissolute writer; and actress Adah Isaacs Menken, wildly successful, unabashedly notorious, and one of the great sex symbols of the nineteenth century. By turns calculating and vulnerable, she was like a sepia-tone Marilyn Monroe.

On the eve of the Civil War, this motley group made the Broadway saloon its headquarters. The Pfaff's Bohemians, as they were known, met here every night to drink, joke, argue, and drink some more. Along the way, they also managed to create startling and original works. Although much of their output is long forgotten, its animating spirit lives on, continuing to have resonance today. The Pfaff's Bohemians were part of the transition from art as a genteel profession to art as a soul-deep calling, centered on risk taking, honesty, and provocation. Everyone from Lady Gaga to George Carlin to Dave Eggers owes a debt to these originals. They were also the forerunners of such alternative artist groups as the Beats, Andy Warhol's Factory, and the abstract expressionist painters who hung out during the 1950s at New York's Cedar Tavern.

If you've never heard of Pfaff's saloon, or its coterie of Bohemian artists, that's not surprising. More than 150 years have elapsed since this scene's heyday, and time moves in mysterious—sometimes heedless—ways. History is not a meritocracy. To reconstruct the lives of Clapp, Ludlow, Menken, and the members of the circle, I did a vast amount of original research, consulting correspondence, contemporaneous newspaper accounts, and old books. Many of these materials were yellowed and musty, yet what began to strike me most was the *aliveness* of my subjects. It shone through. The more I pursued this cast of long-lost artists, in libraries and archives, the more their time seemed to resonate with our own. I felt an obligation to revive them by telling their stories.

Of course, Whitman has not been forgotten. But the importance of his participation in a circle of Bohemian artists has. Despite the sheer volume of Whitman scholarship, conducted over more than a century's time, this has remained one of the least understood periods of the poet's life. Pick up any book on Whitman, and invariably only a few pages are devoted to Pfaff's and its circle, often less. This was no casual association. Between roughly 1858 and 1862, Whitman was at the saloon virtually every night.

Time spent among the Bohemians was crucial to the evolution of his masterpiece, *Leaves of Grass*. In 1860 he published a vastly expanded edition of the work, featuring more than one hundred new poems, many drawn from the experience of being part of this artists' circle. The new edition even included an entire section devoted to romance between men. Pfaff's—permissive place that it was—gave Whitman the opportunity to explore his sexuality in both art and life.

Whitman's barfly years were a vital stretch for him, filled with triumph and torment and intense creativity. It was that critical time *before*—before fame, before myth, before he had been forever fixed as the Good Gray Poet. By focusing on this period, my goal is to provide fresh context for Whitman's life and career. Whitman himself recognized its importance. As an old man, he told Thomas Donaldson, one of his first biographers, "Pfaff's 'Bohemia' was never reported, and more the sorrow."

The outbreak of the Civil War scattered the Bohemians. Pfaff's saloon opened up, loosing its colorful denizens into the world. Famously, Whitman went to Washington, DC, where he tended to wounded soldiers. Others saw battlefield action or traveled across the troubled nation performing theatrical pieces. A couple of the Bohemians even headed out to raucous silver-rush Nevada, where they met up with a promising young writer who only months earlier had adopted the pen name Mark Twain.

Thus, it seems natural to carry on with this tale through the years of the Civil War, to follow the main figures as they fan out across the land, yet keep crossing paths, sometimes in dramatic new settings. In fact, the story continues right on through the assassination of Lincoln in 1865. For the Pfaff's set, this was more than simply a tragic news event. The group had unexpected, even shocking, connections to that fateful evening at Ford's Theatre.

And then everything came crashing down. It's almost as if the darkness surrounding Lincoln's death couldn't be contained, spread out, and infected the Pfaff's set as well. These artists were intimately bound up with their times. Just like that, their times were at an end. Nearly everyone in the circle died young, often under grim circumstances. America's first Bohemians burned brightly, but briefly, then flamed out in spectacular fashion. Whitman was among the few to live on, past that tempestuous era.

By the late 1860s, the group was fast receding into history. But memories of them remained vivid. For many years, it was a given that the famous Bohemian scene would be properly memorialized. "Pfaff's, as it was, has passed away; but the history of it would make one of the most unique and startling books in American literature," states an article in the *Cincinnati Commercial* from March 14, 1874. But the years kept slipping past, then decades . . . then entire centuries. One can easily walk along Broadway and go right past the shoe store, with no idea that Walt Whitman and a group of artists used to meet below in that basement saloon.

But it's not as if the passage of time somehow erased the very existence of the Pfaff's Bohemians. They've been here all along. They're like restless ghosts—elusive, flickering, unsettled. And this is their tale, at last.

CHAPTER 1

Bohemia Crosses the Atlantic

THE STORY BEGINS on November 11, 1814, with the birth of Henry Clapp Jr., on Nantucket Island, off the Massachusetts coast. He would come to be known as the King of Bohemia, but his childhood was spent in a devout family during a highly conservative era.

The Nantucket of Clapp's youth had two beacons: whaling and faith. Though only a small island—a mere forty-eight square miles—it was then a maritime power unto itself, the whaling capital of the world. Its fleet of roughly seventy ships stalked the Atlantic, even rounded Cape Horn and fanned out across the Pacific, relentlessly pursuing their quarry. Local lore held that the first word a baby learned would likely relate to whales. The islanders possessed a vast whaling terminology. For example, *townor* referred to a particular whale spotted for the *second* time.

Nantucket was also a stronghold of Congregationalism, one of the primary religious denominations of the region's original Puritan settlers. H. L. Mencken famously described the Puritans as "desperately afraid that somebody, somewhere might be having a good time." Both of Clapp's parents came from long, distinguished lines. His father could date his New England ancestry to 1630, when his forebears arrived aboard the *Mary and John,* only ten years after the *Mayflower.* Clapp's mother could trace her lineage six generations straight back to Tristram and Dionis Coffin, the original white settlers of Nantucket. Clapp, as one of eight children who lived to maturity, was part of a household that was crowded, strict, and God-fearing. Clapp would remember this upbringing as the "Spare-the-Rod-spoil-the-Child Academy of my boyhood."

Growing up, Clapp attended the Admiral Sir Isaac Coffin Lancasterian School, a unique institution. The school featured America's very first training ship, used to give the older students hands-on experience, preparing them for a life at sea. In 1830 fifteen-year-old Clapp took two voyages on this training ship, the *Clio,* first to the coast of Quebec, then all the way to Rio. He hated the experience. Mostly, he spent the voyages seasick and in misery.

Following graduation, Clapp moved to nearby Boston. He found work that, fittingly, was on dry land yet also tied to the economy of his native Nantucket. He sold whale oil wholesale. But this didn't strike him exactly as a promising career. When a friend of Clapp's landlady died, she asked him to draw up a death notice that could be submitted to the newspaper. For Clapp, the simple act of composing a few brief paragraphs suggested a new career direction. He decided he wanted to try journalism.

During the next few years, he bounced from paper to paper, taking jobs with the *Nantucket Inquirer* and the *New Bedford Intelligencer.* After such a dour upbringing, working for newspapers awakened something in Clapp. He found the world of words to be refreshingly alive, even though, as a young reporter, he was mostly called upon to write short notices about public events or the weather. Sometimes he got to craft a nice turn of phrase, though. In reporting on a parade of Odd Fellows (a fraternal society akin to the Freemasons), he couldn't help but comment on their preposterously colorful uniforms: "I venture the assertion, that the dolls in the royal nursery of Queen Victoria do not have more gaudy pinafores than this body of grown up men." He described Nantucket as peaceful, punning that its citizens were involved in "pacific business, viz:—fitting whale-ships for the Pacific ocean."

Clapp worked his way up as a newspaperman, eventually becoming editor of the *Lynn Pioneer.* Where Nantucket was a whaling powerhouse, Lynn, Massachusetts, was an industrial center during the 1840s, the shoe-making capital of America. The *Pioneer* was owned and financed by a shoe-factory owner, who held radical political views. His paper regularly covered topics such as abolition, temperance, labor reform, and pacifism.

For Clapp, opposing the status quo proved thrilling. He delighted in a newfound freedom to take on powerful people. He "liked to say startling things," a newspaper colleague from these years would recall, "and did not always exhibit the best taste."

One time, Clapp took aim at a local judge named Aaron Lummus, accusing the man of doling out biased justice. According to Clapp's account in the *Pioneer,* the judge gave preferential treatment in his court to rich people over poor people. For good measure, Clapp referred to Judge Lummus as a "lummox." Clapp was convicted for libeling a justice of the peace and sentenced to sixty days in jail. He continued to edit the *Pioneer* from behind bars.

Clapp was short and homely. By his early thirties, he was balding fast, leaving him with a fringe of reddish hair and a too prominent, jutting forehead. His shrill voice was once described as sounding "like snapping glass under your heel." Yet he discovered that he had rare oratorical powers. The *Pioneer* had steeped him in the causes of the day. He began to travel around New England, building quite a reputation and becoming a much-sought-after lecturer.

Involvement in radical causes further opened up the world to Clapp. At the same time, he discovered that many of his fellow reformers were as rigid and dogmatic as anyone he'd encountered growing up. Disagree with them by an inch, he found, and you invited the same wrath as if you were miles apart. There was a kind of absolutism at work here. It reminded him of his Congregationalist upbringing, in which something was either pure or wicked. Clapp even managed to run afoul of William Lloyd Garrison, the abolitionist firebrand. Clapp was all for ending slavery, yet he differed from Garrison over some fine points on how to achieve this aim. Garrison denounced Clapp just the same, calling him "a wily creature, with considerable talent, but not to be trusted or encouraged."

Clapp felt more at home in the temperance movement. Here, he managed to take up with a group called the Washingtonian Total Abstinence Society. This was a very new organization, founded in 1840.

Even though General Washington was known to tipple, the movement took its name from him, as a show of respect. This says a lot about the Washingtonians. In this era, most temperance organizations pursued a two-pronged strategy: fight to ban alcohol so as to prevent future drinking, and let the current crop of drunkards rot. Justin Edwards, cofounder of the American Temperance Society, stated that one of his organization's goals was to let alcoholics "die off and rid the world of an amazing evil." By contrast, one of the tenets of the Washingtonians was "faith in man." The group believed that drunkards could be redeemed and held out hope that it was at least possible for someone to stop drinking and return to society. Washingtonians can be rightly seen as a forerunner of Alcoholics Anonymous.

The contours of Clapp's character were starting to become evident. He was irreverent. He possessed a ready wit. And he was what today would be called a moral relativist, especially given his involvement with the love-the-drunkard-but-hate-the-drink Washingtonians.

In August 1849, Clapp went to Paris to attend a three-day world peace congress. This was his first visit, and after the sessions were over, he decided to stay for a while, even though he spoke only a smattering of French. "I could say *oui*, but couldn't give the native squeal even to that," he'd later joke, and was forced at the outset to resort to "bad English—the American's usual substitute for French."

Clapp chose a fortuitous time. Only one year earlier, France had experienced a revolution that started off with the best utopian intentions, but ultimately devolved into another ho-hum, bureaucracy-as-usual government. In the wake of this incomplete revolution, the boulevards of Paris still thrummed with idealism, slogans, and grand artistic schemes. The city's cafés played host to a thriving scene, known as Bohemianism.

The term *Bohemian* (*Bohémien* with two *e*'s in the original French) dates to roughly 1830. Its coinage is rooted in a misperception, namely, that the Romani people who were wandering into France during the nineteenth century were natives of Bohemia, then a central European kingdom and part of the Hapsburg Empire (today a region of the Czech Republic). It now appears that the Romani originated centuries ago in India and from there migrated through Asia and into Europe. But as a people, the Romani have always managed to sow puzzlement. In England a similar confusion about the Romani people's origins gave rise to the term *Gypsy*, derived from the mistaken notion that they hailed from Egypt.

The French notion of *Bohemian* contains still another layer of complication. From the outset, the word was bandied about loosely and with a kind of willful indiscriminateness. Well-to-do, establishment Parisians—especially those of a conservative political bent—applied it to the Romani, but also to anyone who looked eccentric: flamboyantly dressed artists, scruffy students, women of suspect moral standing. This attitude was rooted in a kind of xenophobia: France was under siege, from the forces of the decadent and odd, and it didn't matter whether they came from a far-off, mystical Bohemia or from within the Republic itself.

Parisian artists and other free-living types seized on *Bohemian*, appropriated it, made it their own. The word made it possible to contrast two opposing forces in society. You had your bourgeois—cautious, smug, and prosperous. And you had their opposite—Bohemians. In France, *Bohemian* quickly became tight-packed with cultural coding. Utter but that single word, and a vivid image unfolded.

Clapp checked into the Hôtel Corneille in the Latin Quarter, smack in the heart of Parisian Bohemia. The Corneille had figured in a Balzac novel and had become the favored quarters for foreign travelers seeking an authentic down-and-out-in-Paris experience. In future years, the painter James Whistler would stay here, as would James Joyce. Clapp got a cheap room on the top floor; he had to walk up seven flights. The room's furniture and other appointments were in such an advanced state of disrepair that, as Clapp put it, "Everything that had an arm, a leg, a knee, a foot, or a back to it, was more or less dislocated." On the wall hung some caricatures of the hotel's proprietress presenting a bill for the cost of a stay, executed in a crude hand by a previous occupant.

Clapp made the acquaintance of some fellow guests at the Corneille, a group of Englishmen who were dabbling in assorted artistic pursuits.

He accompanied several of them to a café, his very first brush with a ubiquitous institution that provided the very lifeblood of Bohemia. (Paris, circa 1849, had an estimated forty-five hundred cafés.) Clapp ordered coffee and also smoked some tobacco. Undoubtedly, Clapp had tried coffee before, and he appears to have had some firsthand familiarity with smoking as well. (Neither was forbidden in Congregationalist New England, so long as one practiced moderation.) Still, he was intrigued by his first taste of Parisian coffee, which he described as having "a consistency between a liquid and a paste. . . . It ran like molasses in the winter." And he enjoyed his first puff of caporal, strong French tobacco, and was intrigued by the practice of smoking it in a little clay pipe.

As a confirmed Washingtonian, however, Clapp stopped short of alcohol. According to his written reminiscence, upon being offered a drink, Clapp dutifully said, "Thank you, gentlemen, I don't drink."

"Don't drink!" was one Englishman's response. "Nonsense, man! Surely you'll take something."

But Clapp was resolute: "I'm a teetotaler."

"A tee-what?"

"A teetotaler." Clapp explained, and his companions were dumbstruck.

"Come, now, that won't do in this country. A teetotaler in Paris? . . . You don't mean to drink Paris water, do you?"

His companions may not have realized it, but for Clapp, simply spending time in a café represented a huge departure. Already, so early in his Paris sojourn, he'd strayed miles from the righteous path. Clapp's New England demanded that every minute of every day be given over to industriousness and vigilance, reform and revival. *Idle hands are the devil's workshop.* The mere act of sitting in a café with no purpose, no agenda, just sipping coffee, smoking a pipe, and whiling away the time, was decadence enough.

On a subsequent evening, Clapp's English companions took him to a *café chantant,* a different type of Paris café. (There were dozens of species of café: *bistros* and *brasseries* and *cabarets*; *bastringues, boîtes,* and *mastroquets*—the list goes on and on, each a subtle variation from the others.) A *café chantant* offers musical performances, burlesque, and dancing. Clapp's group "secured a nice little nook of observation" and ordered coffees all around. He was intrigued to see that even though it was well into the evening, the café was full of unmarried women. It struck him that, by taking up with these Englishmen, he had fallen in with a truly "fast set." His consorts, in turn, got a kick out of schooling Clapp about the various types of French women.

One of Clapp's party pointed out some nearby women, saying that they were *étudiantes* (translation: studentesses). He explained that the name derives "not because of their devotion to study, but because of their devotion to students." The Latin Quarter takes its name from a university established there in the Middle Ages, where Latin was the required language. When Clapp visited, it remained a cheap section of Paris, still crawling with dirt-poor students—and studentesses. The Englishman continued: "But let me describe the studentesses: In the first place, she is what she looks to be—a fast woman. As you see, she dresses in the shabby-genteel style; hangs her bonnet over the chair and makes herself at home; burns brandy in her coffee."

From this point, Clapp's new friends launched into a general discussion of other types of Parisian women, demonstrating in the process a grasp of one of those precise, and uniquely French, systems of nomenclature. There were *grisettes,* often young country girls who had come to Paris in search of factory work and romance. There were *lorettes,* a type of high-class courtesan. And there were the *femmes publiques,* licensed prostitutes and a type of woman that one of Clapp's friends decreed "the lowest round on the ladder."

"Horrible!" exclaimed Clapp. "But what are the characteristics of the *lorette?*"

"The *lorette* belongs to the *Aristocracy of Easy Virtue,*" continued one of the Brits. "She is the finest-dressed woman you meet on the Boulevards, and looks down upon the *étudiante* in her straw bonnet and cheap finery, and the *grisette* in her plain cap and sixpenny calico, with haughty disdain. She resides in the quarter which takes its name, like herself, from the church of Notre Dame de Lorette, where she usually worships."

Throughout the discussion, one of Clapp's newfound companions remained silent, buried in his sketch pad, rendering a French woman at a nearby table. She was someone he had pursued and been rebuffed by, leaving him heartsick. Clapp and his group eventually departed the *café chantant* into the Paris night, where "the air rung with shouts of dissipation and mirth."

If Bohemia was thriving upon Clapp's arrival in Paris, it would soon ratchet up to a whole other level. In late November 1849, only three months after Clapp checked into the Hôtel Corneille, Paris went wild, seeming to lose its collective mind, over a particular artistic creation. In the aftermath, a kind of Bohemian frenzy swept the city.

The unlikely catalyst was Henry Murger. For years, this centime-less writer had lived in a squalid attic room, laboring away in utter anonymity. Occasionally, he had succeeded in placing a piece in a small literary magazine, but mostly he'd been churning out pabulum for hat-making trade journals, second-rate children's magazines, even a novelty publication printed on water-resistant paper and aimed at bathhouse patrons.

Murger was part of a circle of artists and eccentrics who hung out at the Café Momus. Among them were an aspiring musician named Alexandre Schanne, the Desbrosses brothers—one a sculptor, the other a painter—and Marc Trapadoux, a mysterious figure who always wore the same faded frock coat and somehow managed to get by without a discernible occupation. The group was so poor that they often sat for hours at the Café Momus, sharing a single cup of coffee.

Murger's health was terrible. He suffered from purpura, an affliction sometimes caused by extreme malnourishment and characterized by patches of reddish discoloration on the skin. His left eye continually watered, the result of a defective lacrimal gland. Yet somehow, this sickly scribe managed to take a series of lovers, most notably Lucile Louvet. Lucile was employed in a sweatshop, where she put in punishingly long hours making artificial flowers. Her hands were forever covered in colored splotches, stains from the dyes used in her work.

Lucile died of tuberculosis in the paupers' wing of Hôpital de Notre Dame de Pitié, bed number 8. She was just twenty-four—or at least that was the age estimated on her death certificate. Murger didn't even get to say good-bye. Visiting hours were on Sundays only; when the day rolled around, it was too late—Lucile had already expired.

Murger captured the doings of his circle—its high jinks and heartbreaks—in a series of literary sketches published in *Le Corsaire-Satan,* an underground journal. He altered some details, and pumped up a few episodes for effect, but the sketches were a fairly faithful chronicle of his life and the lives of his companions. He did change the names, though. Murger became the main character, Rodolphe; Lucile was Mimi. The mysterious Trapadoux was an inspiration for Colline. But *Le Corsaire-Satan* was a fairly obscure journal, and Murger's sketches failed to make much of an impact.

That all changed after Murger was approached by Théodore Barrière, a successful playwright who had the idea of collaborating on a theatrical version. Their first meeting was in Murger's cramped quarters, and Murger insisted on remaining in bed. Having lent his only pair of trousers to a friend, he thought it best to remain under the covers. From this inauspicious beginning, a dramatic collaboration was born, and the pair crafted a five-act play. Barrière brought professional polish and rearranged the sequence so that certain events would pack a dramatic wallop. A musical score was also added, courtesy of composer Pierre-Julien Nargeot. Even so, the completed work features an extraordinarily free-form plot, particularly by the standards of the day. Mostly, the action consists of a group of artists hanging around, talking, fighting, and scrounging for money. It's an unusual play, but also one that stayed true to the random spirit of Murger's original sketches and to the way of life that inspired them.

La vie de Bohème premiered on November 22, 1849, at the Théâtre des Variétés. It was an instant sensation. "The public is being moved as it has not for a long time," raved the *Journal des Débats.* "Everything is, so to speak, observed, felt and suffered," wrote another reviewer, adding, "One can tell that this work was lived before it was written." Night after night, the play performed to sold-out houses. Audiences were fascinated by its seeming verisimilitude. Charles Perey, the actor who played the impoverished musician Schaunard, had made a point of meeting with his character's real-life counterpart, Alexandre Schanne. Perey had studied Schanne's mannerisms, even borrowing his clay pipe for the production. Despite the specific subject matter, the play achieved a kind of universality. In the first act, for example, a character shouts, "La Bohème, c'est nous" (We are Bohemia). Most of all, the play succeeded in moving audiences, particularly in the famous closing scene, when Rodolphe learns that Mimi has died and wails, "Oh, my youth, it is you that is being buried!"

For some time, Bohemianism had been a fixture of Parisian life. But the play succeeded as nothing had before in defining its myriad compass points: intense passion for art; more talk of art than actual making of art; cafés, strong coffee, stronger alcohol; a near-pathological fear of conventionality and a charming insouciance in the face of impending disaster; no money, no prospects, no qualms about romance—the more and messier the entanglements, the better; and, most vividly, early tragic death, often hastened by damp, chilly garret conditions, typically from tuberculosis.

Murger and Barrière's play would remain a work of enduring appeal. In 1896 Puccini adapted it for his classic opera, *La Bohème*. More recently, it furnished the basis for *Rent*, the long-running Broadway play. Even though *Rent* takes place in a different century and a different setting—New York's East Village at the height of the AIDS crisis—it retains many elements of the original work. Among other things, *Rent* holds on to the names of a couple of Murger's most beloved characters, Collins and Mimi.

There is no evidence that Clapp attended *La vie de Bohème* during its landmark Paris run. What is clear, however, is that he dove ever more deeply into Bohemianism, becoming totally immersed in the mania that swept the city in the play's aftermath.

Clapp decided to stay in Paris indefinitely. He earned a small income by contributing articles to London papers. He didn't require much, as he was paying just fifteen francs (then three dollars) a month for his room at the Corneille. Clapp drifted away from the group of Englishmen who had provided him his entrée into Paris Bohemianism. Over time they started to look to him like mere tourists, and he was seeking a deeper experience.

Clapp began hanging out at a café near the Luxembourg Gardens, always careful to select a table far from the orchestra, where he could overhear people talking in their native language. It was a wise gambit, for, as Clapp observed, the French were utterly "addicted to talk."

He became such a regular that he soon achieved that highest of café honors: the table where he sat became *his* table. The waiters all knew him; they brought him coffee without his even having to ask. The other patrons grew friendly as well and began to visit him at his table. Clapp learned to speak French so fluently, he claimed, that he had to convince natives that he was actually a Yankee. He took up smoking in earnest, even bought his own clay pipe.

And he began to drink. Whiskey proved his liquor of choice. This was a drastic turnabout, particularly for a confirmed teetotaler, and afterward Clapp would always attempt to wave away his decision with humor. "Temperance secured for us all the right *not* to drink. Meanwhile, it left the right to drink intact" was a favorite wisecrack. Clapp also began spending time in the company of young women. He took a special liking to one named Octavie. She was about twenty, hailed from the provinces, and could neither read nor write. But Clapp found her a challenging conversationalist with "more good sense than could be distilled out of a dozen libraries." He added, "Her mind was not lumbered with other people's thoughts. . . . The keenness of such a woman was not to be eluded."

Clapp—in thrall to whiskey and Octavie—fell utterly in love with Paris. "There was a charm about the beautiful city which was inconceivable," he would recall. Paris was so specific. It was so different from anything he'd known before. Yet it felt so right. For Clapp, the boulevards, the bridges, the Seine, even the early-morning yells of milkmaids hocking their goods, all became familiar. As he put it, "A strange home-feeling took possession of me."

Clapp remained in Paris for more than three years. When he finally returned to America late in 1853, it was to New York, not the New England of his previous life, and he was hell-bent on re-creating *la vie Bohème* that had transformed him so completely.

CHAPTER 2

A Long Table in a Vaulted Room

ON MOVING TO NEW YORK, Clapp was able to settle in remarkably quickly. This felt like a spiritual home, as surely as Paris had before. New York's vastness, jumble, and, most of all, its veil of anonymity made the city a welcome departure from the confining Puritan world of his early years. Clapp managed to get piecemeal work as a journalist and also did some translation, French to English.

As he settled into the life of the city, Clapp held fast to his idea of bringing Bohemia to America. In 1856 he happened upon a promising venue for this experiment: Pfaff's Restaurant and Lager Bier Saloon. For Clapp's earliest visits, the establishment may have been located elsewhere on Broadway, but it soon settled into its famous spot, in the basement at No. 647, a few doors north of Bleecker Street.

Pfaff's was situated beneath the fashionable Coleman House. But the saloon had almost no relationship with the hotel above; no stairway descended from the lobby. Instead, it was necessary to find the street entrance, marked by the word *Pfaff* faintly lettered on the hotel's gray brick exterior. (The full name—"Lager Bier Saloon" et al.—appeared only in newspaper advertisements.) Beneath this obscure sign was a hatchway in the Broadway sidewalk. One entered here, like going into a root cellar, proceeding down a steep, narrow metal stairway to the saloon.

Pfaff's was a surprisingly ample space, extending underground for much of the length of the hotel's lobby above. It was also very modestly appointed. Sawdust covered the floors. A handful of wooden tables and chairs were scattered about. Above the conversational din, one could hear the distant clatter and neighs from the horse-drawn coaches on Broadway. The low ceiling hung thick with smoke; a small number of gaslights provided the sole illumination, faint and flickering. The play of shadows was extreme, contorting the saloon's customers so that they looked by turns grotesquely squat or wildly elongated. All of these elements contributed to a kind of spectral, otherworldly feeling. The saloon operated Monday through Saturday with an official closing time of 1:00 A.M., though often patrons were still reveling hard as the sun began to rise over Manhattan's East River. Here, the rules were meant to be broken.

A big enticement for Clapp was the saloon's coffee. It was cheap, just three cents a cup, but also strong and thick, reminding him of the coffee he'd so enjoyed in Paris. He also took a liking to Charles Ignatius Pfaff, the proprietor. Herr Pfaff was a round little man with shaggy eyebrows and chubby fingers. His Old World manner and thickly accented English gave him a courtly and discreet air. He favored a winking, confidential style that seemed to suggest that he would form no judgments whatsoever about his customers. Born in Baden, Switzerland, of German descent, he had arrived in New York in the early 1850s, part of a wave of German immigrants.

Despite the spare ambience, it was possible to get a full meal at Pfaff's. Pfaff employed a cook who specialized in *pfannekuchen,* a type of large, hardy German pancake. Also on the menu were beefsteak, Welsh rarebit, liver with bacon, and the saloon's much-praised cheese plate. The food was good, but—more important—the liquor flowed freely. Pfaff was considered an excellent judge of champagne and offered a large selection of wines, including sauternes, volnays, and white burgundies, later more commonly known as chardonnay. But the big draw, per the establishment's name, was lager. Pfaff and his fellow German immigrants had revolutionized beer making in America. From the old country, they brought brewing and aging techniques that produced beers that were lighter than English-style stouts and ales, to this point the mainstays of American drinking establishments. At Pfaff's, lager was served in large pewter steins. And it was cold, a genuine novelty at a time when most pubs served beer at room temperature. Pfaff availed himself of refrigeration, then a cutting-edge luxury, and arranged for ice deliveries, making it possible both to serve beer cold and to preserve batches longer. A reminiscence of Pfaff's saloon from many years later would describe its proprietor as "one of the first men in New York who thoroughly understood the art of drawing and keeping lager beer."

Clapp had found his Café Momus. He'd discovered a place with the right permissive air, a Manhattan equivalent to the Paris haunt of Henry Murger and friends. Now, it was just a matter of assembling a coterie of Bohemians.

Of course, New York City had its share of Bohemians, even if they didn't designate themselves as such . . . yet. The world was full of such types, always has been. Bohemians—in deed if not name—have existed throughout history, from Diogenes, the eccentric Greek philosopher who slept outdoors in a bathtub, to William Blake, the offbeat but visionary English artist. Such people have tended to live out their strange lives on the margins. Save for the French Bohemians, they haven't been part of any larger movement; their mores and behaviors haven't tended to be codified. Therein lay Clapp's notion: to assemble a group of idiosyncratic New York artists and writers in emulation of the Parisian model that he'd experienced.

His very first recruit was Fitz-James O'Brien, a friend and fellow journalist, followed quickly by a translator, a poet, and a soon-to-be famous cartoonist. There was no better choice to begin the group than O'Brien, the walking definition of Bohemian. To this point, he'd led a colorful and prodigal life. He was born in County Cork to a wealthy family, wealthy enough that they had painlessly weathered the Irish potato famines of the 1840s. Shortly after his twentieth birthday, he set off for London, flush with an £8,000 inheritance, seeking adventure in the big city and planning to become a famous writer. He landed a job at a newspaper that quickly folded. But he had no trouble finding adventure: O'Brien burned through his entire inheritance in only two years, the equivalent of spending roughly $1 million in current dollars. Then the husband of a woman O'Brien was having an affair with came home unexpectedly from a colonial post in India. O'Brien fled England for America, arriving nearly broke. He holed up in a fine Manhattan hotel, ordered bottle upon bottle of wine, stayed thoroughly soused, and then skipped out on a tab that he couldn't possibly begin to cover.

O'Brien was trim and moved with an athletic grace. He was only twenty-seven when Clapp tapped him as charter Bohemian, so his dissipated ways hadn't yet caught up with him. He had a long crooked nose, a brush mustache, and a weak and tiny pointed chin—hardly handsome. But people couldn't take their eyes off him. O'Brien was a peerless raconteur who had earned a reputation around town for spinning out enthralling tales. In all he said, in his every move, he conveyed worldliness and ease. He had this particular way of tilting his head, jutting out that tiny chin; it was extremely mannered, perhaps a vestige of his earlier life as a young Irish scion.

But closer observation revealed that O'Brien had already traveled a vast distance from his youth, psychologically, and was in a very different place. Every time one saw him, he was guaranteed to have a new cut or scrape. O'Brien was a chronic brawler. Frequently, one of his eyes was blackened, the result of his latest drunken fistfight. According to legend, he once got into a fight with a perfect stranger over right-of-way on the sidewalk. He spent plenty of nights in the Jefferson Market jail. In O'Brien's tellings, these set-tos always played as good fun, adventure. But every so often, people noticed an unaccountable look that crept into his eyes—a kind of animal desperation.

O'Brien lived in a succession of ramshackle rooming houses, moving on whenever arrears grew too high and his charms with the landlady wore thin. But he clung to his goal of becoming a famous writer. And he had no trouble drumming up work, as an arresting yarn spinner possessed of a vaguely aristocratic air, face always curiously marred with some fresh scrape. Editors couldn't resist; this was a man with stories to tell. But newspapers paid very little, and O'Brien had expensive tastes (he liked to treat his friends to steaks at Delmonico's whenever he scored a payday) as well as a staggering alcohol tab to be met on a daily basis. Thus, he worked in a kind of fever. During his first years in New York, O'Brien had tried his hand at everything—short fiction, poems, criticism, editorials, society puff pieces, and hard-hitting reportage—for a dizzying array of publications, some solid, some very short lived:

the *American Whig Review, Putnam's, Harper's New Monthly Magazine,* the *Home Journal,* the *Knickerbocker,* the *Leisure Hour.* "Haste is evident in all that he wrote," a friend recalled, adding that O'Brien saw no reason to "labor at a story, or a poem, when he could sell it as it was."

O'Brien recycled the names of his fictional characters, using Miss Halibut, Mrs. Honiton, and Croton Poole in several stories each. He penned a poem called "Helen Lee" and one equally hackneyed called "Dora Dee." O'Brien even wrote a moralistic anti-boxing poem—despite his own proclivities—because an editor wanted it for the benefit of female readers. Another time, he landed an assignment with the *New York Picayune* to write a serial tale entitled "From Hand to Mouth." The story was to cover familiar territory, featuring poverty-addled characters in seedy rooming houses. O'Brien was able to deliver only some of the installments, and the serial was left dangling.

Rarely, very rarely, O'Brien was able to banish the noise from his head and achieve a kind of productive calm. On such occasions, it became clear how talented he really was. In 1854 he'd written a play, *A Gentleman from Ireland*, which enjoyed a successful run at Wallack's Theatre in New York. And not long after that first visit to Pfaff's, O'Brien began work on a fantastical short story. It was the tale of a man who uses a microscope to peer at a single droplet of water and spies a tiny world, complete with a beautiful woman. Through the magic of the lens, tantalizingly, the woman appears human size to him, and he falls in love with her. But there's no way to bridge their worlds; the man can't even figure out how to communicate his presence. As the droplet evaporates, he looks on helplessly as the object of his desire withers and dies. It was a masterful story, one that suggested the literary heights of which O'Brien was capable. But the moment would be fleeting. "No American writer ever had such chances of success as Fitz-James O'Brien," that friend would recall, " . . . and but one American writer ever threw such chances away so recklessly."

Just as Clapp had found success in his earlier career as a public speaker—despite being a slight, homely man with a thin, grating voice—he proved adept at assembling a devoted collection of Bohemian artists.

He possessed a surprising charisma. A contemporary describes him as having "a certain kind of magnetism that drew and held men, though he was neither in person nor manner, what would be called attractive."

Besides O'Brien, among the early notables Clapp invited into his circle were Charles Halpine, George Arnold, and Thomas Nast. Halpine was a journalist who, among other jobs, translated articles from French papers for publication in the *New York Herald*. Despite a pronounced stutter, he was considered a sparkling conversationalist. Halpine regularly amazed and amused his companions with revealing new constructions such as "Harriet Be-seecher Be-stowe." Arnold was a genial man who made a paltry living writing poems for newspapers, a career that's unimaginable today. He employed a variety of pseudonyms such as "Pierrot," "George Garrulous," and "Chevalier M'Arone." Known for composing light verse at lightning speed, he tossed off the following poem while drinking at Pfaff's:

> Here,
>   With my beer
> I sit,
> While golden moments flit:
>   Alas!
>   They pass
> Unheeded by.
> And, as they fly,
> I,
> Being dry,
>   Sit, idly sipping here
> My beer.

As for Thomas Nast, he frequented Pfaff's before becoming famous. He first showed up as a teenager, maybe sixteen or seventeen (there was no drinking age), and worked for five dollars per week as an apprentice at *Frank Leslie's Illustrated Newspaper*. Nast, small for his age and chubby, was known as the "fat little Dutch boy," thanks to an unfortunate haircut. During his visits to Pfaff's, he simply sat on the periphery of Clapp's group in silent, red-faced intimidation. In a few years, however, he would emerge as the preeminent political cartoonist of nineteenth-century America, producing enduring caricatures of Boss Tweed and assorted robber barons for *Harper's,* where he worked for more than two decades. A master at visual shorthand, he's often credited with creating the elephant and donkey symbols for the Republican and Democratic Parties. Nast also illustrated Clement Moore's classic *A Visit from St. Nicholas,* helping popularize the image of Santa Claus.

During this earliest period, Clapp's Bohemian group was fairly amorphous. On a given night, whatever people happened to show up would take over a table or two at the saloon and then fall into conversation about life and work and art. Many of them Clapp invited from his circle of acquaintances, which included a number of journalists. But others happened upon Pfaff's as they walked along Broadway. Despite the obscure sign and sidewalk-hatchway entrance, people just seemed to find the place. Clapp quickly discovered that Pfaff's very location, Broadway and Bleecker, was itself a great recruiting tool, drawing people that were curious—in both senses of the word.

Broadway was then one of the world's preeminent streets, described in a story in *Putnam's* as "altogether the most showy, the most crowded, and the richest thoroughfare in America." It was still a couple of years before Frederick Law Olmsted and Calvert Vaux would begin work on Central Park. New York City had only a handful of small parks and precious few places for people to congregate. Given the lack of attractive public space, Broadway filled that role, and filled it admirably. While most New York streets were crabbed and narrow, Broadway was an ample road with wide sidewalks, making it an ideal place to stroll. People derived immense pleasure, and could be thoroughly entertained, simply by walking around. "Saints and sinners, mendicants and millionaires, priests and poets, courtesans and chiffoniers, burglars and bootblacks, move side by side in the multiform throng," according to *The Great Metropolis*, a nineteenth-century guidebook to New York City.

The heart of Broadway was a two-mile stretch, from Chambers Street to Union Square. It had everything. In addition to Coleman House, there were about twenty other large hotels, including the stylish St. Nicholas and the modern New York Hotel, boasting indoor plumbing on every floor. This stretch was also the theater district, catering to every taste, highbrow to gutter. Laura Keene's Varieties—a venue offering Shakespeare and other serious fare—had recently opened at 622 Broadway, across the street from Pfaff's. But it was also possible to see a risqué play at one of the many concert saloons that lined Broadway or take in a blackface minstrel show at the Odd Fellow's Opera House. (Nowadays, a play that's "on Broadway" would likely be farther uptown, in an area developed during the twentieth century, where the street passes through Times Square.)

Broadway was also the shopping district. There was a velocipede dealer, a chandelier maker, and Huyler's candy store. There were numerous large emporiums such as Hearn Brothers and a particularly fancy and famous one run by the retail mastermind A. T. Stewart. A few years hence, Mary Todd Lincoln, in the grip of a shopping mania, would scour Broadway, wildly overshooting the $20,000 appropriated for White House decorations. She would then try to browbeat a lowly Washington bureaucrat, pushing him to shuffle around some funds to cover the overage, but the man refused.

Perhaps most significantly, where Clapp was concerned, Pfaff's was only about a ten-minute walk north along Broadway from newspaper row, home to dozens of dailies and specialty sheets. This meant that along with gawkers and shoppers and strollers, Clapp could also count on a steady stream of writers wandering into Pfaff's.

And then there's Bleecker Street. "'I lodge in Bleecker street' is a biography in brief," according to *The Great Metropolis*. By the 1850s, Bleecker Street, once a fashionable address, had gone completely to seed. "It more resembles some of the streets in Paris than any other in New-York," continues the guidebook. "Bleecker Street is the place of rendezvous for countless illegitimate lovers. Husbands meet other men's wives; wives meet other women's husbands. . . . Many representatives of art of some kind repair to Bleecker street for the cheapness of its accommodations as well as for the freedom of its life. Poor scribblers and scholars, painters and engravers, actors and poets may be found in its lodgings."

Pfaff's: at the intersection of Broadway and Bleecker. One way or another, plenty of people—the desired Bohemian types—discovered that subterranean saloon. Clapp lay waiting in his dusky lair, ready to pull them in.

Soon, Clapp's circle included people involved in all variety of creative pursuits. There were journalists, actors, and illustrators; there were poets, playwrights, painters, and sculptors. But one common trait that cut across many in this set was poverty, crushing poverty. To make it as an artist in New York has always been tough, but never more than during the 1850s. In this way, it was very similar to Paris of the same era. By virtue of being thriving mercantile and cultural hubs, both cities lured in far more artists and writers than could possibly be supported.

Matters grew still more dire when, early in the life of Clapp's group, the economy was slammed by the Panic of 1857, one of the most severe downturns in US history. It left an estimated one hundred thousand New Yorkers out of work. By day, men formed long lines in the vain hope of landing temporary jobs; by night, feral former pets, released by households that could no longer afford them, roamed the streets, looking for food. According to legend, Cornelius Vanderbilt—hoping to catch some sleep—hired a personal exterminator to thin the army of stray cats that yowled through the night.

Clapp's circle wasn't much better off. Even after the panic subsided, many remained both homeless and unemployed, a circumstance for which the Bohemians had a slang term: *on the rock*. Herr Pfaff was unusually lax about credit. He knew his clientele well, recognized that as soon as they earned any money they'd be back to settle the tab, and start a new one.

O'Brien frequently found himself *on the rock*. Often, he was so destitute that he couldn't afford the tools of his trade such as paper and ink. He would go to Pfaff's hoping to connect with someone in better straits who could help him out. He'd charm the person into taking

him home, usually to some nearby tenement. O'Brien would hole up
and remain awake several days, scrawling furiously with a borrowed
quill. Then he'd walk from magazine office to magazine office, peddling
his story, sell it, return to Pfaff's, buy everyone celebratory drinks, go
broke, repeat.

One time O'Brien showed up at the *Harper's* office, demanding a
$25 advance for a story the magazine had commissioned. This was un-
heard of; magazines paid on publication—and often not even then.
The editors flatly refused. So O'Brien burst into the bindery depart-
ment, grabbed a board, and scrawled a message on it. He marched
back and forth in front of the magazine's office with a makeshift sign:
"One of Harper's Authors. I Am Starving." He was mollified with a
$5 advance.

Another trait that defined Clapp's artists' circle, even in its earliest
days, was a fixation on all things bleak and morbid. For some, this
was simply posturing. The artists recruited by Clapp tended to be very
young. Exploring morbid themes was a way to signal that one had
privileged insight into some cold truths about the human condition:
*I'm no stranger to darkness, and to prove it I've chosen a skull as the subject
of my poem/painting/sculpture.* Stephen Fiske, an aspiring playwright
and a teenager when he first showed up at Pfaff's, nicely sums up this
attitude: "Just at that period death was very dear to all of us."

For some members of Clapp's circle, however, the morbid fixation
would prove more than a pose. Living the life of an artist carried gen-
uine risks, including alcoholism, drug abuse, tuberculosis, madness,
and suicide. Among the Pfaff's set, some of those who grew most com-
mitted to Bohemianism would suffer those very fates, the same as their
Parisian counterparts—or Edgar Allan Poe.

Clapp and his coterie held Poe in special veneration. In fact,
O'Brien's story in progress, about viewing a tiny world through a
microscope, had a decidedly macabre tone—a debt to Poe. Many in
the crowd drew charcoal sketches on the walls of their decrepit flats,
something that Poe had reputedly done. By now, Poe was long gone;
he had died back in 1849. In his day, he wasn't referred to as a "Bohe-
mian." But he certainly lived the life (drunken, dissolute, aflame with

creativity) and died the death (penniless, insane, only forty years old). Poe would serve as a kind of patron saint for the Pfaff's Bohemians.

Clapp was creating something truly radical. Convening his group in a dingy, underground lager house was a striking departure from the drawing rooms and salons where artists of the day tended to congregate. More typical for the times was the Calliopean Society, an august collection of New York City writers that included Peter and William Irving, Washington Irving's brothers. One of its bylaws spelled out that absolutely, under no circumstances, were "controversial subjects" to be discussed. Or consider the Saturday Club. Founded in Boston in 1855—the year before Clapp started his group—it took its name from a dinner held on the fourth Saturday of every month at the tony Parker House hotel. Even the names of the members sound formal and stuffy: John Lothrop Motley, Henry Wadsworth Longfellow, Oliver Wendell Holmes Sr.

The notion of the rebel artist hadn't really taken hold yet in America. If one hoped to be successful—rather than some wild-eyed Bleecker Street debauchee—it was necessary to be presentable. As Joseph Wood Krutch, one of Poe's earliest biographers, noted: "He might have had the good fortune to be born, like Baudelaire, in a world a little more tolerant of outcasts than that of literary America in the early nineteenth century."

In the years ahead, Clapp and his circle would do a great deal to change the standing of the outsider artist and to romanticize the role as well. They gathered in a saloon, not a salon.

As it grew, Clapp's group did at least become more organized (though *organized Bohemia* is certainly an oxymoron). Proprietor Pfaff set aside a dedicated area in his lager house, reserved for Clapp and his group. This quirky space, at the front of the establishment, extended out underneath the Broadway sidewalk. Casks of wine lined one wall. Here, the ceiling was even lower and vaulted. Small glass bull's-eyes, placed in the pavement, let in the faintest gloaming and also made it possible to pick up a kind of shadow tally of the foot traffic on the pavement above. It was a rather smelly spot—right near a privy. But this curious little vaulted space also had the advantage of being set apart. Where before the Bohemians had met in the saloon's main room, now they had their own private area.

Pfaff furnished Clapp with a long table, capable of seating a large group of people. A little niche in the wall became the dedicated spot for Clapp's collection of clay pipes, an affectation from his Paris days. Once again, Herr Pfaff proved a canny saloon keeper. He recognized that catering to a group of regulars was simply good business. Clapp's crowd were his favorites, and he made a point of waiting on them personally. Rotund, radiating good cheer and discretion, Pfaff would take orders all around.

Clapp took up a position at the head of the long table. He was now in his early forties, making him at least twice the age of many of his newfound acolytes. They treated him with due deference, referring to him as the "King of Bohemia." Clapp pretended not to like the title, though it was exactly what he'd wanted. His wit was sharper than ever, honed now by whiskey, which remained his drink of choice. He referred to Wall Street as "Cater-wall Street" and punned that its bankers had outsized "lie-abilities." He dismissed a writer of middling talent by saying the man "aimed at nothing and always hit the mark precisely."

Clapp reserved some of his sharpest jibes for newcomers. There were roughly thirty spots at his long table; the vaulted room was a cramped, little space. While some people made only sporadic appearances, others were becoming regulars. Clapp was forced to become selective. Toying with the mix, trying to get just the right collection of people at his table, seems to have given Clapp a special, even sadistic, thrill.

When someone showed up for the first time, Clapp would engage the person in a verbal battle, a kind of hazing ritual. An old article in the *American* magazine describes how Clapp "spied the intruder" and "shot a remark at him over the shoulder of another." Sometimes Clapp would even toss out a comment in French. Newcomers who responded faced the considerable challenge of trying to parry with Clapp in a language he'd mastered while in Paris. Any prospective member, according to that article, was "treated with scant courtesy until he had won a position by an intellectual tilt." Plenty of failed aspirants to Clapp's group beat a hasty retreat from the vaulted room.

Those who remained couldn't exactly rest easy. In the ferocious little ecosystem that Clapp had set in motion, he had his favorites, such as O'Brien and the poet Arnold. Naturally, this left others feeling insecure. Many felt they had to constantly work to curry the King of Bohemia's favor. They also had to contend with one another. This was an artists' circle, after all, brimming with competition, raw ambition, and egos as large as they were delicate.

Still, this uneasy atmosphere had its upside. Being an artist can be a solitary pursuit; at the very least, the saloon offered fellowship. Pass muster with Clapp, hold one's fellow artists at bay, and there was pride in belonging to an exclusive group, albeit an impoverished one—the Pfaff's Bohemians. There were professional advantages, potentially: a writer might meet an editor who was seeking to publish new voices; a sculptor might learn about art dealers looking for fresh talent. There was even the opportunity to share works in progress. Members of the circle brought in novels, plays, even paintings for critique. William Winter—a young, aspiring writer in these earliest days—would recall that during a critique, his fellow Bohemians "never spared each other from the barb of ridicule." But he would also remember it as "a salutary experience" for artists, "because it habituated them to the custom not only of speaking the truth, as they understood it . . . but of hearing the truth, as others understood it, about their own productions."

Underneath everything, a terrible tension always hummed in that little vaulted room. Here, it was necessary to live by one's wits—or, rather, wit. But with the right mix of people (the proper level of inebriation also helped), Clapp frequently achieved a kind of social alchemy. "Those were merry and famous nights," recalls an 1868 account, looking back wistfully on those first shining moments. There were clever puns and bawdy jokes; people told rambling stories and delivered toasts that went all rococo in their sentiment and complexity. As the evening drew on, the bon mots fairly flew. The long table was the site "of quip, and quirk, and queer conceit, of melancholy mirth and laughing madness," according to another old account.

Clapp had found a home at Pfaff's. He was quickly assembling his circle of Bohemian artists. He was their king, no less. But Clapp longed to pull a singular talent into his orbit, someone who could deliver the glory he craved.

CHAPTER 3

Whitman at a Crossroads

WHEN WHITMAN FIRST wandered into Pfaff's cellar, likely sometime in 1858, he'd already published two editions of *Leaves of Grass,* a collection of experimental poems. But the work had generally been ignored. Between the two editions, he'd sold only a handful of copies. Whitman was lost and in considerable torment.

Part of him was so certain that fame was his rightful station. Not merely fame: Whitman's ambitions were boundless, and on a good day, becoming the "greatest poet" of his age, America's representative bard, an immortal artist—all seemed inevitable. He could even marshal a tantalizing piece of evidence, an endorsement he'd received from Ralph Waldo Emerson, then one of America's leading artistic tastemakers. But his work had received only a small number of reviews, typically filled with puzzlement and derision. Mostly, he'd been met with the worst thing for an artist: terrible, soul-deflating silence. So Whitman also had all the proof he needed that failure and anonymity would be his destiny. He wasn't altogether sure that he shouldn't abandon poetry and move off in some radical new direction.

When he started frequenting the saloon, Whitman was thirty-nine years old. He stood roughly six feet, tall for the era, but weighed less than two hundred pounds. He wasn't yet the beefy, shaggy poet of legend. His hair was cut short, a salt-and-pepper mix of brown and gray. His beard was trimmed. Only later would he put on weight, the wages of stress and illness and advancing age. Only later would he grow his hair long and let his beard go thick and bushy.

But he was already an eccentric dresser. Whitman favored work-ingmen's garb, such as his wideawake, a type of broad-brimmed felt sombrero. He liked to wear it well back on his head, tilted at a rakish angle. His trousers were always tucked into cowhide boots. He wore rough-hewn shirts of unbleached linen, open at the collar, revealing a shock of chest hair. Whitman had a rosy complexion, almost baby-like, and quite incongruous for a big man. Because he was meticulous about hygiene, he always smelled of soap and cologne. His manner of dress often struck people as more like a costume. Or maybe it was a kind of armor, protecting the vulnerable man underneath.

Whitman wasn't much of a drinker. In fact, no one at Pfaff's would ever recall seeing him so much as tipsy. He would sit hour upon hour, nursing a single lager, intrigued by the spirited banter. "I think there was as good talk around the table as took place anywhere in the world," he would say.

He appears to have viewed the proceedings as a kind of conver-sational white-water rapid that he either was afraid to enter or per-haps didn't care to. As a poet, Whitman is celebrated for language that moves—soaring, swooping, singing—but his manner of speaking offered such a contrast: slow . . . deliberate . . . earthbound. He pro-nounced "poems" as "pomes," drawling it out, his eyelids drooping. That was another of his characteristics—those drooping eyelids, which lent a kind of impassivity to many of his facial expressions.

It wasn't as if his mind were slow; clearly, it was quite the oppo-site, but maybe all the connections and contradictions lighting up his synapses were best worked out on the page. At any rate, he steered clear of the "rubbing and drubbing," as he called those infamous ver-bal battles. "My own greatest pleasure at Pfaff's was to look on—to see, talk little, absorb," he would recall. "I never was a great discusser, anyway—never."

Once, at a birthday dinner, Clapp sat at the head of the table, col-lecting lavish toasts all around from his acolytes. When it came Whit-man's turn, the poet raised his stein and managed only to offer: "That's the feller!" The other Pfaffians couldn't believe it. "The ravishing charm of Walt Whitman's colossal eloquence," sneered William Winter. But what was it really: Was it shyness or sadness? Was it hauteur, or a willful and affected show of inarticulateness?

Regardless, Clapp—for so many reasons—was thrilled to have Whitman, even a reticent Whitman, at his table. The poet was five years his junior, while so many in the circle were decades younger. He'd achieved a measure of acclaim, outstripping most of the other Bohemians. Clapp sensed that Whitman could act as a kind of calling card, conferring legitimacy, drawing other more established artists into his ambit.

At the same time—and this is crucial—Whitman had thus far fallen short of fame. Clapp considered himself an unerring judge of talent. He was certain he could detect the poet's genius where others had mostly failed. The fact that what little acclaim Whitman had received was typically more like notoriety made the situation very nearly perfect. Here was a chance to provoke people; there's nothing the King of Bohemia liked better. Clapp would emerge as Whitman's great champion. In due time, thanks to a publication Clapp founded called the *Saturday Press,* he would publish, promote, and defend Whitman's work. Whitman would later state, "I have often said to you that my own history could not be written with Henry left out: I mean it—that is not an extravagant statement." It's worth noting that this comment was uttered years in the future, to a biographer, by an entirely transformed Walt Whitman. It was a Whitman who still recognized his debt to Clapp's ceaseless evangelism.

People tend to think of Whitman as the Good Gray Poet, up in a pantheon somewhere, holding celestial court with Dante and Homer. But in 1858, none of this was assured. Upon first arriving at Pfaff's, grand ambitions notwithstanding, Whitman was decidedly mortal. So far, he'd led a bewilderingly varied life, soaking up experience. The catholic nature of his formative years is a key to understanding the Whitman that first showed up at the saloon and the towering figure that he was to become.

Born in 1819, Whitman grew up living mostly in Brooklyn. His father was a speculative home builder with abysmal business instincts, and the family was forever skating on the brink of ruin. By age eleven, Whitman was done with formal schooling and went to work to help his large family, which included seven other siblings. Whitman worked as an office boy for a law firm, then for a doctor. He found intermittent work out on Long Island as a country schoolteacher. This was one of many places in those days that had no official certification—and required only the most minimal qualifications—for teachers. He tended to classrooms as large as eighty kids, some older than he, for a rock-bottom salary. He also tried his hand selling pencils and inkstands out of a small Brooklyn storefront.

But his primary occupation was journalism. At age twelve, he got his first newspaper job as an apprentice at the *Long Island Patriot.* Over the next quarter century, in an era when the profession was remarkably unstable and unremunerative, he worked for a wild array of publications in Brooklyn, Manhattan, and Long Island: the *Daily Plebian, Evening Tattler, Statesman, New World,* and *New York Mirror,* to name just a few. He did every possible job, from operating a bed-and-platen hand press to writing articles. At age twenty-two, he landed his first editorship with a big-city daily, taking charge of the *Aurora,* a Manhattan paper that competed—not very effectively—with about twenty others. He even founded a couple of newspapers, including the *Long Islander.* For this paper, he wrote most of the articles and sold all the advertisements, often trading ad space for potatoes or firewood. He delivered the paper himself, traveling the thirty-mile route once a week on a horse named Nina.

Whitman wrote about everything. He covered a baseball game between New York and Brooklyn, separate cities in those days; he reviewed *Omoo,* an early novel by Herman Melville, an exact contemporary, though the two never met; he tried his hand at medical advice: "To cure a tooth ache, plunge your feet in cold water." At one paper, he wrote a regular column on murders in New York City. At another, he produced profiles of city characters like coopers and butchers. He wrote editorials against capital punishment, in favor of stricter rules on ferryboats, and against dueling, which he denounced as "honorable nonsense."

The papers where he worked often received complimentary passes to various entertainments. Even as a young apprentice, Whitman got to use those tickets. On rare occasions, he was able to get someone else to join him, often one of his brothers. There was a set-apartness to Whitman from early on; for all the people he met, he would always lack for intimates. But viewing performances alone had its advantages. It allowed him complete focus. He gained a thorough knowledge of Shakespeare, developed a particular passion for opera. When Whitman went to see contralto Marietta Alboni, he was utterly transfixed, even though he didn't speak a word of Italian. She did something like forty performances during her New York stand; Whitman caught them all.

Over the years, Whitman spent time enough in Manhattan to become the ultimate Broadway rambler—small wonder that he eventually found his way to Pfaff's. He grew to know the two-mile stretch from city hall to Union Square probably better than anyone ever. He had his own peculiar collection of spots he enjoyed visiting. There was Dr. Abbott's Museum of Egyptian Antiquities, where he passed untold hours looking at mummies and artifacts. There were several daguerreotype studios on Broadway, including one run by the celebrated Mathew Brady. Creating daguerreotypes was a new process, and getting one's picture taken was a novelty, sweeping the nation. Whitman regularly made the rounds, studying the portraits. At the Broadway Temple, meanwhile, Whitman attended learned lectures on a huge array of subjects. He was exposed to the latest thinking on geology and astronomy, which held that the earth was very old and space unfathomably large.

Broadway was an infinity unto itself. Whitman loved the street for its bizarre contrasts and unexpected harmonies. Here, it was possible to attend a play about pirates and also to meet a coach driver named One-Eyed Joe. Owing partly to his own humble roots, Whitman felt a rapport with coach drivers and other workingmen. He would greet the drivers who constantly traversed Broadway with a kind of downward salute, like a chop. They invariably returned his greeting. When Whitman took a coach, he liked to ride up front, sitting beside the driver. He didn't necessarily talk much on the ride; he was always sparing with spoken words, most content to listen. But in the company of drivers, he felt at ease, while among his fellow artists he would be forever wary.

Over time, Whitman developed his sartorial style in emulation—pretentious imitation, some of his contemporaries would argue—of such workingmen. He even compiled a dictionary, full of slang such as *bender, bummer, spree,* and *shin-dig,* picked up from coach drivers and blacksmiths and stevedores. Though never published, Whitman's *Primer of Words* was intended as an update to Noah Webster's landmark work. A sample entry for *so long,* then still a slang term, goes as follows: "a delicious American—New York—idiomatic phrase at parting."

At times, Whitman would simply stand on Broadway, studying his reflection in a shop window and marveling at how his image blended with the multitudes passing behind him. To Whitman, the result was a highly satisfying optical illusion: Manhattan was coursing through him.

But perhaps his favorite place to visit was a shop with a supremely Gothic-sounding name: the Phrenological Cabinet of Fowler & Wells. Address: 286 Broadway.

Phrenology is a pseudoscientific theory that holds that the brain is extremely compartmentalized, consisting of a huge number of different centers. The centers control various attributes, such as destructiveness or the capacity to love. These can be built up through use or can atrophy through neglect, just like a muscle. The center for destructiveness, for example, was thought to be right above the ears. Someone who is destructive could be expected to have a pronounced swelling in that area. By examining the shape of people's skulls, reading the bumps, it was thought possible to determine their character.

Thousands of nineteenth-century Americans had their skulls read, including Horace Greeley and Edgar Allan Poe. In *Moby-Dick,* Ishmael attempts to gain phrenological insight into the great whale. Employers sometimes even asked prospective hires to submit to a phrenological reading. In some ways, phrenology was extremely prescient. Scientists now recognize that the brain truly is divided into discrete regions that govern various functions. But phrenology's fine-grain divisions (supposedly, there were centers devoted to love, anger, benevolence, and countless other traits), not to mention the notion that a person's propensity for such traits can be revealed by bumps on the skull, is now viewed as bunkum. At best, phrenology can be seen as the crazy granddad of modern neuropsychology.

In its day, however, phrenology was taken quite seriously, and the contribution of Fowler & Wells to the field was considerable. Brothers Orson and Lorenzo Fowler, along with their associate Samuel Wells, succeeded in wedding phrenology's concepts with America's burgeoning self-help movement. "Know thyself" was the business's official slogan. Through a phrenological reading, the proprietors promised, not only could one gain self-awareness, but by exercising deficient traits, one could also achieve personal growth.

Whitman haunted the Phrenological Cabinet of Fowler & Wells. It featured a gallery of plaster casts of the skulls of murderers and thieves—miscreants one did not want to emulate, bump-wise—as well as celebrities and other desirable types. Whitman enjoyed browsing the store's collection of books such as *The Philosophy of Electrical Psychology,* a text that held that people's power to connect with one another was based on harnessing electrical currents that flowed through all the universe's matter. Fowler & Wells were also big advocates of the idea that sex is a natural function, nothing to be ashamed of. Titles such as *Love and Parentage* counseled that sex was not only procreative, but also something to be enjoyed.

On July 16, 1849, Whitman paid three dollars to have his skull read by Lorenzo Fowler. On a scale from 1 to 7, Whitman rated an exemplary 6.5 on such traits as benevolence, self-esteem, and firmness. He received one of his lowest marks for acquisitiveness, the pursuit of money and material gain. The low rating sat fine with Whitman, struck him almost as a veiled compliment. In his report, Lorenzo noted, "Size of head large . . . a certain reckless swing of animal will, too unmindful, probably, of the conviction of others." He added, "You are yourself at all times." Overall, Fowler painted a flattering picture of Whitman, casting him as a well-rounded modern man. (The phrase *well rounded* derives from phrenology and is based on the notion that an actualized person has a nicely shaped head, without any distortive bumps.) The results greatly pleased Whitman.

Up and down Broadway, in and out of journalism, taken by daguerre-otypes, transported by opera, gathering gathering gathering experience—but for what? By the early 1850s, Whitman began to feel what he later described as a "great pressure, pressure from within." With his thirty-fifth birthday fast approaching, he grew pained by the notion that at the same age Shakespeare was "adjudged already to deserve a place among the great masters," having by then written such plays as *Romeo and Juliet, A Midsummer Night's Dream, The Taming of the Shrew, The Merchant of Venice,* and *Richard III.*

Yet Whitman remained unsure where his area of mastery might lie. He'd tried such a variety of endeavors, yet failed to distinguish himself in any single one. By now, Whitman had drifted out of journalism, save for the occasional freelance piece. He was currently involved in building and flipping houses with about the same luck his father had managed. He'd even published a handful of poems, none of them memorable, none of them showing much originality or promise.

But a fresh pass at poetry yielded very different results. This time the ideas came pouring out of Whitman. He wrote in mad haste, seeking to capture what he called "the gush, the throb, the flood, of the moment—to put things down without deliberation." Before long, he had covered myriad scraps of paper with scrawled fragments and half-formed notions. These he collected in an envelope. And then he set to the task of crafting this raw outflow into finished poems, a process as meticulous as what came before had been spontaneous. As Whitman put it, he "wrote, rewrote, and re-rewrote."

By 1855—three years before he first showed up at Pfaff's—Whitman had a collection ready. "Remember," he would state many years later, "the book arose out of my life in Brooklyn and New York from 1838 to 1853, absorbing a million people, for fifteen years, with an intimacy, an eagerness, an abandon, probably never equaled."

The title he chose, *Leaves of Grass,* was a treble entendre. On the one hand, *leaves* simply means "pages." It was frequently used in 1850s book titles, such as Fanny Fern's widely read *Fern Leaves from Fanny's Portfolio.* As a veteran newspaperman, Whitman was also playing on *grass* as journalistic lingo for filler, articles that could be held for a slow news day. But he also meant his title to work on a more profound level, as an assertion that the whole of something and its parts are indivisible: grass consists of countless individual leaves, yet each is part of the whole.

Leaves of Grass was like no collection of poetry the world had ever seen. It consisted of twelve untitled poems, flowing inexplicably one into the next, propelled by lengthy, comma-less sequences and bursts of ellipses. Whitman mixed elevated language with slang such as *tushes, blab,* and *foofoos* (vain people). And he sprinkled in plenty of the day's pseudoscience, things like electricity traveling via "instant conductors" from one person's body to another.

Much about *Leaves of Grass* was groundbreaking. Whitman wrote the poems in free verse, a form for which he is acknowledged as the innovator. This was a complete departure from the rigid meter and rhyme of his contemporaries. Many of the poems also featured a kind of universal first person that shape-shifted and swung wildly through time and space. Sometimes *I* could be taken simply as Whitman, but this was an outlandishly fluid *I* that switched in an eye blink from male to female and with the greatest of ease assumed various identities: a slave, a witch being burned at the stake, a cholera sufferer, a clock.

With *Leaves of Grass,* Whitman laid out for himself an ambitious mandate: "The proof of a poet is that his country absorbs him as affectionately as he has absorbed it." The techniques he employed—free verse, fondness for idiom, the universal *I*—were in service of trying to express the full nature of America. He was out to capture the country's teeming, democratic vastness:

> Do I contradict myself?
> Very well then. . . . I contradict myself;
> I am large. . . . I contain multitudes.

Whitman chose to self-publish his collection, not unusual in that era. He hired the Rome brothers (Andrew, James, and Thomas), who ran a print shop in Brooklyn. The brothers' only experience was with legal forms. Thus, Whitman's poems were typeset in tiny ten-point letters on extra-large pages. The oversize work was bound and given a green cloth cover; the title, *Leaves of Grass,* was rendered so that the individual letters flowed together, sprouting roots and tendrils.

Because Whitman was paying to publish his own work, the first run was limited to 795 copies. He arranged to have his poetry collection sold, of all places, through the Phrenological Cabinet of Fowler & Wells. The books were available in the outfit's New York, Boston, and Philadelphia locations. Otherwise, the work could be found at only a few other places, such as William Swayne's bookstore on Fulton Street in Brooklyn.

Nevertheless, Whitman had massive hopes for *Leaves of Grass.* He envisioned the initial run selling out quickly. Money would keep flowing in, enough to fund the larger and then larger printings necessary to meet public demand. This was a time when poetry was a proven route to fame and fortune. Longfellow's *Song of Hiawatha*—published only a few months after *Leaves of Grass*—got off to a quick start, selling 30,000 copies during its first six months in print. Martin Farquhar Tupper, a wildly popular poet (yes, such a thing once existed), managed to sell 300,000 copies of his work *Proverbial Philosophy.* But the country wasn't yet ready to absorb Walt Whitman. No reliable numbers exist for the first edition of *Leaves of Grass,* but according to the poet's own bitter accounting, sales were minuscule.

It's actually surprising—a tribute to how truly radical the work was—that it still managed to receive a handful of reviews. Most were not sympathetic. *Putnam's* described *Leaves of Grass* as "a curious and lawless collection of poems. . . . The introduction of terms, never before heard or seen, and of slang expressions, often renders an otherwise striking passage altogether laughable." The *Boston Intelligencer* said of Whitman: "There is neither wit nor method in his disjointed babbling, and it seems to us he must be some escaped lunatic, raving in pitiable delirium." Harsher still was a London publication called the *Critic:* "Walt Whitman is as unacquainted with art, as a hog is with mathematics. His poems—we must call them so for convenience—twelve in number, are innocent of rhythm and resemble nothing so much as the war-cry of the Red Indians."

Whitman also sent copies of *Leaves of Grass* to various literary lions. Poet John Greenleaf Whittier delivered perhaps the most concise verdict. Supposedly, he hurled Whitman's book into the fireplace.

A copy also went to Ralph Waldo Emerson. Back in the 1830s, Emerson had emerged as the leading light of transcendentalism, the profoundly influential movement centered in New England and dedicated to such precepts as the infinite potential of humankind and the need for self-reliance. Arguably, Emerson remained *the* arbiter of literary taste in America. He had a very different response to Whitman's work than the critics. On July 21, 1855, Emerson wrote Whitman a five-page letter that contained the following: "I am not blind to the worth of the wonderful gift of 'Leaves of Grass.' I find it the most extraordinary piece of wit and wisdom that America has yet contributed. . . . I find incomparable things said incomparably well, as they must be." And the kicker: "I greet you at the beginning of a great career."

On receiving the letter, Whitman was wonderstruck. For several months, he carried the folded letter around in his pocket, secret confirmation of his singular talent. He felt that he had received the blessing of "an emperor." Soon, Whitman heard from Emerson again. Emerson planned to travel from his home in Concord, Massachusetts, to New York City and hoped to meet Whitman in person.

It's hard to imagine two people more mismatched in terms of physical appearance, temperament, everything. Whitman was earthy and robust; Emerson, fifty-two, sixteen years the poet's senior, was thin, with a ramrod patrician bearing. Where Whitman's formal education ended at eleven, Emerson was a graduate of Harvard Divinity School. Whitman placed a high value on physically demanding jobs such as carpentry. Emerson once attempted a manual labor regimen as a kind of spiritual experiment. But it left him exhausted, and he delivered the following maxim: "The writer shall not dig." Whitman was deeply emotional. Emerson was cerebral to the core, even once describing himself as a "cold, fastidious" person.

Despite these differences, however, there existed an unexpected af-
finity, one that prompted the Sage of Concord to seek out an obscure
Brooklyn poet. In his essays, Emerson maintained a steady drumbeat
about the need for homegrown, nativist art. It was high time, he ar-
gued, for America to quell its cultural insecurities and stop the slavish
imitation of Old World models. Ignore "the courtly muses of Europe,"
he famously urged. Yet Emerson was in no position to heed his own
call. As an essayist, he was unrivaled—eloquent, urbane, powerfully
persuasive. As a poet, however, Emerson was not nearly as talented
or inspired. In Whitman, he believed he'd discovered that vaunted,
authentic American voice.

For Emerson's visit to New York, Whitman took him to the Fire-
man's Hall, a raucous club on Mercer Street. It was a strange choice.
Whitman, it seems, was trying to make a calculated impression. "He
shouted for a 'tin mug' for his beer," Emerson would recall. Emerson
emerged from that first meeting with a sense that Whitman was odd,
but sublimely gifted—just as the poet had hoped.

In 1856, Whitman self-published a second edition of *Leaves of Grass*.
He made numerous changes. The book was now printed in a far more
sensible size, one that was portable (roughly seven by three inches). He
added twenty new poems. And this time around, Whitman gave the
poems titles. What's more, he added *Poem* to all thirty-two titles, just
to be certain that people knew exactly what they were reading. It made
for some awkward verbiage, for along with "Poem of the Road" and
"Burial Poem," there's the glaringly self-evident "Poem of the Poet."
Whitman also cleaned up his unruly syntax, becoming a bit more
sparing with ellipses and more generous in his use of commas. Oddly,
Whitman chose to include his own phrenological reading in the appen-
dix. Even in the nineteenth century, it was unusual for a new edition
of a book to differ so greatly from the previous one. But then, nothing
about *Leaves of Grass* is typical.

For the second edition, the most striking change appeared on the
book's spine, where the following was stamped in gold: "I Greet You at
the Beginning of a Great Career R. W. Emerson." Inside the volume,

Whitman reprinted Emerson's letter in full. Taking matters still further, Whitman crafted a kind of open letter to Emerson. He didn't mail it to him; rather, the letter was simply published in the book, where it served as a canny device to help position the new volume. Whitman's open letter begins: "Here are thirty-two Poems, which I send you, dear Friend and Master." The implication was clear: not only had Emerson endorsed the twelve poems in the first edition, but his blessing extended to the new poems as well.

Upon receiving a copy of the new edition in the mail, the cold, fastidious Emerson was overcome with hot passion. Friends reported that they had never seen him so angry. Whitman had overstepped his boundaries and succeeded in pushing away his benefactor.

It was a moot point, however. Despite Emerson's unauthorized endorsement, the new volume of *Leaves of Grass* was another abject failure. In fact, it is said to have sold even more poorly than the first, if that's possible. Around this time, Whitman scrawled the following in a notebook, under the heading "Depressions": "Every thing I have done seems to me blank and suspicious.—I doubt whether my greatest thoughts, as I had supposed them, are not shallow—and people will most likely laugh at me.—My pride is impotent, my love gets no response.—The complacency of nature is hateful—I am filled with restlessness.—I am incomplete.—"

This was the Walt Whitman who first showed up at Pfaff's. Poetry wasn't paying the bills, so he had fallen back into journalism and was working for the *Brooklyn Daily Times*. Then, in June 1859, Whitman lost that job, supposedly due to a pair of controversial editorials, one urging licensing for prostitutes, the other suggesting that women, so as to ensure compatibility with potential marriage partners, should have the option of premarital sex. Unemployed, he started going to Pfaff's nearly every night.

By now, Whitman had turned forty. The poet was living at home with his mother in a basement apartment at 106 North Portland Avenue in Brooklyn. (Whitman's father had died four years earlier.) Crowded into the quarters were Whitman's youngest brother, Eddy, who was both mentally slow and emotionally disturbed, and eldest brother, Jesse, a disabled former sailor slipping ever deeper into insanity, the result of syphilis caught from a prostitute while on a shore leave in Ireland. Present, too, was George, a carpenter and easily the most practical Whitman sibling, a doer rather than a feeler. Walt and George shared a special bond, rooted in the fact that they were opposites. A fourth brother, Jeff, had just moved into the apartment with his new wife, and they would soon have a child. Fortunately, Walt's two sisters, Mary and Hannah, had made lives for themselves outside this cramped and impoverished household.

Often, Whitman simply loafed the day away, before setting out in the late afternoon for Pfaff's. From Brooklyn and back was a six-mile trip by foot, ferry, and coach, so frequenting this particular saloon was quite a commitment. But as an unemployed poet, facing bleak prospects, Whitman found that Pfaff's was a place where he could be among other artists. It provided him with a desperately needed identity. The belief that Clapp showed in him must have been extremely heartening.

Clapp's deference had a downside, however, at least where the others in the group were concerned. This could be a tough crowd; there was the perpetual jockeying for the favor of the King of Bohemia. Many in the set held themselves above Whitman. As Elihu Vedder, an illustrator and Pfaff's habitué from this period, recalls, "He had not become famous yet, and I then regarded many of the Boys as his superiors, as they did themselves." Sure, Whitman had that Emerson endorsement—indeed clung to it—but his few reviews were mostly bad and his sales paltry.

Sometimes, Whitman found himself the target of the verbal sparring that he worked so hard to avoid. At Pfaff's, nobody was spared. A caustic comment might issue from somewhere along the table, and Whitman would realize it was directed at him. "I don't know if you ever realized it—ever realized what it means to be a horror in the sight of the people about you," Whitman would recall, "but there was a time when I felt it to the full—when the enemy—and nearly all were the enemy then—wanted for nothing better or more simply, without remorse, to crush me, to brush me, without compunction or mercy, out of sight, out of hearing: to do anything, everything, to rid themselves of me." The comment is hyperbolic, most certainly paranoid, but also captures something of the flavor of being on the receiving end of the Pfaff's slings and arrows.

Sometimes Whitman fired back. He couldn't help himself. While he prided himself on staying above the fray, the rubbing and drubbing sometimes wore him down, managed to find his raw spots. Given his languid style of speech, Whitman didn't go in for elaborate mind-game put-downs. But he had his ways. "I like your tinkles," Whitman told a Pfaff's regular named Thomas Aldrich, referring to the man's poems. The sting lay in the blasé, utterly dismissive way that he delivered the line. (No, this wasn't the benevolent, mist-shrouded Whitman.) On the attack, he possessed a "bovine air of omniscience" that could be maddening, according to William Winter. Winter was well acquainted with it, for Whitman once slammed him with "Willy is a young Longfellow." The jibe was brief, pithy, and a direct hit: where Poe was this crowd's patron saint, Longfellow was its bête noire. As a sentimental poet, Longfellow was anathema to many in the Pfaff's set. They snidely referred to him as "Longwindedfellow." Then again, Longfellow had outsold Whitman and the rest of the Pfaffians put together.

Whitman grew so frustrated that he began to think about giving up poetry. "It is now time to *stir* first for *Money* enough, *to live and provide for M.*—" (M. being his mother). One option that he considered, though he was shaky on specifics, was delivering lectures on politics. Whitman, far more than many in the Pfaff's circle, was engaged by the subject, which he approached in his own highly intuitive fashion. Whitman had a poet's grasp of politics, one might say, and his insight could be almost eerily keen. He'd even once written a pamphlet on the subject. It included a savage attack on the political climate of the 1850s, in which Whitman resorted to outlandish rhetorical flourishes such as his statement that President Franklin Pierce "eats dirt and excrement for his daily meals, likes it, and tries to force it on The States." The pamphlet was not published in Whitman's lifetime. But it is notable for one prescient passage, in which Whitman imagines the ideal candidate to lead the country: "I would be much pleased to see some heroic, shrewd, fully-informed, healthy-bodied, middle-aged, beard-faced American blacksmith or boatman come down from the West across the Alleghanies, and walk into the Presidency." Incredibly, these words were written in 1856, several years before a beard-faced candidate, in from the West, was even a glimmer in the eyes of America.

As for Whitman's plan to be a "wander-speaker," vague though it was, he actually drew up a circular, entitled *Walt Whitman's Lectures.* Never mind that he wasn't even much of a talker, let alone a gifted public orator. "I desire to go by degrees through all These States," he announced, "especially West and South." He came up with what seemed like a proper price for his services. Where Emerson commanded upwards of $50 per lecture, Whitman proposed to charge 10 cents a head. In the circular, Whitman stated that lecturing on political issues would be "henceforth my employment." But the notion of lecturing was really no more than a lark, a distraction from the real work at hand.

In the dim light of Pfaff's, Whitman was discovering that he couldn't shake poetry so easily. It was inspiring to be among artists, even if they could be irksome, even if he mostly just looked on. "What wit, humor, repartee, word wars, and sometimes bad blood!" Whitman marveled. It goaded him on. Soon he was writing fresh poems. Even after two editions of *Leaves of Grass,* he had so much more to say. His new work was quite a departure from what he'd done previously. It showed the kind of assurance that comes with maturity and the experience of loss. He was tackling fresh subjects and highly controversial ones, too.

Sometimes, just sometimes, if the evening's mix at Clapp's long table was right, if the roiling sea of egos that surrounded him had achieved momentary calm, then Walt Whitman—this wounded, prideful man—in a voice quiet and slow, would read one of his new poems to the crowd at Pfaff's.

CHAPTER 4

Hashish and Shakespeare

"WE WERE ALL VERY MERRY at Pfaff's," wrote Thomas Aldrich in his poem "At the Café." But just a few lines later, he asks: "Did you think . . . that my heart, as I passed the Rhine wine to the boys, was as black as the midnight and bitter as gall?"

The poem mines that vein of darkness, one of the most distinctive traits of Clapp's circle. Of course, it's partly self-conscious posturing. Aldrich—yet another representative of the Pfaff's youth brigade—was only twenty-three when he wrote it. But he was also tapping into forces in the world around him that were disquieting, pressing, and undeniably real. There was darkness aplenty to draw on at this particular time.

While the Bohemians gathered in that little vaulted room beneath the Broadway sidewalk, the world above them was fast slipping into disarray. The fact that Clapp was able to launch an American Bohemia during the 1850s is not mere happenstance. Conditions were ripe. Just as revolutionary rumblings had caused Paris's Left Bank scene to blossom in the 1840s, America was going through paroxysms of its own in the decade that came to be known as the Fiery Fifties.

This was an agonizing time in US history, as tensions ratcheted up between the North and South. There was a pervading sense of doom; it seemed that at any moment, things might spin out of control. At the same time, America's glorious founding years remained a fresh memory. Plenty of people were around who had grown up during the presidencies of Washington, Adams, Jefferson, and Madison. Even a smattering of Revolutionary War veterans were still alive. The contrast

made it all that much more painful. Facing a mounting crisis, America
was saddled with some of its worst, most uninspiring leadership ever.

During the latter part of the 1850s, James Buchanan was president.
He was an even less capable executive, if that's possible, than his prede-
cessor, Pierce. Buchanan was a so-called doughface, a Northerner sym-
pathetic to the interests of Southern slaveholders. The term suggests a
highly changeable person, capable of molding his features to curry the
favor of varied constituencies. Duality ran deep in Buchanan's nature.
Before becoming president, he had been a wealthy lawyer who owned
a sprawling estate in Lancaster, Pennsylvania, called Wheatland, mod-
eled after a Southern plantation. Predictably, he pleased no one during
his presidency.

Congress was simply nonfunctional. Throughout the country's his-
tory, Americans have bemoaned the lack of cooperation in Congress,
but in the 1850s it reached epic proportions. Sessions degenerated into
exchanges of invective and slander, North pitted against South. A par-
ticularly deranged episode occurred on February 5, 1858, during a late-
night debate in the House of Representatives. Laurence Keitt of South
Carolina called Pennsylvania's Galusha Grow a "Black Republican
puppy." (Representative Grow was white; "Black Republican" was a
popular insult of the day, a slap at the party's avowed sympathy for
slaves.) Returning the insult, Grow told his Southern colleague, "No
negro-driver shall crack his whip over me."

At this point, Keitt rushed at Grow and started to throttle him. A
melee erupted on the House floor, and roughly fifty representatives
swarmed together, kicking and punching and hollering. Wisconsin's
Cadwallader Washburn took a swing at William Barksdale of Missis-
sippi. The punch grazed Barksdale's skull, knocking off his wig. Barks-
dale hastily replaced the hairpiece and continued to scuffle. Duly noted,
however, was the fact that the distinguished congressman from Missis-
sippi had put his wig on backward. The floor erupted again, this time
with howls of laughter. Keitt unhanded Grow, and the melee ended.

Outside the halls of Congress, there was violence in abundance.
This was an era of widespread rioting; in Boston, Louisville, Baltimore,
mobs took to the streets, often driven by a sense of outrage that was

vague, inchoate, but killing dozens just the same. Bleeding Kansas was the scene of sectarian tensions that resulted in as many as two hundred deaths; Americans were treated to the spectacle of two competing Kansas territorial legislatures, proslavery in Lecompton and free-soil in Topeka.

By the late 1850s, there didn't exist a single official US institution that wasn't in crisis: Congress, an actual battleground; territorial governments, a farce; the Supreme Court, utterly suspect following the *Dred Scott* decision. Scott was a slave who sued for freedom on the grounds that his master had moved with him to Wisconsin, a free territory. But the Court ruled that a black person had no right to sue. Further, the Court handed down a ruling so broad as to make it difficult to arrest the spread of slavery into the Northern territories. Buchanan worked secretly behind the scenes, obtaining his desired outcome for the case by pressuring a couple of justices, an egregious violation of the separation of powers. In this way, Buchanan, arguably the worst president in US history, played a role in *Dred Scott*, often considered the nadir of the US Supreme Court. The ruling led to rampant uncertainty about the nation's future. That uncertainty, in turn, was a major factor in sparking the Panic of 1857. On top of everything else, the economy was in shambles.

Among the Pfaff's set, Whitman was especially caught up in the Fiery Fifties. He filled his private notebooks with comments, lamenting the era's "hot passions" and "inertia." In his political pamphlet, he asked, "What historic denouements are these we are approaching? On all sides tyrants tremble, crowns are unsteady, the human race restive, on the watch for some better era, some divine war." As part of his blurry plan to become a "wander-speaker," he even contemplated whether the president or perhaps the Supreme Court might require his services, and whether he might be called upon "to dart hither or thither, as some great emergency might demand." Whitman always held grand—grandiose, his detractors in Clapp's coterie might say— notions about his capacity to soothe a troubled nation.

Other Pfaffians tended to be less overtly consumed by the big events of the day. But that doesn't mean they were unaffected. Being a writer or artist in the 1850s, according to one account, was like being an "overcharged Leyden jar." (A Leyden jar is an old-fashioned device used to conduct experiments with static electricity.) It's hard to imagine O'Brien, say, the impoverished writer in an unholy hurry, getting involved in a political discussion. Politics was not a subject he ever showed interest in or explored in his work. But simply as citizens, and further as people of sensitive artistic temperament, the Pfaff's crowd registered the chaos of the Fiery Fifties just the same.

A common stance among Clapp's set was a kind of sly cynicism. Every aspect of American society seemed so eroded, so diminished; drinking, carousing, and trading witty barbs in a subterranean bar—what else even made sense? That's part of the tension in "We were all very merry at Pfaff's." This much was certain: the status quo was a sham. The term didn't exist in the 1850s, but the Pfaffians were forming what today is called a counterculture.

It's only fitting, then, that Fitz Hugh Ludlow found his way to that underground saloon on Broadway. Ludlow first showed up at Pfaff's in 1858, as the wunderkind author of *The Hasheesh Eater*. The book—a literary sensation that had been published the previous year—details Ludlow's drug experiences starting as a teenager and on through college. This was fresh and shocking territory. It was also the perfect book for an era of widespread disillusion, a time when tired old rules and failed authority were being questioned.

Ludlow, pale and slightly built, looked even younger than his twenty-one years. But he was also a formidable conversationalist. Well versed in the classics, he was comfortable ranging across a huge variety of subjects, many of them arcane or occult. He possessed an absurdly large vocabulary, enjoyed sprinkling his everyday speech with five-dollar words such as *barathrum* (an abyss), *omphalopsychite* (a navel gazer), *sacerdotal* (relating to priests), and *sesquipedalia* (a word for very long words). Due to a surfeit of jittery energy, he spoke with great animation, making wild, staccato gestures with his hands.

Ludlow's rare conversational powers quickly earned him a regular place at Clapp's long table. He brimmed with ambition, like a schoolboy intent on getting the best marks. Having made such an audacious start with *The Hasheesh Eater,* he was certain that still greater literary heights awaited him.

Ludlow had grown up in Poughkeepsie, New York, the son of a Presbyterian minister. At age three, he taught himself to read. He was a sickly youth, a dreamer; rather than playing outside, he was content to remain indoors with a book. By seven, he was studying Latin and Greek with his father: "the smartest and most learned boy I ever saw," recalled a cousin. Ludlow was so nearsighted that, while still a child, he was fitted with spectacles, very unusual for the time. The other kids taunted him with what would become the classic insult aimed at glasses wearers: "four eyes."

After his mother died, everything took a turn. Ludlow became rebellious, developing a fondness for what he'd later call "childhood's sweetest flavor—the taste of disobedience." He bounced from school to school. Often his father was forced to interrupt his sermons, pointing up at the church's gallery and saying, "Fitz Hugh, I mean you."

At age sixteen, Ludlow started frequenting an apothecary shop in Poughkeepsie. Ludlow sampled the various drugs available "until I had run through the whole gamut of queer agents within my reach." The concept of illegal drugs didn't exist yet. Young Ludlow appears to have viewed these dabblings as scientific inquiry, or at least that's how he would play it in *The Hasheesh Eater.* As for the apothecary, maybe he was simply charmed by Ludlow's enthusiasm and willing to share samples of his potions and patent medicines with a teenager. Ludlow tried ether and chloroform, various opiates and stimulants. "When the circuit of all the accessible tests was completed," Ludlow recalled, "I ceased experimenting, and sat down like a pharmaceutical Alexander, with no more drug-worlds to conquer."

Then, one afternoon, Ludlow happened to visit the shop when the apothecary was unpacking an enticing new arrival. It was a box from Tilden & Company of New Lebanon, New York, filled with little vials of *Cannabis indica* extract. This plant (common name: Indian hemp) can be cultivated for marijuana, or a sticky resin can be collected from its leaves and concentrated, producing hashish. While recreational use

goes back centuries in places such as China and India, hashish was
viewed strictly as a medicinal agent in nineteenth-century America. It
was prescribed in small doses and taken orally as a remedy for a variety
of ailments. "A most pleasurable and harmless stimulant," promises an
old advertisement in *Harper's Weekly*. "Cures Nervousness, Weakness,
Melancholy, &c."

For his first foray, Ludlow took a massive dose. He rolled the tar-
like green resin into a fat pellet, what he called a "bolus," and then
chewed it up. At first nothing happened. But then Ludlow noticed that
time seemed to have ground to a halt. He checked his watch, allowed
his mind to meander a bit, and then checked again. A mere thirty sec-
onds had passed. Ludlow went home and hid in his bedroom, safe from
his preacher father. Later that evening, still very much under the influ-
ence, he sneaked out of his room and stood at the top of the stairway.
The stairs appeared to stretch endlessly downward. "My God!" Ludlow
thought. "I am in eternity."

Ludlow continued to experiment with hashish. When he enrolled at
Union College in Schenectady, New York, one of the first things he did
was arrange to buy Tilden's extract directly from the company. He in-
troduced several of his friends and dorm mates to hashish in this form.
None of them were as taken with the drug as Ludlow. Already, he was
a veteran sensation seeker. Back in grammar school, he had once been
punished for chewing cloves to stay awake in class, and his sister would
recall that as a two-year-old he liked to eat cayenne pepper directly
from the shaker. At Union, Ludlow took heroic doses of hashish, eating
as much as four grams at once, the equivalent of smoking six joints at
an impossibly fast clip.

Ludlow had many of the classic experiences of cannabis users, such
as giggle fits, ravenous hunger, and extreme receptivity to music. While
high, Ludlow went to see an orchestra and was enthralled when the
music began to separate into its component parts and he was actually
able to pick out the sound issuing from each individual violin. Be-
cause he was taking such massive doses—and also due to his delicate
nature and unbridled imagination—Ludlow had vivid hallucinations
more closely akin to those experienced on mushrooms or LSD, a drug

that would not be synthesized until nearly a century later. Solid walls melted and reconstituted in front of Ludlow's eyes, squat little buildings sprouted into fantastical Moorish castles, the physical features of his classmates mutated (a whist enthusiast's face fanned out like a hand of cards) in ways that seemed to reveal their underlying characters. During one hash-blissed perambulation, Ludlow came upon a little brook that trickles through the Union campus. In his altered state, the brook looked like a mighty river. Filled with awe, he began shouting, "The Nile! The Nile!"

Ludlow downed a "bolus" every day for six months. "Life became with me one prolonged state of hasheesh exaltation," he recalled. His grades suffered, and he was fined $1.12 one semester and $2.40 another for repeatedly missing morning-prayer recitations. (These were not small amounts considering that tuition was then $19 per semester.) Over time, Ludlow also began to have his share of bad experiences while on hashish. Once, he lay curled in his bed as a "hot and hissing whisper" repeatedly urged him, "Kill thyself!" Soon the command was taken up by an infernal chorus, and "unseen tongues syllabled it on all sides and in the air above me." At times, Ludlow felt a piercing, near-cosmic sense of aloneness, as if he'd been banished by God—a terrifying perception for a preacher's son: "Slowly thus does midnight close over the hasheesh-eater's heaven."

Around the time Ludlow graduated from Union, he decided to quit hashish. But no sooner had he sworn off the drug than he began to pine for its effects. He missed the way that hashish animated the world around him. Sober existence was so blasé, "like a heavy tragedy seen for the fortieth time." Ludlow added, "I tried in vain to detect in the landscape that ever-welling freshness of life which hasheesh unveils; trees were meaningless wood, the clouds a vapory sham. I thirsted for insight, adventure, strange surprises, and mystical discoveries."

Ludlow became a heavy tobacco smoker. He tried blowing bubbles and watching the play of rainbow colors over the soapy surface. Both activities proved a sorry substitute for a hashish reverie. Ludlow was so very alone in his experience, suffering from psychedelic drug withdrawal at a time when Sgt. Pepper, logically, could only be a military man, Timothy Leary an Irish gent, and the phrase *turn on* would have been gibberish—people didn't even have electricity.

At the suggestion of a doctor, as a kind of therapy, Ludlow decided to write his unique personal story. In four fevered months, Ludlow hammered out a 365-page manuscript, which he then submitted to Harper & Brothers, one of the most eminent publishers in the United States. They jumped on it, rushing into production with *The Hasheesh Eater: Being Passages from the Life of a Pythagorean*. (The subtitle derives from Ludlow's pet theory that Pythagoras used hashish. Given the ancient Greek thinker's outré ideas, he posited, how could it be otherwise? This is possibly the first instance of a speculative game that has occupied the drug cognoscenti ever since: *To have such perceptions, Shakespeare, Da Vinci, Hieronymus Bosch—fill in the blank—simply must have gotten high.*)

Ludlow's book was one of the publishing sensations of 1857. Sales were strong and, given the subject matter, the reception surprisingly positive. (He was denied entry into the snooty Century Club, but Pfaff's was more his style anyway.) It helped that Ludlow opened his book with assurances that he had used hashish with the object of "research," not "indulgence," signaling that this was no callow tale glorifying drug use. Further, Ludlow's narrative spent ample time on the dark side of hashish—graphically detailing some of his nightmare experiences—and concluded with his decision to quit using the drug.

Predictably, many readers ignored Ludlow's note of caution, taking away a different message: *there's a drug out there that promises a path to enlightenment.* In fact, the publication of Ludlow's book led to something of a fad for hashish. A reporter for the *New York World* ingested the drug and then wrote about his experiences, concluding, "For me, henceforth, Time is but a word." As a student at Brown, John Hay—later Lincoln's personal secretary and secretary of state under Presidents Theodore Roosevelt and William McKinley—was also inspired to try the drug. "*The Hasheesh Eater* had recently appeared (1857)," a classmate reminisced, "and Johnny must needs experiment with hasheesh a little, and see if it was such a marvelous stimulant to the imagination as

Fitzhugh Ludlow affirmed." Hay himself would look back on Brown as a place "where I used to eat Hasheesh and dream dreams."

After getting to know Ludlow, several of the Pfaff's set felt compelled to celebrate hashish, at least in their literary efforts. O'Brien worked the drug into one of his snap-and-its-done short stories, Aldrich wrote a poem called "Hascheesh," and Whitman included allusions in some of his poetry from this time. Given his moderate drinking habits, Whitman in particular is unlikely to have indulged. Always ultrareceptive to societal trends, more likely Whitman used hashish imagery to reflect the current vogue for the drug.

Despite the success of Ludlow's book, he made very little money. *The Hasheesh Eater* went through three printings in rapid succession and sold about five thousand copies. By the terms of his contract, Ludlow earned roughly $500. On becoming a Pfaff's fixture, he was a dirt-poor celebrity—a not-so-unusual combination in nineteenth-century America. At this time, he also got married.

Ludlow's wife was the former Rosalie Osborne. She was eighteen years old and stunning, with dark eyes and delicate features. Rosalie was the kind of woman men couldn't tear their gaze from, lest they miss an instant of the ever-unfolding drama of her beauty. "Her form, the freshly blossomed woman," is how Ludlow described his new bride, "her complexion, marble struck through with rose flush."

To others, however, Ludlow and Rosalie seemed almost comically mismatched. She was far too striking, the poet Aldrich's wife noted, for such a bookish young man. It was an opinion widely and sniggeringly shared by the Pfaff's set. On marrying Ludlow, the boy writing wonder, Rosalie seems to have expected that Manhattan would open up before her. For now, the couple was living in a run-down, $5-a-week rooming house on Clinton Street.

Ludlow contributed short stories and criticism to various magazines, all the while casting about, hoping to find a worthy—and lucrative—follow-up to *The Hasheesh Eater.* The pressure of the New York literary game was immense. George Curtis, an editor at *Harper's,* described Ludlow as "slight, bright-eyed, alert." But there was also something subtly off in his manner. Years later, Curtis stated that he was also sure

that he "recognized in the young man" a thirst for the "peculiar temp-
tations for men of a certain temperament."

By the time he became a Pfaffian, Ludlow had succeeded in kicking
hashish. For the rest of his life, he would resist the drug's pull—or so
he claimed. That may well be true. But what few people knew was that
not long after he arrived in New York, Ludlow began to secretly dabble
in a far more dangerous substance.

Another member of the growing Bohemian set was Edwin Booth, a
talented and troubled young actor. He didn't necessarily hang out at
Pfaff's. But he moved in this same circle and became friends—in some
cases very close friends—with Clapp, Aldrich, Winter, and others.
During the autumn of 1858 he was living in New York City and in the
midst of a colossal drinking binge.

Booth, who turned twenty-five that November, had pale skin and
long curly black hair. His eyes were his most striking feature: deep-
brown irises and startlingly white whites, framed by thick, upturned
lashes. These were arresting eyes, a shared trait of the Booth family,
though Edwin's seemed mostly filled with sorrow. People who knew
him noticed that he never laughed—the closest he came was a wan
smile and slight heaving of his chest.

Booth was born in Maryland, a circumstance that would have a
profound influence on the course of his life. Perhaps the only influence
that loomed larger was his father, the legendary Junius Brutus Booth.

The elder Booth, a short, bow-legged man with a booming voice,
was considered one of America's premier actors in the first part of the
nineteenth century. During this rough-and-tumble theatrical era, ac-
tors toured relentlessly, playing makeshift theaters in tiny towns in
front of audiences who might be sitting on wooden crates, crunching
on peanuts, and hissing and whooping. To hold such crowds, Junius
had perfected what's known as the blood-and-thunder school of acting.
He hammed outrageously, making incredibly broad gestures.

For the duel scene in *Richard III,* his signature role, he'd often chase
the actor playing his rival, Richmond, right off the stage and out into
the street. Before death scenes, Junius would hide a carmine-soaked

sponge in his costume. At the critical moment, he'd slip the sponge into his mouth, bite down, and—red froth bubbling on his lips—flail and lurch, spasm and twitch, before finally lying still. Junius developed a reputation for utterly inhabiting his roles, and on good nights audiences found these performances electric. In his youth, Whitman saw Edwin's father on such an occasion, and he never forgot it. "His genius was to me one of the grandest revelations of my life," the poet would recall, "a lesson of artistic expression."

But there were many, many bad nights. Junius lived his life on a knife-edge between creativity and utter insanity. Drinking—something he did frequently and with gusto—served only to blur the line further. For inexplicable reasons, he once played the role of Julius Caesar entirely on his tiptoes. During a performance of *Hamlet* in Natchez, Mississippi, when the curtain rose for act 5, the crowd was treated to rooster-like crowing coming from the rafters above the stage. Someone had to climb a ladder and convince Junius to rejoin the production. The stories of his erratic behavior were legion, and he came to be known as "crazy Booth the mad tragedian."

Booth sired twelve children—seven survived to maturity. All but one of them lived in a shambling house on a large spread near Bel Air, Maryland. There was one child by a woman other than Edwin's mother, whom Junius also helped support. A whole lot of people were dependent on the mad actor. When Edwin was thirteen, a fateful decision was made: he would accompany his father on the road, keeping him off drink and out of trouble. Edwin dropped out of school, intending to continue his studies on a piecemeal basis while traveling.

Chaperoning his father turned out to be a full-time job, though. Edwin spent hours preparing Junius's elaborate costumes and brushing his wigs. Whenever they'd check into an inn, there would be a constant stream of visitors, many of them enraged—Booth had failed to keep a commitment, say, or maybe he owed the aggrieved party money. Often, Junius hid under the bed, and young Edwin was left to make excuses. Following performances, Junius would be lit up, emotionally, and he'd demand that Edwin play a banjo to calm him so he could drift off to sleep.

Other times, Junius would sneak out of the room, and it fell to Edwin to find him. Edwin knew that a late-night round of nearby taverns would likely turn up his father. On being confronted, however, Junius would really ham it up, making shooing motions with his hands, exchanging glances of puzzlement with the other patrons, pretending for all the world that Edwin was some irritating stranger, not his son. All this took a terrible toll. One of Junius's fellow actors noted that teenage Edwin appeared neglected, exhausted, and filled with anxiety.

Still, there was recompense for this lonely and itinerant life. By spending hours running lines with this father, by watching Junius's every performance from the wings, Edwin received a crash education in acting. Soon he began to appear in plays alongside his father, doing smaller roles, such as Gratiano in the *Merchant of Venice*. By his late teens, Edwin had graduated to major roles. He'd seen these plays countless times; he knew all the lines by heart. Once, he was even a last-minute substitute in the demanding role of King Richard after ever-capricious Junius decided to take a nap right before showtime. Edwin pulled it off, and as the final curtain fell he was met with clamorous applause. The theatrical manager took him by the elbow and led him out to take another bow, announcing to the audience, "You see before you the worthy scion of a noble stock."

When Junius died, Edwin was ready to step in. The circumstances of his passing were fittingly bizarre: While chugging up the Mississippi aboard a steamboat, Junius grew thirsty and impulsively drank a glass of river water, something travelers were vigorously warned against. He became violently ill and died a few days later, on November 30, 1852, age fifty-six. Edwin was now nineteen. He set out on the theatrical circuit alone, playing many of the same houses that his father had. Comparisons between the two were only natural, and smart promotion to boot. A billboard in Chicago is typical: "Come see Edwin Booth, the world's greatest actor, the inheritor of his father's genius!"

For Edwin, however, there would be no carmine-drenched fits. He relied on a new, more naturalistic acting style that was starting to come into fashion. In fact, he would grow to be one of the style's leading lights. Edwin was well suited for a subtler kind of acting. His expressive face—the dark eyes against pale skin—could telegraph minute shifts of emotion, and he was especially good at rendering shades of pain and grief. His voice was soft, but commanding. Onstage, he relied on careful modulation and phrasing to make a scene come alive. Asked to compare his approach to his father's, he once said, "I think I am a little quieter."

But in other ways, Edwin was very much Junius's son. Early in his career, particularly, he had terrible problems with alcohol. "I was neglected in my childhood and thrown into all sorts of temptations and evil society," Edwin would recall. "Before I was eighteen I was a drunkard, at twenty a libertine." Like his father, Edwin was mesmerizing on a good night, mortifying on a bad one. A review from a Sacramento paper of an 1856 performance by Edwin in *The Corsican Brothers* includes the following: "Mr. Booth, who was cast to sustain the principal character, could hardly sustain himself, but he struggled through it, dragging everything down to the depths of disgust. Speaking mildly, he was intoxicated. . . . The audience was indeed small, but a few more such nights will cause it to be even smaller."

The year 1858 found Edwin living in New York City and drinking very hard. In fact, an entire slate of his scheduled performances had to be canceled. Edwin was still many years—and untold emotional distance—from the discipline that would ultimately lead him to be hailed as nineteenth-century America's greatest tragedian.

Among the Bohemian set, Booth became particularly close to Ludlow. Both were in their early twenties; both were considered prodigies. Each had been privy to adult-world decadence at a tender age, though Ludlow actively sought out drugs, where Booth had no say about being thrown into the company of reprobate actors. Ludlow called his friend a "splendid savage," a reference to the fact that this Shakespearean actor had been raised under such deprivation. Booth admired Ludlow's vast erudition (everyone did) and admitted, "I wish I could write as well as he."

Two of Edwin's brothers also went into the family business, acting. As of the late 1850s, his older brother, Junius Jr., was out in California, managing a theater and taking roles in the productions it staged. John Wilkes was only just getting his career under way.

John was five years younger than Edwin. Following their father's death, he'd been left to run amuck on the Maryland homestead, pretty much raising himself in his own eccentric fashion. He became a devotee of Agesilaus, the ancient Spartan king, and took to sleeping on the floor on a painfully hard mattress. On the wall of his bedroom, he mounted a deer's head, and from the antlers he hung swords and daggers, even a rusty blunderbuss. Sometimes, he'd set out on horseback, shouting heroic slogans into the empty woods, while carrying a lance, a gift to his late father from an old soldier who had fought in the Mexican-American War.

Some of John's strongest notions were formed by simple geography, by the fact that the Booths' home was in Maryland. Even in the antebellum era, the state's residents had varied allegiances—some identified with the Northern United States, others with the South. Deep divisions existed on the all-important issue of slavery. As a so-called border state, Maryland would ultimately play it both ways, never seceding, remaining in the Union throughout the Civil War, while maintaining the institution of slavery during the first years of the conflict. The Booth family was itself divided. While hardly an abolitionist, Junius had been opposed to slavery, and Edwin shared this view. But John—owing partly to the fact that he attended school with the sons of some plantation owners—grew deeply enamored of the idea of Southern aristocracy and was an avid defender of slavery.

While Edwin tried to make it in New York, John was getting his career started in Richmond, Virginia. He joined the Marshall Theatre company. As he told his sister, Asia Booth, he aimed to establish himself as a Southern actor, and she perceived that he "wanted to be loved of the Southern people above all things." But on another occasion, he revealed what was perhaps his heart's truest desire, his deepest calling: "I must have fame, fame!"

John shared the Booth trait: those dark eyes. While Edwin was extremely charismatic, John was considered more handsome. He was also viewed as the inferior actor, with a style very different from Edwin's. He was more of a classic scenery chewer. When John played Hamlet, it was duly noted, there was no subtlety, no sense of progression: the prince was a raving madman from the moment the curtain rose. Clara Morris, an actress who worked with both brothers, once offered this comparison: "There was that touch of—strangeness. In Edwin it was profound melancholy; in John it was an exaggeration of spirit—almost a wildness."

And so it was, that—on a whim—John abandoned his troupe at the Marshall Theatre in the middle of a run of *Smike,* a dramatization of the Dickens novel *Nicholas Nickleby.* The reason: he had just learned about the capture of John Brown. He took up with a militia that planned to guard Brown until he could be tried for treason and executed.

In what was perhaps the defining event of the Fiery Fifties, Brown—avenging abolitionist to some, bloodthirsty lunatic to others—had led a raid on a federal armory at Harpers Ferry, Virginia, in an attempt to seize a large cache of weapons. He planned to distribute them to slaves in the hopes of fomenting an armed insurrection in the South. A force led by Colonel Robert E. Lee captured Brown, but not before ten of the raiders were killed, along with a US Marine and six civilians. Brown, age fifty-nine, tall and lean with a shock of white hair and that Old Testament beard, was placed under heavy guard at a jail in Charlestown, Virginia. From his cell, Brown composed the note that contained his last words: "I John Brown am now quite *certain* that the crimes of this *guilty, land: will* never be purged *away*; but with Blood."

Upon arriving in Charlestown, amid all the commotion, John did little more than mill around. He wore a borrowed uniform, but had brought along his own pistol and knife. He camped and cooked, and at night he entertained his fellow militiamen by reciting Shakespeare. On December 2, 1859, he looked on as Brown was hung at the scaffold. Then John Wilkes Booth returned to Richmond and resumed his acting career.

Meanwhile, back at Pfaff's, Clapp continued to build an American Bo-
hemia. There was Whitman, of course. Still unemployed, he was just
barely scraping by. "Poor Walt!" he would recall of this period in his
life. "Poor most everybody! Always hard up!" In lieu of money, how-
ever, he was luxuriating in time, having attained a kind of temporal
wealth. He had time enough to hang out at Pfaff's and ample time left
over in which to write.

As a consequence, Whitman was now in the midst of another cre-
ative cloudburst, the equal of the one that had produced the first edi-
tion of *Leaves of Grass*. He was working on a number of new poems. As
yet, he wasn't submitting any of them for publication. Whenever the
mood proved placid and conducive, however, he continued to read his
poems in progress to the assembled artists.

Besides Whitman, there was no telling who else might show up at
Pfaff's. That was part of the fun, the intrigue. These were Bohemians,
after all—things were free and loose, and the crowd varied from one
night to the next. Sometimes O'Brien and Arnold were there, some-
times Ludlow and Aldrich. Other regulars in the saloon's early days in-
cluded sculptor Launt Thompson, playwright Ned Wilkins, and Count
Adam de Gurowski, an eccentric, one-eyed Polish nobleman in exile.

Clapp, an editor by both trade and temperament, applied his nat-
ural gifts to the composition of his table, constantly fiddling with the
mix. He was forever driving away Bohemian hopefuls with cruel jibes
so as to make room for writers and artists he held in greater esteem.
He could be ruthless, but it was in service to an ideal—the perfect
combination of clever drunken revelers. On any given night, one was
guaranteed to meet some interesting men at Clapp's long table.

CHAPTER 5

Bold Women and Whitman's Beautiful Boys

ALSO WOMEN. One of the notable things about Pfaff's was that the saloon welcomed them at a time when American society was extremely segregated by gender.

During the 1850s, there were considerable constraints regarding where a woman could go in public. A proper woman could accompany her husband or a serious beau to a church social or to an institution of betterment such as a library or museum. She could go for a stroll along a promenade, maybe take in an evening at the opera. But a woman who was unaccompanied by a man had to be very careful, lest she convey the wrong impression. A lone woman out on the town raised questions, invited suspicion. In fact, there's a term from this era that says it all: prostitutes were commonly called "public women."

To avoid even the appearance of impropriety, to stave off unwanted advances from men, women frequently went on outings in groups. Many American cities accommodated this custom by providing spots exclusively for women. New York featured an array of these places, such as the Ladies' Reading Room, Ladies' Oyster Shop, and Ladies' Bowling Alley. There was even a large women-only eatery on Broadway called Taylor's, which fed three thousand female customers on an average day in the 1850s. It was "the restaurant of the age," said the *New York Herald*. When Central Park opened in 1858, a separate section of the lake was set aside for unaccompanied women who wished to ice skate in peace.

There were also public institutions that were decidedly male domains—taverns chief among them. McSorley's, a legendary Manhattan watering hole and contemporary of Pfaff's (it opened in 1854), had the slogan "Good Ale, Raw Onions, and No Ladies." It wasn't as though women didn't drink. Rather, they had their own conventions in this gender-split society. Often, they consumed alcohol as the active ingredient in tonics and patent medicines, touted as mood elevators or means to calm frazzled nerves. Or a woman might purchase a "growler," an ale-to-go that could be consumed in the privacy of her own home. To order a growler, a woman would enter a saloon via a separate doorway, if possible. A lady's entrance was a common feature of drinking establishments of the time. That way, a respectable woman could be spared the embarrassment of walking through the barroom proper and being subjected to stares and lewd comments.

But Herr Pfaff hailed from Europe, where different rules applied. He was also a smart businessman, who recognized an opportunity in catering to females, especially in populous Manhattan, where there were many different kinds of people, not all of them slavishly devoted to the prevailing mores of the day. Even in the 1850s, in other words, there were women who were happy to hang out in a bar. Pfaff's was their place.

As for Clapp, he was simply a man ahead of his time. In his youth, he'd become an esteemed lecturer on issues such as temperance and abolitionism, but also women's rights. Nearly a century before the passage of the Nineteenth Amendment, Clapp had been an advocate of women's suffrage. Of course, he'd also had his own taste of European mores, visiting Bohemian Paris and hanging out in cafés where the sexes freely mingled. There, Clapp had spent time with women such as Octavie, enchanted by their conversational skills. No surprise, then, that when it came to assembling his coterie, Clapp was keen to include women. Unlike so many of his contemporaries, he respected women, considered them his equals—provided they could match wits with him. Once, Clapp even took a swipe at the *Nation* magazine, calling it "Stag-Nation"—a well-aimed jab that, among other things, captured the fact that in those days the publication had male contributors, almost exclusively.

One of the women who found a place at Clapp's table was Ada Clare. Clare was born into a wealthy cotton dynasty that traced its Charleston, South Carolina, lineage back to the years before the Revolutionary War. Her given name was Ada Agnes McElhenney, and her family was related to some of the South's most distinguished figures. She was a grandniece of Robert Hayne, a senator from South Carolina during the 1820s and 1830s. She was a distant relative of John Calhoun, one of the most outspoken advocates of states' rights and slavery in the antebellum period.

When Clare was still a young girl, both her parents died from illnesses, succumbing only a few years apart. She was raised by her grandparents. Every effort was made to prepare her to be a proper planter's wife. The fine points of etiquette were ceaselessly drummed into her. To quell her appetite and keep herself slim, Clare was urged to drink a glass of vinegar in the morning. In the presence of eligible young gentlemen, Clare was encouraged to be mostly silent, restricting herself to a supportive laugh or a coquettish glance. None of this really took. By her teen years, she considered herself a "spirituelle," a term often used (before the advent of *Bohemian*) to describe a woman who led a free and easy life in pursuit of art. Already, she longed to escape a future that threatened to be, as she put it, "a series of little acts, a dead level of vapid monotony."

At twenty, Clare set off for New York City to try to make it as an actress. In the eyes of her respectable southern family, there was shame enough in the choice. But she managed to pile on further scandal by stealing a private fund her relations had raised, earmarked for a monument to recently deceased John Calhoun. She used the money to get settled in Manhattan (and would later pay back the sum with interest). Around this time, she also transformed from Ada McElhenney into Ada Clare. The latter struck her as a fitting stage name, easier to remember and easier to pronounce than her given name. "Ada Clare" also happens to be a character in Dickens's novel *Bleak House*. The fictional Clare is an orphan, something her real-life counterpart saw as a meaningful parallel, since she had first lost her parents and then broken with the values of her South Carolina upbringing.

Her acting career did not get off to a good start. Clare was petite and had a lovely voice, mellifluous with a pronounced southern lilt. But unlike an Edwin Booth, say, she was unable to project. On a nineteenth-century stage, she simply came across as a petite woman with a weak voice. For one of Clare's first roles, Ophelia in *Hamlet,* a critic rated her performance as "passable." Clare made far quicker inroads as a writer. (Along with Whitman, the poet/wander-speaker, many at Pfaff's had dual aspirations, a hedge against the uncertainty of the artist's life.) Clare became a frequent contributor of essays and verse to the *New-York Atlas,* a widely read Sunday-only newspaper. Upon publication of her work, "Lines to ___," an *Atlas* editor sent her a note, praising it as "one of the most beautiful poems in the language."

At Pfaff's, Clare brought a needed touch of refinement to the proceedings. She organized "common-purse" suppers, at which impoverished artists pooled their money to buy a decent shared meal. And she always made a point of remembering the birthdays of the members of the circle. Clare acted as a kind of counterweight to Clapp's "evil influences," as one Pfaffian put it. Soon she was given a title of her own, Queen of Bohemia.

As queen, however, she could be equally as fierce and uncompromising as King Clapp. Clare was a sparkling conversationalist, who placed a high value on spontaneity. She had a particular aversion to canned jokes, which she called "a tyrant and slayer of conversation." She once described herself as having "a frankness of speech and manners with men, a talent to dress becomingly, a good appetite, a cheerful expression, an acquaintance with rouge, an aversion to lying, and the ability to think for myself!"

Clare was very striking. Upon sitting down at Clapp's table, it was duly noted that she always chose a place where she'd be flatteringly illuminated by a gas lamp. She wore her blonde hair in a way that was highly idiosyncratic for the time: short and parted to the side, like a man. The hairstyle combined with her small stature gave Clare a pixie-ish look. She had wide-set blue eyes and a pointed nose, once described as the "right nose for a trim little person with a past."

The *with a past* is a reference to one of the most notable—and for the time shocking—things about Clare: she was raising a child who was born out of wedlock. The father was believed to be Louis Moreau Gottschalk, a man with whom she had carried on a torrid affair. Gottschalk was a New Orleans–born pianist, noted for working American idioms such as slave spirituals and folk songs into his compositions. During the 1850s, he became an international celebrity, the first American composer to achieve a stature to rival a Liszt or a Verdi.

Gottschalk was darkly handsome and had a world-weary Lord Byron manner that drove women to distraction. Supposedly, a crazed female piano devotee kidnapped him after a concert in Switzerland and held him captive for five weeks, a love slave. That was part of the Gottschalk myth. But Gottschalk's reality may not have lagged too far behind. His diaries are full of entries such as this: "an amiable audience warm, intelligent, elegant, the majority composed of young girls whose charming physiognomies are made to turn the heads of pianists!" Or this: "the most charming types of young women that ever crossed the dreams of an old bachelor" were visible as he scanned a different audience while playing his piano.

Clare kept the details of her fling with Gottschalk a closely guarded secret. But a likely result was her son, named Aubrey. While out in public with Aubrey, she relished shocking people by introducing herself as "Miss Ada Clare and son." Her meaning was instantly and provocatively clear: she had a child, but a missus she was not. Aubrey was by this time a toddler. Clare always had to arrange for a babysitter before going to Pfaff's.

A number of other women also became part of the Bohemian circle at Pfaff's. Among them were journalist Jenny Danforth; Marie Stevens Case, a novelist and French translator; and Dora Shaw, an actress and poet.

Inspired by Ludlow's infamous book, Stevens Case and Shaw once ate hashish together. The two women slipped into a shared hallucinogenic state in which everything took on a sinister ancient Egyptian pall. Stevens Case had the sensation that her head was growing and growing; she was turning into a giant stone Sphinx. "I thought I was an oracle, doomed to respond through all Eternity," she reported. Shaw, convinced that they had been bitten by an asp, à la Cleopatra, kept shrieking: "We are poisoned! We are poisoned!" In modern parlance, the women had a bad trip. They never ate hashish again.

That little alcove room also kindled its share of dalliances. O'Brien paired off for a time with Jenny Danforth. During a brief separation, she sent him a letter in which she commanded: "Remember me while I am away. Come when I return." Given his well-known penchant for alcohol, she added, "Be good. And let the festive cup alone." Instead, she urged him, "Drink me silently."

Clapp, meanwhile, took a romantic interest in Ada Clare, a development that was carefully observed by the other Bohemians at the long table. She was queen to his king, after all. She did not, however, return the sentiment. When Clapp was pursuer rather than the pursued, he could transform from a snapping turtle into a puppy dog. So it was with Clare. He settled into an uneasy role as her friend and protector. If someone made a disparaging comment about her out-of-wedlock child, Clapp would invariably pipe in with, "It was an immaculate conception." No doubt, this was wishful thinking on his part. Given Clare's aversion to canned humor, she surely grew tired of this line.

And then there's the outrageously charismatic woman who first became a fixture at Pfaff's in the summer of 1859. Clare gets credit for introducing her into the Bohemian circle. This latest addition was an actress whom Clare had met while making the rounds of auditions. Among Clapp's set, she would soon earn the distinction as the wildest, most brazen, and most colorful. Given the volume of personality in the vaulted room, that's saying a lot. Underneath it all, the newest Pfaffian was also a deeply vulnerable person. Nothing was ever simple, nothing ever straightforward, about Adah Isaacs Menken.

On first arriving at Pfaff's, she no doubt had a different story for every single person at that long table. She was a self-mythologizer par excellence, who, with complete abandon, spun out assorted and conflicting fantastical stories about her life: *She was born Dolores Adios Los Fuertes, the offspring of Spanish royalty. She was the granddaughter of a Revolutionary War hero. She was raised an orphan in a convent in Rome and escaped by climbing over the wall. She translated the "Iliad" into French at the age of twelve. She was the adopted daughter of Sam Houston.* An 1860 profile in the *Wisconsin Daily Patriot* guilelessly relays some of her questionable claims: "She speaks French, Spanish, and English; can ride, hunt, shoot, dance, and act; has been taken prisoner by the Indians; has learned the art of war from Gen. Harney."

About Menken's earliest years, precious little is known with any degree of certainty. Her name at birth may have been Ada Berthe Théodore. It most certainly was *not,* as she was fond of claiming, Marie Rachel Adelaide de Vere Spenser. No question, she was a young woman in her Pfaff's days. As to her exact age—who knows? (No birth certificate has ever been located.) June 15, 1835, is considered her birth date, by tradition, and because it's the one most commonly professed by Menken herself. That would mean she turned twenty-four in 1859, the year she showed up at Pfaff's. She may have been born in Milneburg, once a town on the shores of Lake Pontchartrain, subsequently absorbed into the city of New Orleans.

It seems likely that she was the child of a mixed-race couple. Maybe her father was African American, or perhaps it was her mother. Possibly one parent was Irish—on the issue of ethnicity, the details are hazy once again. On this matter, however, there was also a sound, logical reason for Menken to keep things vague. This was an era when interracial children faced intense stigma, along with questions (varying from region to region) about whether they were free citizens or by legal status potential slaves. A bizarre and highly specific nomenclature existed, featuring terms such as *mulatto* (one black parent, one white parent), *quadroon* (one-fourth black heritage), and *sambo* (a heritage more black than white).

Menken made her first stage appearance as a teenage chorus girl at the French Opera House in New Orleans. She joined the troupe, she would later say, to help support her family, which had slipped into poverty. Then, in the early 1850s, she took up as a bareback rider with Victor Franconi's Imperial Hippodrome, a circus that toured through Texas. This was an extremely challenging gig, requiring her to strike acrobatic poses on a moving horse. For the circus stint, at least, there's some support, including the recollection of someone who saw her perform. (As her life progresses, Menken's story—while remaining crazily colorful—also becomes documentable.)

In 1856, she married Alexander Isaac Menken, scion of a well-to-do Jewish family. He was conducting an orchestra in Galveston, Texas. He started out as her voice teacher, but things quickly turned romantic. What he almost certainly did not know: his new wife had already been married once before to Nelson Kneass, a member of a minstrel group called the New Orleans Serenaders. That marriage lasted only a few months, and she had left without even bothering to get a divorce. Alexander Menken and his new bride stayed on in Texas for a while. Soon enough, the family dry goods business beckoned, and the couple moved to his hometown of Cincinnati.

During the mid-nineteenth century, Cincinnati was the center for Reform Judaism in the United States. This was due to Queen City resident Rabbi Isaac Wise, leader of the movement in America. Wise was also the editor of a highly influential newspaper called the *Israelite*. It helped connect American Jews, many of them living in small groups that were greatly isolated geographically one from the next. Rabbi Wise's newspaper kept them informed on matters of doctrine and faith. The paper also featured notices in which Jewish communities in various cities advertised for people to play vital religious roles. Memphis's Congregation B'nai Israel, for example, placed a notice searching for a rabbi and also for a kosher butcher.

Upon settling in Cincinnati, Menken—master of reinvention—embraced Judaism with a rare fervor. (She would often maintain that she was born Jewish, as opposed to having adopted her second husband's faith.) She started to contribute poems to the *Israelite*. Her poems tend to have rather obvious, basic titles such as "Sinai" and "Moses." And the versifying is far from inspired.

Will He *never come?* Will the Jew,
  In exile eternally pine?
By the idolaters scorned, pitied only by few,
Will he never his vows to JEHOVAH renew,
  Beneath his own olive and vine?

"She is a sensitive poet who, unfortunately, cannot write," Charles Dickens would one day remark. (Menken was destined to travel in some rarefied circles.) But though her poetry was rather prosaic, some of her work did at least manage to address vital concerns of the time such as the discrimination faced by Jews in the Ottoman Empire. As an added touch, she assigned many of her poems dates from the Hebrew calendar such as 11. Tishri 5618 (September 29, 1857).

Menken longed to return to the stage. Apparently, this became the source of considerable marital tension. Alexander Menken liked the idea of a steadfast wife, who regularly contributed verse to an esteemed religious publication. Eventually, she wore him down. She began to perform at theaters around Ohio in cities such Cincinnati and Dayton. However, the more she acted, the harder he drank. He seems to have realized she was going to be difficult to hang on to. Acting—with its odd hours and opportunities to meet strange men—promised to hasten the process. Ultimately, the couple would get divorced. She walked away with only one thing: a stage name. By tacking on an *h,* Ada became Adah. And by adding an *s* to Isaac (her ex's middle name), her new full name had a more harmonious flow. Now, and through three subsequent marriages, she would forever and always be known as Adah Isaacs Menken.

As an actress, Menken lacked the traditional skills of the trade. She wasn't collaborative, didn't really care to play off her fellow thespians. She certainly lacked the subtlety of acting's new, naturalistic school. Menken was already a character. She had devoted her considerable talent and intelligence to creating herself—in real life. Exploring other characters, well, that held less interest. But Menken possessed a couple of formidable theatrical attributes that entirely compensated for whatever she lacked. She was absolutely fearless. And she had a drop-dead sexiness that projected deep into the cheap seats. By modern standards, Menken might be described as zaftig. To a nineteenth-century eye, she was alluringly, almost excruciatingly, curvaceous. "Adah was a symbol of Desire Awakened to every man who set eyes on her," according to one of her husbands. "All who saw her wanted her immediately."

James Murdoch, one of the era's finest actors, offers the following description of Menken's approach to stagecraft, such as it was: "A woman of personal attractions, she made herself a great favorite. . . . She dashed at everything in tragedy and comedy with a reckless disregard of consequences, until at length, with some degree of trepidation, she paused before the character of Lady Macbeth!"

Through steely ambition worthy of Lady M herself, Menken managed to land that plum role in an 1858 production staged in Nashville. She starred opposite the great Murdoch. This was a fast-and-loose era in American theater; skilled actors were expected simply to know certain popular roles, such as teenage Edwin Booth stepping in as King Richard III. Often productions were mounted on short notice with few or even no rehearsals. That's one reason Shakespeare was so popular. It was part of a shared repertoire.

Only a few hours before the play was set to open, Menken approached Murdoch, sheepishly revealing that she didn't know her lines. She begged him to teach her, and he did his best to prepare his co-star.

When the curtain rose, however, Menken's mind went blank. So she simply shadowed Murdoch, standing very close to him throughout the play. He fed Menken her lines in a whisper. For Lady Macbeth's soliloquies, once Menken got rolling, she simply improvised. According to Murdoch, "She poured out such an apostrophe to guilt, demons, and her own dark purposes that it would have puzzled any one acquainted with the text to guess from what unlimited 'variorum' she could have studied the part." A Nashville paper described Menken's Lady Macbeth as "full of southern passion," but "devoid of Shakespeare or, for that matter, any known playwright." The audience, however, met her performance with clamorous applause.

Menken was wise enough to quit while she was ahead. She would never again attempt Shakespeare. Upon moving to New York, she concentrated instead on so-called protean comedies. These were better suited to her particular skills. Protean comedies were a type of drama, popular at this time, where actors demonstrated versatility by playing a large number of different roles. The plots fell somewhere between broad and nonexistent; for audiences, the pleasure lay in watching rapid-fire character changes. An actor might play a dandy, then a lady, then a doctor, and so on. Menken starred in such protean standbys as *The Little Corporal* and *Satan in Paris*. Sometimes, she was called upon to do as many as nine costume changes in a single play. It helped that Menken looked fetching, whether dressed as a nurse or as a filthy street urchin.

At Pfaff's, Menken and Clare became close friends. Both hailed from the South, and they were close in age. Menken's supposed birth date made her one year younger. They formed a kind of mutual-admiration duo. Menken aspired to be like Clare, an effervescent wit, taken seriously as a writer. Clare could only dream of having Menken's magic onstage. While the men puffed their pipes, in obeisance to King Clapp, Menken and Clare enjoyed smoking cigarettes together at Pfaff's, a verboten activity for proper women. Menken, following Clare's lead, even cut her black hair short and parted it like a man. Given Menken's figure, however, the effect was very different.

Of course, the two women also shared the same first name, though Menken had added an *h* to the end of hers. (Ada was a fairly popular name in the mid-1800s; Ada Clifton, also an actress, was an occasional visitor to Pfaff's.)

Whitman became very partial to Menken and Clare. Clapp would remain his primary ally in the circle, but he also valued Ada and Adah, once saying of them, "The girls have been my sturdiest defenders, upholders." Pure Whitman: he was forever sizing up fellow artists by the measure of whether *they* held *him* in sufficient esteem. But he also felt genuine affection for Menken and Clare—they weren't merely two women who had his back. And he truly enjoyed talking with

Clare—quite a tribute. Despite his efforts to remain above the con-
versational fray at Pfaff's, he was drawn in by Clare's easy, graceful
manner. He made a point of sitting by Queen Clare at the table and
once described her as having "no inconsiderable share of intellect and
cultivation."

Still, there was only so long he could keep up the banter. Soon
enough, he was guaranteed to lapse back into silence. Whitman was
a hard man to fathom. His manner was laconic, often he was nearly
mute, yet he managed to emanate a sense of vastness—a vastness of
experience. One of the things the Pfaff's set noticed was that he kept
the pieces of his life (people too) in separate compartments.

During the late 1850s, he could be found at the saloon nearly every
night. When he sat down to Clapp's table, he was guaranteed to be
the honored guest, or, as one account aptly put it, Whitman was "the
shrine to which Clapp led the faithful." But here's the thing: Whitman
may have been a regular at Pfaff's, but he was not always at Clapp's
table. That vaunted vaulted room, crackling with intellectual tension,
was tight-packed, almost claustrophobic. Beyond it lay an ample sub-
terranean space, dim lit and expansive, with other reaches to explore.
"There was no formality—'Bohemia' sat around in groups," Whitman
once observed of Pfaff's. " . . . In fact, a portion of that 'Bohemia' did
not recognize another portion of visitors as 'Bohemians.' It took hard
work and merit to have full membership."

Whitman sought full membership. As it happened, Pfaff's main
room was a gathering place for other types and stripes of Bohemian.
Though these patrons were not members of Clapp's official and vigor-
ously curated Bohemian circle, they had been drawn to Herr Pfaff's es-
tablishment for the same reason: the wild and welcoming atmosphere.
Among the denizens of the saloon's larger room were assorted rebels
and societal outliers, including plenty of gay men. Pfaff's was a place
where gay men could meet, in an era when such matters were not so
clearly defined and delineated.

Café Lafitte in Exile, a fixture in the New Orleans French Quarter
since 1953, touts itself as "America's Oldest Gay Bar." There are other

claimants to the title, such as Seattle's Double Header, which opened in 1933. Perhaps the honor rightly belongs to Pfaff's, an establishment from a whole other century. Given its two separate rooms and diverse clientele, however, Pfaff's is actually a semigay bar. What's more, *gay* meant "lighthearted" in the 1850s. Even the term *homosexual* wouldn't come into wide usage for another thirty years.

During its time, then, Pfaff's might best be described as a "semi-adhesive bar," though that doesn't exactly roll off the tongue. In the quirky language of phrenology, "adhesiveness" was the capacity for intense and meaningful same-sex friendship. Its symbol was two women embracing. By contrast, "amativeness" referred to romantic love between a man and a woman. Whitman, who took great pride in his phrenological reading, received one of his highest scores for adhesiveness. (He rated a 6.) Whitman loved to twist words and phrases, appropriating them, lending them new meaning. In his poetry, he employed a number of coded terms for passionate attachments among men such as "comrades" and "adhesiveness."

When Whitman first started going to Pfaff's, he was in a serious relationship with a man named Fred Vaughan. Often, he and Vaughan would sit together at a table in Pfaff's other, larger, room. Vaughan was in his early twenties, nearly two decades younger than Whitman. He was of Irish descent and worked as a stage driver. It appears the two men even lived together for a time on Classon Avenue in Brooklyn. During that giddy stretch when Whitman walked around with Emerson's letter burning a hole in his pocket, one of the people he showed it to was Vaughan.

Not long after the couple began going to Pfaff's, however, their relationship started to sour for reasons that are unclear. It's possible their problems stemmed from the fact that Vaughan had reached an age when he was expected to find a proper mate, that is, a woman. Vaughan ended up getting married and settled into a rather conventional life. He worked a series of jobs such as insurance salesman and elevator operator and with his wife raised four sons. He also became a terrible alcoholic. In the early 1870s, after roughly a decade of silence,

Vaughan reconnected with Whitman, writing him several letters, one of which includes the following heart-rending passage: "I never stole, robbed, cheated, nor defrauded any person out of anything, and yet I feel that I have not been honest to myself—my family nor my friends." In the letters, Vaughan never spells out the source of his anguish. Perhaps it was the result of living in a state that felt unnatural to him. One letter includes, "My love my Walt is with you always."

Even as his relationship with Vaughan faltered, Whitman continued to visit the larger room at Pfaff's. Here, Whitman spent time in the company of a group of young men that included Fred Gray, son of a prominent New York doctor; Hugo Fritsch, son of the Austrian consul; and Nathaniel Bloom, a cart driver. Whitman described them as "beautiful" and credited this circle with providing the "quiet lambent electricity of real friendship." He addressed them as "my darlings and gossips" and "my darling, dearest boys."

It's striking how different Whitman's manner was with this group of men. One can scarcely imagine him using words such as *darling* or *gossip* at the long table in that vaulted room. As everyone does, Whitman revealed different sides of himself to different kinds of people. The two sections of Pfaff's appear to have served separate social needs for Whitman—as a poet and as a gay man. Where Clapp's circle offered artistic fellowship, albeit met by Whitman with much standoffishness, the poet showed a warmer, more playful side to his beautiful boys.

Even the act of traveling to and from Pfaff's provided an opportunity for Whitman to meet men. It was, after all, a six-mile round-trip from his Brooklyn home, requiring a variety of different conveyances. All along the way—while walking, riding in coaches, and aboard ferries—Whitman encountered men, all different kinds. But he was especially drawn to workingmen such as stage drivers. Edward Carpenter, a friend of Whitman's during his later years, once described the poet's tastes, saying "the unconscious, uncultured, natural types pleased him best, and he would make an effort to approach them."

Whitman's notebooks are filled with brief descriptions of the men he encountered, often during his ambles to and from Pfaff's:

Tom Egbert, conductor Myrtle av. open neck, sailor looking

Mark Graynor, young, 5 ft. 7 in, black mustache, plumber

Saturday night Mike Ellis—wandering at the cor of Lexington av. & 32d st.—took him home to 150 37th street,—4th story back room—bitter cold night—works in Stevenson's Carriage factory.

Dan'l Spencer . . . somewhat feminine—5th av (44) (May 29)—told me he had never been in a fight and did not drink at all . . . slept with me Sept 3d.

A failed romance. A restless sense of longing. As it's always been, these are raw ingredients that get mulled, weighed, processed—and ultimately transformed into art.

CHAPTER 6

The Saturday Press

POETS, JOURNALISTS, ACTRESSES, and a gifted hashish eater: Clapp had assembled quite a collection of talented eccentrics. But he wasn't content merely to preside over an artists' circle. As it happened, Clapp had a ready means for extending his reach. He was founder and editor of a journal called the *Saturday Press*. During its brief, impecunious existence, it would become one of the most influential publications in America.

The *SP* was a weekly journal devoted to culture and the arts. It was also a showcase for work by members of the Pfaff's set. American Bohemianism had been born in a basement saloon. But Clapp's journal brought the movement out into the light, revealing it to a curious world. Thanks to the *SP*, the Pfaff's Bohemians even achieved a moment of cultural zeitgeist. Most significant, perhaps, the *Saturday Press* played a major role in rescuing Walt Whitman from anonymity, helping establish him as a poet for the ages. (Clapp—an editor with brilliant instincts—would revive his journal in 1865 for a handful of issues, once again achieving an impressive, outsize impact.)

The debut issue of the *SP* is dated October 23, 1858. To start up the venture, Edward Howland, a friend of Clapp's, sold his personal collection of rare books, netting $1,000. It wasn't much, but it qualified Howland as the *SP*'s initial "investor." Thomas Aldrich, the poet who crafted the line "We were all very merry at Pfaff's," served as Clapp's deputy editor. The journal occupied a small, dingy office in a nondescript building at 9 Spruce Street in Manhattan, directly behind the headquarters of the *New York Tribune*. Clapp referred to Horace Greeley's *Tribune* as being "next door to the *Saturday Press* building."

While the *SP*'s offices were humble, Clapp was not. On returning to America from Paris, he had abandoned New England for New York, certain that the latter would provide more fertile soil for growing a Bohemian movement. Clapp held an enduring grudge against New England, blaming the region for an upbringing that he considered too earnest, too reverent, too narrow. Upon creating his journal, he was eager not only to poke fun at the region, but also to challenge the cultural primacy of Boston.

By the late 1850s, New York's population had just topped a million, making it five times the size of Boston. Teeming and hectic, New York was America's commerce center, yet to a great degree Boston remained the nation's cultural capital, often referred to in those days as the "American Athens." The city looked the part; during the 1850s, Boston went on a neoclassical jag, raising a series of stately Doric-columned buildings. But its eminence went much deeper than appearance. Boston was home to Harvard, the country's first university. The Boston Public Library, opened in 1854, was the world's first free municipal public library. The city's Handel and Haydn Society scored coup after coup, presenting the US premieres of everything from the *Messiah* to works by Bach and Mozart.

When it came to so-called high culture, Boston reigned supreme. New York had its share of book publishers, but Boston was the seat of such high-tone houses as J. P. Jewett, which issued the abolitionist masterwork *Uncle Tom's Cabin,* and Ticknor & Fields, official American publishers (they paid foreign authors, rather than pirating their work) of Dickens and Tennyson. New York had its share of writers, but most of the real forces in American letters lived within a day's carriage ride of the Massachusetts State House. While simply walking around Boston, San Francisco writer Bret Harte once quipped, "It was impossible to fire a revolver without bringing down the author of a two-volume work."

Boston also had the *Atlantic Monthly*. The magazine debuted in 1857, only one year—no coincidence here—before Clapp launched the

Saturday Press. The *Atlantic* was "born mature," in the words of cultural historian Van Wyck Brooks. The inaugural issue alone contained work by Oliver Wendell Holmes, Harriet Beecher Stowe, Emerson, and Longfellow. James Russell Lowell, the *Atlantic's* editor, contributed a short poem, a sonnet, and an essay to that first number. An article about the Panic of '57, by New York–based writer Parke Godwin, was the sole contribution by a non–New Englander. This would prove an enduring pattern: over its first fifteen years of existence, according to one count, two-thirds of its pieces were the work of New England writers.

It's hard to imagine two publications more opposite in temperament than the *Atlantic* and the *SP.* The *Atlantic's* editorial meetings were often held at the elegant Revere House. For one such meeting, Stowe, a temperance advocate, requested that no alcohol be served. According to T. W. Higginson, a frequent contributor, "conversation set in, but there was a visible awkwardness. . . . The thawing influence of wine was wanting." By contrast, the *SP's* raucous editorial meetings were often held at Pfaff's, the journal's spiritual home. For meetings at the Spruce Street office, Clapp often lugged a bucket of beer from Pfaff's. He published a manuscript submissions guideline in the *SP,* stating that he was "firm but courteous in accepting drinks and declining articles."

The *Atlantic's* first issue included a kind of mission statement, asserting, among other things, that the magazine "will not rank itself with any sect of anties." In other words, it aimed to be sober, balanced, above the fray. By contrast, Clapp was all about *anties.* Here's a description of Clapp, courtesy of William Winter, who served for a time as a subeditor at the *SP:* "He was brilliant and buoyant in mind; impatient of the commonplace; intolerant of smug, ponderous, empty, obstructive respectability; prone to sarcasm; and he had for so long a time lived in a continuous, bitter conflict with conventionality that he had become reckless of public opinion. His delight was to shock the commonplace mind and to sting the hide of the Pharisee with the barb of satire."

When the opportunity came to start a journal, Clapp formed it in his image. According to Junius Henri Browne, a contemporary New

York writer who did not contribute to the *SP*, the journal "often spar-
kled with wit, and always shocked the orthodox with its irreverence and
'dangerous' opinions."

The *SP* sold for five cents an issue (two dollars for a year's subscrip-
tion) and featured essays and arts criticism as well as poetry and the
occasional work of fiction. Heavily represented in the editorial mix
were pieces written by the Pfaffians, prompting the *Philadelphia Ex-
press* to dub the journal "the organ of Bohemia." O'Brien, for exam-
ple, acted as the *SP*'s first drama critic, a gig that—like most of his
gigs—held his focus for only a few issues before he failed to turn in a
column that was due and then quit altogether. But first, he managed
to review his own 1854 play, *A Gentleman from Ireland,* then in revival
at Wallack's Theatre. "I had not seen it played for a couple of years,"
he explained, "and I think viewed it from as impartial a point of view
as any dramatic critic in the city." O'Brien then proceeded to pan his
own work: "I discovered that it is not a comedy, although announced
to be such. It is simply a sort of farce in two acts. The dialogue is
sometimes smart, but never witty, while occasionally it rises into the
realms of fustian. The ending of the first act is weak and nonsensical.
There is no characterization in it from beginning to end, and every-
body talks like everybody else."

During his brief *SP* tenure, O'Brien also reviewed a production of
Hamlet—from a distinctly Pfaffian perspective. Had Hamlet not been
a nobleman, had he not been wealthy and privileged, O'Brien contends
that the "prince would most undoubtedly have been a Bohemian."
O'Brien then proceeds to catalog the Dane's supposed Bohemian at-
tributes, such as "Hamlet was at times a roysterer," and "he is famil-
iar with the carousal and the wassail . . . the wild revel, the midnight
debauch," adding that he "has a stupendous contempt for all kinds of
sham and humbug."

Indeed, the *SP* devoted ample space in every issue to Bohemianism
itself: defining, defending, celebrating, and mythologizing the move-
ment. This was necessary. The word *Bohemian* hadn't yet appeared in
Webster's or other dictionaries. As of the late 1850s, an American was

most likely to encounter this still exotic term, say, when reading Balzac in translation. Clapp worked tirelessly, pushing *Bohemian* into popular usage in American English, scattering its tenets far and wide.

The *SP* was the vehicle. Sometimes, the journal acted almost like a primer, covering the subject in simple, easily digestible ways. It offered a poem by James Hammond, "Ode to a Tobacco Pipe," which extols the pleasures of one of Clapp's favorite indulgences. It published George Arnold's poem "Beer," quickly knocked off at Pfaff's during a drunken reverie. An essay signed only with the initials D. D. and entitled "Bohemia" simply wends its way among various historical figures, designating them as either worthy or unworthy of the designation. Chaucer, Sophocles, and Sappho—Bohemians. Henry Knox, Alexander the Great, and John Winston Spencer-Churchill, Seventh Duke of Marlborough—decidedly not. The essayist even makes the following assertion: "All of Washington's greatness came from his Bohemianism." Nothing further is offered to substantiate this bold claim about the Revolutionary War hero and father of the United States. Then again, creating a galling sense of insiderism (some are worthy of the club; others aren't) seems to be the essay's primary purpose anyhow. Ada Clare provides a more straightforward take on Bohemianism in the February 11, 1860, issue:

> The Bohemian was by nature, if not by habit, a Cosmopolite, with a general sympathy for the fine arts, and for all things above and beyond convention. The Bohemian is not, like the creature of society, a victim of rules and customs; he steps over them all with an easy, graceful, joyous unconsciousness, guided by the principles of good taste and feeling. Above all others, essentially, the Bohemian must not be narrow-minded; if he be, he is degraded back to the position of a mere worldling.

Clare was also an *SP* regular, with a column called "Thoughts and Things." Clare ranged widely, attending to numerous subjects. As a defiant single mother, one of her most frequent concerns was feminism, though the term didn't yet exist. She railed against the prevailing styles in women's clothing, asserting that bonnets, hoop skirts, and heels were male-sanctioned fashions, designed to slow women down and keep them servile. "The number of things she is obliged to put on and take off," writes Clare, "involves a sacrifice of time and patience to which the martyrs were utterly strangers."

In one column, Clare mulled over a puzzling double standard. Why are brave men deemed *virtuous*, she asked? Why is the word *chaste* invariably applied to maidens? Doesn't virtue imply an active personal discipline, while chastity suggests a mere passive condition? In other words, a virginal woman gets no credit for her actions—or rather, lack of actions. The clear implication, Clare concluded, was that women weren't believed to have any control over their sexuality. They needed to be reined in by society's mores. "As it is," writes Clare, "the great body of men persist in believing, against all record and the witness of their own eyes, that the woman who can accept one man can accept all men."

As with so many of the Pfaffians, there's something startlingly modern about Clare. In one "Thoughts and Things" column, she even addressed the issue of the way the media—the nineteenth-century media, that is, of novels as opposed to glossy fashion spreads—pressured women about their weight. Clare was on intimate terms with this topic, given her own southern belle upbringing, complete with a morning glass of appetite-stymieing vinegar. Clare writes, "There is a horribly pernicious sentiment prevailing among novel-writers, which always represents the interesting heroine as being fragile, delicate, and unhealthy. This sentiment has found its way into boarding-schools, so that the fat and healthy girls are regarded with an insulting pity, by their dyspeptic companions."

Clapp was also a frequent contributor to his own journal, mostly as a critic, a role for which he was spectacularly well suited. He expended buckets of ink on Edwin Booth, following his career in exhaustive, worrying detail: *Was Booth's latest Hamlet an improvement on earlier Hamlets? Was he fulfilling his potential as an actor?* But with the exception of his own Bohemian circle—most especially Whitman, as will become clear—Clapp wasn't what could be called a constructive critic.

Destructive criticism was more his style. In one issue of the *SP*, for example, he reprinted "War," a new poem by Tennyson, explaining that had the work been originally submitted to his journal, it would have been summarily rejected. The reason, Clapp explained, that the poem was appearing at all (no doubt without remuneration for Tennyson) was simply as "a specimen of what the most gifted poets can do when they are not in earnest."

Clapp wrote as he spoke, lashing his subjects with cruel invective. He thrilled at coming up with novel conceits for lambasting his targets. Once, Clapp gave a wretched review to a book while withholding the name of the author and the title. Clapp explained that he'd already "wasted two hours and fifty minutes reading it." To identify the work, he explained, would provide publicity, wholly unmerited publicity, to the author.

But Clapp reserved his greatest critical animus for . . . Boston. The pages of the *SP* fairly swim with insults meant for the city he had once called home, where he had sold whale oil as a young man. "New York is such a big city," goes a typical jibe, "and that it excites so much envy and uncharitableness on the part of its sister cities—and especially Boston, which is such a quiet little place, that it always reminds us of an inscription we once saw on the Canal de l'Ourcq, near Paris—'Here may be found tranquility and fish in abundance.'"

Characteristically savage is Clapp's review of the collected papers of Boston eminence Edward Everett. "A most frightful mass of weak and wearisome platitude" is Clapp's verdict on the entire lifetime literary output of this author, statesman, and onetime Harvard president. "All is prim, precise, regular, respectable, austere, reverend," Clapp continues, adding, "Had this book been written by a person less stately and pretentious than Mr. Edward Everett, had it proceeded from one of the disciples rather than from the lord and master of respectable twaddle, we suppose it would have received little attention from the public." Clapp was only getting warmed up. He called Everett an "inflated bladder" and suggested that he possessed "well-cultivated but quite ordinary mental faculties," before working up to his gravest insult. He accused Everett of "conventionality" (*the* cardinal sin in Clapp's canon). For good measure, Clapp added that "most of the literary men congregated in and about Boston are of this kind."

Predictably, one of Clapp's favorite targets was the *Atlantic*. "The December [1858] number of the *Atlantic* was very heavy, and conferred on us, at best, the somewhat doubtful benefit of a few hours sound and unexpected sleep." Of the next issue, he had this to say: "The leading article—on 'Olympus and Angard'—is very learned, doubtless, but it is so full of the mythic, the eddaic, the cosmogonic, the telluric, the cryptogalmic, the eupeptic, and, especially, the ethnic and the chronic, that it makes us almost dyspeptic to think of it."

Born mature, the *Atlantic* elected simply to ignore Clapp.

In a way, the *Saturday Press* can be seen as the *New Yorker* with a malevolent streak. There are marked similarities between Clapp's journal and Harold Ross's magazine, launched in a subsequent century. Both publications make a cult of Manhattan. Both strike a studied pose of urbanity, esteem the arts above all, and share a fondness for the second-person regal, as in "us" and "we." There are echoes of Clapp's long table, too, in the Algonquin Round Table, a salon legendary for its high-wire quip bandying among *New Yorker* writers such as Dorothy Parker, Robert Benchley, and Alexander Woollcott. Even so, the connection between the Pfaff's Bohemians and the Algonquin wits is not as close as it might appear. Call it an ethereal influence as opposed to a direct one. Clapp was certainly one of the originators of that maddening Manhattan hauteur. But by the 1920s, his set was mostly forgotten.

If the *SP* was a kind of proto–*New Yorker,* it was one with decidedly shallow pockets. Clapp quickly burned through the proceeds from Howland's rare book collection. So he brought in a series of other investors, what he called "fresh blood," but their contributions were also quickly exhausted. Running a journal is expensive. Advertising revenue was never enough, though there were plenty of advertisers.

Among the businesses that regularly placed ads in the *SP* were A. W. Faber pencils, Delano's Improved Life-Preserving Vest, and Mathew Brady's ambrotype and daguerreotype studio, with three locations, one on Broadway. Nearly every issue of the *SP* also carried the following advertisement for Pfaff's:

Go to Pfaff's! At Pfaff's Restaurant and Lager Bier Saloon, No. 647 Broadway, New York, You Will Find: The Best Viands. The Best Lager Bier. The Best Coffee and Tea. The Best Wines and Liquors. The Best Havana Cigars. The Best of Everything at Moderate Prices N.B.—You will also find at Pfaff's the best German, French, Italian, English, and American papers.

Most issues also included a plea from Clapp for subscribers. He managed countless variations on the theme: *If you enjoy this publication, please, please subscribe.* This regular feature showed none of Clapp's characteristic wit. In fact, these pleas for money were quite earnest, with a whiff of desperation thrown in.

The *SP* didn't have a bookkeeper—Clapp couldn't afford to hire one. He didn't even bother keeping books. Instead, Clapp and deputy Aldrich worked out an informal system for handling finances. Whoever showed up first at the office on any given day appropriated whatever money came via mail such as subscription payments and advertising revenues. Clapp was in his forties and a confirmed insomniac, so he often arrived at the crack of dawn, while Aldrich—in his twenties—might roll in hours later. This meant Clapp got to attend to his list of priorities: paying the printer, making rent on the *SP*'s offices, and using whatever pittance remained for his own needs— usually buying drinks at Pfaff's. Paying contributors was considered optional, an afterthought.

One time, William Winter was sitting in the *SP* office with Clapp. The editor was complaining bitterly about money, or the lack thereof— it was a lean time, even by *SP* standards. In fact, Clapp had taken the precaution of locking the front door to stave off creditors. Suddenly, they heard footsteps in the hallway. Someone began banging on the door. Clapp motioned to Winter to remain silent. The pounding continued for a few minutes, accompanied by a series of muttered oaths. Then they heard retreating footsteps. Clapp sat still for several more minutes, ear tilted toward the door, puffing on his pipe. "'Twas the voice of *the Stoddard*," Clapp finally announced to Winter (Richard Stoddard was a regular contributor).

Despite the *SP*'s shaky finances, Clapp built a small but intensely loyal readership. A letter from the October 29, 1859, issue provides some flavor: "You may not know it, dear Editor, but in Oswego, the *Saturday Press* is an institution—indeed, I may say a peculiar institution."

The *SP*'s circulation was maybe five thousand, tops, yet it managed a reach that's simply amazing. This was thanks to a kind of magnifier effect. Items that ran first in the journal were sometimes reprinted in as many as two hundred publications around the country. The *SP* benefited from a US Postal Service policy, allowing editors to mail their publications free of charge to other editors. The policy was a holdover from the early days of America, when it was recognized as prudent for editors—many of them living in great isolation—to be able to trade information. During the 1850s, publications continued to build so-called exchange lists; the *SP* was on hundreds of them. While a publication virtually never paid to reprint an item from another, the convention was to properly credit the source of a piece. And so it was that across the nation—in Houston, Cincinnati, and San Francisco—even nonsubscribers to the *SP* were treated to the journal's articles, in the process learning about Clapp's vicious opinions and O'Brien's latest fistfight or getting a glimpse at the life of the lovely Ada Clare.

Thanks to the *SP*'s ubiquity, Bohemianism became a full-blown cultural phenomenon. While some publications were content to reprint *SP* articles, others wished to do their own original explorations of the subject. Many of these pieces also have a decidedly introductory quality. The public was hungry for the basics: *What exactly was a Bohemian? Did they bathe? Did they bite?* "Men of an indomitable irregularity and indolence, who live by their wits and for self-indulgence, are Bohemians," explained *Harper's New Monthly Magazine,* adding, "They are shaggy as to the head, with abounding hair." According to the *New York Times,* "The true Bohemian has either written an unsuccessful play, or painted an unsalable picture, or published an unreadable book, or composed an unsung opera." The piece ended with a warning: "Still, the Bohemian cannot be called a useful member of society." Predictably, these cautions only made Bohemianism all the more seductive.

Some publications even dispatched intrepid reporters to Pfaff's to provide firsthand accounts. After entering the inner sanctum, a writer for the *Boston Saturday Express* provided the following breathless, mixed-metaphor-laden account: "This is the capital of Bohemia; this little room is the rallying-place of the subjects of King Devilmaycare; this is the anvil from which fly the brightest scintillations of the hour; this is the womb of the best things that society has heard for many-a-day; this is the trysting-place of the most careless, witty, and jovial spirits of New York,—journalists, artists, and poets."

William Dean Howells was one of those people out in the hinterlands versed in Bohemia and all things Pfaffian. During the latter half of the nineteenth century, he would emerge as one of America's most celebrated novelists, the foremost practitioner of the realist school of fiction. His most famous work is *The Rise of Silas Lapham*. He would also serve as editor of the *Atlantic* for a decade, from 1871 to 1881.

In the summer of 1860, though, Howells was just twenty-three and hoping to crack the competitive East Coast literary market. His father was editor of the *Ashtabula (OH) Sentinel,* a newspaper that had an exchange-list relationship with the *SP* and frequently reprinted its items. Howells had also managed to get a half dozen of his poems accepted by the *SP*.

Howells traveled East, hoping to bolster some of his literary connections. His first stop was Boston, where he'd arranged to meet with Lowell, the *Atlantic*'s editor. They had lunch at Parker House, commencing at two—the hour for bankers and other genteel sorts. To Howells's amazement, they were joined at the table by both Oliver Wendell Holmes and James Fields, a principal of the publishing house Ticknor & Fields. In the course of lunch, Howells mentioned that he admired Nathaniel Hawthorne. To his further amazement, then and there, Lowell drafted a letter of introduction and suggested that Howells go and meet with the famous author. He did so, and it was the highlight of his whirlwind visit.

Following the Boston adventure, next stop was New York, where Howells went directly to the offices of the *SP*. The trip East had gotten off to a great start, and now he hoped to firm up his relationship with Clapp. As Howells would recall, "It is not too much to say that it was very nearly as well for one to be accepted by the *Press* as to be accepted by the *Atlantic,* and for a time there was no other literary comparison. To be in it was to be in the company of Fitz James O'Brien, Fitzhugh Ludlow, Mr. Aldrich, Mr. Stedman, and whoever else was liveliest in prose or loveliest in verse at that day in New York."

Right from the start, however, Howells's New York visit took on a very different tenor. Where the Parker House luncheon had been a rarefied affair, there was a distinct looseness to the meeting at the *SP*'s Spruce Street offices. In fact, the mood was downright unhinged. Clapp paced about, saying the most provocative things he could think of. Howells had the distinct impression that the editor was trying to shock him. Several minions—Howells took them for copyboys or assistant editors—were present, and they goaded Clapp on. That Howells had come to visit the *SP* by way of Boston and the *Atlantic* seemed to get Clapp particularly exercised. "The thought of Boston made him ugly as sin," explained one assistant.

Maybe it was defensiveness, or a desire to set the record straight, but when Howells finally got a chance to speak, he felt compelled to relate some details from his visit there. Clapp listened, his face a rictus of skepticism. Howells told him about the meeting with Hawthorne, adding that he had been shy in the presence of his idol and that—to his great surprise—Hawthorne had also been shy. Clapp pulled his pipe from his mouth, waited the perfect measure, before delivering: "Oh, a couple of shysters."

Clapp's minions roared.

The meeting had not gone so well. Nevertheless, that evening, Howells made a second requisite stop, Pfaff's. "I felt that as a contributor [to the *SP*] and at least a brevet Bohemian I ought not to go home without visiting the famous place." Howells took a seat at that long table. He neither drank nor smoked, but he ordered a *pfanne-kuchen,* a German pancake. As he dug in, what struck him most was the leadenness of the conversation, nothing like he'd anticipated.

Everybody was trying overhard to be clever—at least that was his view. As Howells recalled, "We were joined by some belated Bohemians whom the others made a great clamor over; I was given to understand they were just recovered from a fearful debauch; their locks were still damp from the wet towels used to restore them, and their eyes were very frenzied. I was presented to these types, who neither said, nor did anything worthy of their awful appearance, but dropped into seats at the table, and ate of the supper with an appetite that seemed poor."

Howells stuck around only until eleven. He was especially disappointed that Ada Clare had failed to make a showing at Pfaff's that evening. From Ohio, he'd closely followed the Queen of Bohemia, and he'd hoped to meet her in person. The New York leg of his eastern trip had been a real bust—what's more, he would never again contribute to the *SP*. As Howells exited Pfaff's, he was able, at least, to make the acquaintance of a different Bohemian eminence, Walt Whitman:

> I did not know he was there till I was on my way out, for he did not
> sit at the table under the pavement, but at the head of one farther
> into the room. There, as I passed, some friendly fellow stopped me
> and named me to him, and I remember how he leaned back in his
> chair, and reached out his great hand to me, as if he were going to
> give it to me for good and all. He had a fine head, with a cloud of
> Jovian hair upon it, and a branching beard and mustache, and gentle eyes that looked most kindly into mine, and seemed to wish the
> liking which I instantly gave him, though we hardly passed a word,
> and our acquaintance was summed up in that glance and the grasp
> of his mighty fist upon my hand.

Whitman, as described by Howells, is almost godlike, what with his "mighty fist" and "cloud of Jovian hair." But here's the thing: he wasn't yet perceived that way at the time of their meeting. Howells's account is a recollection, published in an 1895 *Harper's New Monthly Magazine* article, so everything is filtered through the haze of three and a half decades gone by. Thanks to the vagaries of memory, Howells's description mixes the Whitman of Pfaff's with another Whitman—the celebrated poet of the people, the lofty figure that he slowly became over time.

The *SP* played a crucial, early role in this transformation. It started with the publication of Whitman's sensational new poem "A Child's Reminiscence," in the journal's December 24, 1859, issue. (He would later rechristen the poem with the name by which it's now known, "Out of the Cradle Endlessly Rocking.") Clapp had heard him read it out loud and had hungrily seized it. For Whitman, this represented a return to public life after a lengthy silence. It was his first piece of published poetry in several years, since the second edition of *Leaves of Grass* in 1856. An editor's note announced the poem: "Our readers may, if they choose, consider as our Christmas or New Year's present to them, the curious warble, by Walt Whitman."

What's striking about the poem are a newfound maturity and sense of loss. The poem relates a boy's pleasure at encountering a pair of mockingbirds while walking on the beach. During a storm, one of the birds disappears, never to return. Its mate remains, sending terrible anguished cries out to the vast, empty sea. And then, time collapses, as the adult version of the boy looks back, blurring the pain of his own life with that of the lone mockingbird. But he recognizes that there's recompense to being a "solitary singer," for from pain comes beauty— the creative spark.

The poem is notably darker than Whitman's earlier work. In creating it, he seems to have drawn on the blackness that moved through those gatherings in Pfaff's basement:

> Answering, the sea,
> Delaying not, hurrying not,
> Whispered me through the night, and very plainly be-
> fore daybreak,
> Lisped to me constantly the low and delicious word
> Death,

And again Death—ever Death, Death, Death,
Hissing melodius, neither like the bird, nor like my
    aroused child's heart,
But edging near, as privately for me, rustling at my
    feet,
And creeping thence steadily up to my ears,
Death, Death, Death, Death, Death.

After appearing first in the *Saturday Press*, "A Child's Reminiscence" was reprinted in numerous papers. It reached thousands of readers—for many, it served as their introduction to the poet. Through the agency of Clapp's penniless yet mighty journal, Whitman's darkly beautiful new poem was broadcast across the land.

CHAPTER 7

Leaves, *Third Edition*

Dr Sir. We want to be the publishers of Walt. Whitman's poems—
Leaves of Grass.—When the book was first issued we were clerks in
the establishment we now own. We read the book with profit and
pleasure. It is a true poem and writ by a *true* man. . . .

Now *we* want to be known as the publishers of Walt. Whitman's
books, and put our name as such under his on title pages.—If you
will allow it we can and will put your books into good form, and style
attractive to the eye; we can and will sell a large number of copies; we
have great facilities by and through numberless Agents in selling. We
can dispose of more books than most publishing houses (we do not
"puff" here but speak *truth*).

We are young men. We "celebrate" ourselves by acts. Try us. You
can do us good. We can do you good—pecuniarily. . . .

Are you writing other poems? Are they ready for the press? Will
you let us read them? . . .

Yours fraternally, Thayer & Eldridge

THIS LETTER is dated February 10, 1860, shortly after Whitman's poem
ran in the *Saturday Press*. It appears that the principals of a book pub-
lishing company had seen his new effort and were eager to work with
him.

The firm Thayer & Eldridge was a partnership of William Thayer,
age twenty-nine, and Charles Eldridge, age twenty-one, both former

clerks at a Boston-based publisher. Following the bankruptcy of their employer (a casualty of the Panic of 1857), they had bought up its stock, plates, and other assets. As is fitting for a publisher run by "young men," the new company was committed to producing books on progressive—even radical—subject matter. Thayer & Eldridge had recently scored its first big hit with James Redpath's *The Public Life of Capt. John Brown,* a biography—or, more precisely, a hagiography—of the man who had attempted to spark an armed slave insurrection. Redpath's book casts Brown in near-saintly terms. As North-South tensions continued to ratchet up, the title would be increasingly in demand, eventually selling a remarkable seventy-five thousand copies.

Flush with cash, Thayer & Eldridge was busily making other acquisitions. Among its planned titles was a rush-job biography of William Seward, due out in May 1860. It was an election year, and, as of February, Seward was a favorite to be the Republican candidate (Lincoln still faced long odds) and very possibly the next president. To leaven its book list, to mix in some experimental literature with the progressive political fare, Thayer & Eldridge was also seeking some Bohemian authors. After all, Bohemians were the current rage. Around the time the publishers contacted Whitman, they also approached Ada Clare. They signed her right up, agreeing to bring out her forthcoming novel.

"Are you writing other poems," Thayer and Eldridge had asked Whitman in their letter. "Are they ready for the press?" The answers: yes and yes. Being unemployed left him with ample time to write, to rewrite, and to get his efforts into publish-ready form. Since 1856, the date of his last published collection, Whitman had written more than one hundred poems.

He was aiming to create a monumental work. Whitman once requested that a friend, Hector Tyndale, provide a brutally candid critique of the second edition of *Leaves of Grass.* Tyndale, who had recently visited England, told the poet that *Leaves* needed to be more like York Minster cathedral. One of the major shortcomings of the collection, his friend suggested, was that it lacked a sense of scale, of grandness. That criticism stuck with Whitman. From then on, he came to think of the first two versions as "inchoates," as he put it, or "little pittance editions." *Leaves*—as Whitman conceived it—was anarchic and organic; it subscribed to no particular rules. He had followed the first edition with a second, and nothing said there couldn't be further editions—so he'd thrown himself into the task of revising, reordering, and, most of all, enlarging the work.

Many of the one hundred new poems show the influence of spending time at Pfaff's. For example, Whitman had recently written a set of poems portraying love between men. He intended these as a kind of sonnet cycle, though not in any formal way (the poems didn't hew to the classic fourteen-line, ten-syllable-per-line scheme). Rather, Whitman was seeking the spirit of an Elizabethan sonnet sequence, a celebration of male-male romance.

Whitman had even taken the step of having many of his poems professionally set. The typewriter hadn't yet been invented. This was a way to have polished, non-handwritten versions of one's work. Whitman enjoyed looking over the new poems in printed form. It pleased him to think that this was how they would look to readers. Then again, he hadn't been certain that his new work would find readers.

Even as Whitman amassed a huge amount of fresh poetry, he had continued to seesaw between moments of grandiosity and moments of grave self-doubt. He jotted the following notation to himself: "Founding a new American Religion (?No Religion)." At other times, though, he was filled with worry:

> Shall I make the idiomatic book of my land?
> Shall I yet finish the divine volume [?]
> I know not whether I am to finish the divine volume . . .

Thayer and Eldridge's letter carried the weight of prophecy for Whitman. To someone who had self-published a couple of poetry collections, the idea of a genuine publisher was thrilling. To a poet who had so far earned scarcely a penny, the assurance that "we can do you good—pecuniarily" must have been like a dream. From Whitman's standpoint, the fact that Thayer & Eldridge was based in Boston was an unalloyed positive. He shared none of Clapp's antipathy for the city.

A real publisher in the nation's cultural hub had sought him out. That this was a newish Boston outfit run by a pair of progressive-minded young men, as opposed to an old-line firm—which might take a more conservative approach to publishing—made the prospect all the more appealing to Whitman.

Within a month of receiving Thayer and Eldridge's letter, Whitman had temporarily relocated to Boston to oversee the printing of an expanded third edition of *Leaves of Grass*. He rented a room in a shabby lodging house for two dollars a week. Each day, he headed over to the Boston Stereotype Foundry on Spring Lane. This was the finest such facility in Boston; eight years earlier, it had created the plates used for *Uncle Tom's Cabin*. Whitman was given a temporary office on the top floor. It was stiflingly hot, and the air hung thick with a metallic stench. Six floors below, furnaces blasted and trays sloshed with molten lead as stereotypes were created for printing books.

Because Whitman was an old hand at the process—he'd done every job from compositor onward—young Thayer and Eldridge gave him a remarkable degree of control. The typefaces for the volume were hand-picked by Whitman, who suggested an array of fonts: *Saxon ornate shaded* for this poem, *pica ornamented No. 7* for that one. He provided meticulous instructions about the spacing between words, line breaks, and where to use italics.

He also opted to arrange his poems in groups (what he called "clusters") representing common subject matter, although with Whitman, it can never be quite that boiled down. A poem might be placed in a particular cluster because of its mood, or the way it harmonized with another poem, or just *because*. Among the clusters Whitman specified were "Chants Democratic and Native American" (broadly, poems about the commonweal), "Enfans d'Adam" (poems about a desired Edenic state that was innocent and natural), and "Calamus" (the sonnet sequence). Calamus is a plant native to the United States that features a long, phallic bloom.

In a curious way, Whitman's clusters mirror the rigorous segregation he maintained between parts of his own life. He liked to keep people in separate compartments. At Pfaff's, he sometimes joined Clapp's crowd at the long table in that exclusive vaulted room, where he mostly listened, absorbing the chatter. Other times, he could be found in the saloon's main room, conversing with his "beautiful boys."

Whitman worried over every detail in his book's production. He even grew fixated on the blank spaces. Often, when a poem ended on the early part of a page, it was followed by a stretch where there was nothing. In such a busy book, achurn with wildly varying fonts and packed with dashes and exclamation points—favorite Whitman devices—the blank stretches looked glaring. So Whitman decided to fill them with illustrations. Three different ones pop up at intervals throughout the book: a butterfly lighting on an extended finger; the earth, viewed from the vantage of space, and partially obscured by clouds; and the sun over the sea, ambiguously either rising or setting.

Leaves quickly grew to be the most costly book project that Thayer & Eldridge had ever undertaken. "The printers and foremen thought I was crazy," Whitman reported in a letter to his brother Jeff, "and there were all sorts of supercilious squints (about the typography I ordered, I mean)." But when pages started to come off the press, Whitman continued, the skepticism evaporated. The foreman had pronounced *Leaves* "in plain terms, the freshest and handsomest piece of typography that had ever passed through his mill." In another letter, Walt expressed to Jeff his amazement that the new edition was truly under way. A book was so permanent. The publication of *Leaves,* he wrote, "seems to me, like relieving me of a great weight—or removing a great obstacle that has been in my way for the last three years. . . . It is quite curious, all this should spring up so suddenly, aint it."

Jeff wrote back, assuring Walt that he couldn't wait to see the finished book: "I quite long for it to make its appearance."

Emerson soon learned through the grapevine that Whitman was in his midst. He had never forgiven the younger man for taking liberties with his letter, for splashing "I Greet You at the Beginning of a Great Career" across the spine of the second edition of *Leaves*. At the same time, Emerson felt an intellectual obligation to Whitman and held out hope that the poet could yet emerge as that pure and true American voice.

While down from Concord to deliver a lecture in Boston titled "Moral Sentiment," Emerson decided to pay a visit. First, Emerson stopped by the lodging house, but was informed that Whitman was out. So Emerson went to the offices of Thayer & Eldridge. Charles Eldridge walked him to the nearby stereotype foundry and conducted him to the sixth floor, where Whitman was busily reading proofs. Whitman's cramped temporary office was stiflingly hot as always. So he and Emerson decided to go for a walk on the Boston Common.

As the two men strolled beneath the elms, they discussed the planned edition of *Leaves*. Emerson broached the subject that maybe Whitman should consider toning down—maybe even cutting—some of the racier content. Whitman offered a few mumbled protestations. Then Emerson launched into a discussion of all the reasons this made sense. He was nothing if not thorough. "It was an argument-statement, reconnoitering, review, attack, and pressing home," Whitman would recall, likening Emerson's discursive style to "an army corps."

Yet it troubled Whitman that Emerson seemed most concerned that the inclusion of certain poems might hurt the work's financial prospects. Could sales truly be Emerson's chief concern? Whitman asked if the book would be as good minus certain portions. Emerson frowned; the question appeared to throw him slightly. But then he continued, allowing that it would certainly still be a *good* book, if not *as good* a book.

Around and around the Common they walked, for two full hours, on a cold March Saturday. Emerson talked and talked; Whitman mostly listened.

A short time afterward, Whitman received a letter from Clapp. "I need not say, we are all anxious to see you back at Pfaff's,—and are eagerly looking for your proposed letter to the crowd." It's unlikely that Clapp was aware of the recent stroll with Emerson. Still, Clapp seems almost to be checking on Whitman, maybe trying to ensure that Boston wasn't exerting too much pull on the poet. (Whitman's letter to the Pfaff's crowd, if he wrote one, has sadly been lost.)

Clapp also promised Whitman that he'd enlist the *Saturday Press* in the promotion of *Leaves*: "What I can do for it, in the way of bringing it before the public, over and over again, I shall do, and do thoroughly— if the S.P. is kept alive another month. We have more literary influence than any other paper in the land."

A battle for Whitman's soul was taking shape. On one shoulder was Emerson, counseling prudence. On the other perched devil Clapp. Whitman chose Clapp. He decided to press ahead with *Leaves,* refusing to make a single change. Whitman would later say, "Emerson's face always seemed to me so clean—as if God had just washed it off." For his part, Emerson would state that he had "great hopes of Whitman until he became Bohemian."

Whitman continued to oversee the production of *Leaves,* in unexpurgated form. Typically, he spent at least a few hours each day in the stereotype foundry. But that left ample time to explore Boston. Sometimes, he simply walked up and down Washington Street, the city's equivalent of Broadway. He wore his wideawake and heavy boots, a getup that often drew stares, much to Whitman's amusement. In Boston, he stood out in a way that he didn't in anonymous New York. He was surprised, too, by the city's high prices. In a letter home, he complained, "7 cents for a cup of coffee, and 19 cts for a beefsteak—*and me so fond of coffee and beefsteak.*"

One of Whitman's favorite spots to visit was the Seamen's Bethel, a chapel near the harbor featuring a congregation that consisted mostly of sailors. Here, Whitman got to listen to Father Edward Taylor, a legendary sermonizer and the model for Father Mapple in *Moby-Dick*. For Whitman, a good sermon was one of life's great pleasures, right up there with opera. It was never about religious instruction for him; matters of belief and doctrine were strictly secondary. Rather, Whitman thrilled at the flow of words, the rhythm, the transformative magic of language. "For when Father Taylor preach'd or pray'd," Whitman wrote many years later, "the rhetoric and art, the mere words, (which usually play such a big part) seem'd altogether to disappear, and the *live feeling* advanced upon you and seiz'd you with a power before unknown."

Whitman visited the Seamen's Bethel repeatedly. Besides Father Taylor's sermons, there were other draws. He liked to sit by himself in a pew appreciating the "physiognomies, forms, dress, gait" of the sailor parishioners. Never averse to mixing the sacred and profane, he found that this little chapel offered a prime opportunity for man watching.

One other notable event from Whitman's Boston stay was attending an extradition hearing for Frank Sanborn. Sanborn, a local teacher and fervent abolitionist, had provided financial and moral support to John Brown as he planned the Harpers Ferry raid. Whitman attended the hearing at the invitation of Thayer and Eldridge. Redpath, their best-selling author and Brown's biographer, was also present.

The two young editors were in a state of high dudgeon for the hearing. They even sneaked pistols into the courthouse. Were the judge to rule against Sanborn, they had hatched a plan to spring to his aid, escorting him to a waiting carriage that would carry him to safety. Thayer and Eldridge took seats at the front of the packed courtroom and sat there, armed and fidgeting. They were much relieved when the judge ruled that Sanborn should not be handed over to the authorities.

Whitman watched the proceedings from the rear of the courtroom, showing his usual detachment. Defendant Sanborn would recall spotting the poet, "wearing his loose jacket and open shirt collar." The hearing and the frenzy surrounding it were, to Whitman's view, just more of the era's "hot passions." He was no slavery sympathizer, but neither was he enamored of John Brown's violent methods. He was a pacifist. A Quaker meetinghouse was one of the places he'd worshipped during his varied upbringing.

Late in the spring, Whitman departed Boston by boat, returning to his Brooklyn home and his Manhattan home-away-from-home: Pfaff's.

The official publication date of *Leaves of Grass,* third edition, was May 19, 1860. Originally, Thayer & Eldridge had planned to pair this literary title with a political title, the biography of Seward. But on May 18, the final day of the Republican convention held in Chicago, there was a surprise turn of events, as Lincoln pulled ahead of Seward to become his party's presidential nominee. (In those days, parties chose the nominee at the convention, not before.) Thayer & Eldridge immediately pulled the Seward biography, which had instantly been rendered irrelevant. They undertook a rush-job book on Lincoln instead. Thayer & Eldridge would become the first house in America to produce a bio of the nominee. But for now, Whitman's title would have to stand on its own in the marketplace.

The latest *Leaves* was a vast, sprawling work. It clocked in at 456 pages and contained 146 poems, 114 more than the previous iteration. Where the first *Leaves* had been a tall, thin volume, Whitman had specified that the new edition be small and thick, giving it roughly the dimensions and the heft of a Bible. For Whitman, this was a highly significant choice: he was going for grandeur, heeding his friend's advice to construct the literary equivalent of a cathedral. The book was supposed to be so much more than a mere poetry collection. Perhaps it could even serve as a spiritual guide, spelling out a "new American religion" or maybe "no religion," as he had scrawled in a notation to himself several years earlier. How better to convey these outsize aims than with a suitably holy-looking tome?

But if Whitman's new work was a Bible, it was a decidedly bawdy one. On the title page, the words *Leaves of Grass* are rendered with little spermatozoa swimming among the letters. Plenty of risqué content can be found in the poems, some of which were carried over from the earlier two editions. There's "love-flesh swelling and deliciously aching" and a "slow rude muscle" and "delirious juice" and "limitless limpid jets of love hot and enormous" and "bellies pressed and glued together with love." Because some of the most libidinous passages appear in the "Enfans d'Adam" cluster, it has often been speculated that these were the poems that Emerson suggested cutting. There's something strident about this group, featuring men and women proudly copulating, glorying in their bodily fluids and functions.

By contrast, the "Calamus" cluster—dedicated to attachments be-
tween men, romantic and otherwise—is less frenzied, more nuanced.
While "Enfans d'Adam" consists of what might be termed "message
poems," celebrating the sanctity of the human form, both male and
female, "Calamus" is where Whitman appears to be exploring his deep-
est feelings. This section contains some of the most beautiful poems he
would ever write. Some are deeply erotic, but the sequence explores a
range of feelings, love and pain and desire and loss. One of the finest is
the brief but lovely "Calamus, number 29":

> One flitting glimpse, caught through an interstice,
> Of a crowd of workmen and drivers in a bar-room,
>   around the stove, late of a winter night—And
>   I unremarked, seated in a corner;
> Of a youth who loves me, and whom I love, silently
>   approaching, and seating himself near, that he
>   may hold me by the hand;
> A long while, amid the noises of coming and going
>   —of drinking and oath and smutty jest,
> There we two, content, happy in being together,
>   speaking little, perhaps not a word.

It is quite possible that the "youth" in this poem is Fred Vaughan,
the man with whom Whitman once lived, the serious romance that
went painfully awry. And maybe the barroom setting is Pfaff's.

Taken in total, *Leaves,* edition three, feels as epic as Whitman in-
tended—almost elemental. It's gorgeous and obscene, earthy and tran-
scendent. Many of the poems feature Whitman's signature first-person
universal, shape-shifting, careening through time and space. Once
again, Whitman demonstrates his fondness for slang, weakness for
bizarre syntax, and fascination with phrenology and other pseudosci-
ences. Terms like *electric, adhesive,* and *magnetic* appear throughout.
Moments of supernatural clarity follow muddied stretches of utter ar-
tistic chaos.

Yet somehow, thanks to Whitman's genius, an overarching theme shines through, the theme of *union*. There is union of past and present, good and evil, life and death. (The poem from the *Saturday Press*—in which the sea repeatedly whispers "death"—was prominently featured in the new collection, positioned by itself, outside of the various clusters.) The theme of union, of course, extends to sexual union: between men and women, men and men. And perhaps most significant, there's political union—between the states.

In the first edition of *Leaves,* Whitman had deemed the United States "essentially the greatest poem." Now, he called on this body politic to remain whole. "And a shrill song of curses on him who would dissever the Union," goes a line in one of the poems. And in another the poet chides, "States! Were you looking to be held together by the lawyers? By an agreement on a paper? Or by arms? Away!" He even makes the connection—pure Whitman here—between the states and paramours: "Inextricable lands! the clutched together! the passionate lovers!" The third edition was published in May 1860. Given what was about to befall America, Whitman, who always approached politics with a poet's intuition, demonstrates a deep prescience.

On the title page, Whitman even went so far as to list the publication date of *Leaves of Grass* as "Year 85 of the States." He was dating his new Bible, it seems, using a new Whitmanian calendar. Accordingly, if 1860 was year 85, then year 1, the moment of origin, began on July 4, 1776, with the birth of the United States of America. This highly idiosyncratic dating system, one of the book's many striking features, grew directly out of Whitman's near-mystical fixation on *union*.

The third edition of *Leaves* was both a demanding and a provocative work. Predictably, critics tended to focus on the controversial passages. The headlines speak volumes. "'Leaves of Grass'—Smut in Them."— *Springfield (MA) Daily Republican*. "Walt. Whitman's Dirty Book"— *Cincinnati Daily Commercial*. "Mr. Whitman sees nothing vulgar in that which is commonly regarded as the grossest obscenity," wrote a *New York Times* critic, adding that the poet "rejects the laws of conventionality so completely as to become repulsive; gloats over coarse

images with the gusto of a Rabelais." In the *Boston Wide World,* a re-
viewer wrote, "Why, these 'poems' (prose run crazy) are the veriest
trash ever written, and vulgar and disgusting to the last degree. There
never was more unblushing obscenity presented to the public eye than
is to be found in these prurient pages and how any respectable House
could publish the volume is beyond my powers to comprehend."

In an unusual turn, the *Westminster Review* placed the onus on
Pfaff's, holding the saloon responsible for the deficiencies of Whitman's
latest effort. For several years now, the critic stated, the poet had spent
his time drunk in a "cellar," and it had blunted his skills.

Many of the bad reviews were tempered, with the critics allowing that
Whitman had promise and talent. There were plenty of good reviews,
too. In fact, Whitman garnered more notices than for his previous two
editions combined. But it still wasn't enough. Even in the nineteenth
century—when far fewer choices vied for people's entertainment
time—to get a book to take flight commercially required publicity, a
steady, relentless drumbeat of publicity.

"What I can do for it," Clapp had promised, ". . . I shall do, and do
thoroughly." In the weeks following its publication, the *Saturday Press*
ran dozens of items on Walt Whitman and *Leaves of Grass.* Clapp en-
listed the Pfaff's circle to write essays, appreciations of the poet, bits of
gossip; his journal even reviewed the book on three separate occasions.
Every issue also carried an advertisement for the title from Thayer &
Eldridge. "Clapp seemed almost to have founded the *Saturday Press*
for the purpose of forcing Whitman upon the balking public," writes
Frances Winwar in a 1941 biography of the poet.

Clapp also ran a number of *Leaves* parodies. Given the jealousy and
ill feeling harbored by some in the Pfaff's circle toward Whitman (he
was so clearly Clapp's favorite), writing a parody must have been a
more palatable assignment. Certainly, there was no love lost between
Whitman and Winter. Whitman once called him "little Willie, weakest
of the New York lot." Winter would refer to *Leaves* as "that odoriferous
classic." Writing a parody for the *Saturday Press* must have come quite
naturally to Winter. And his is spot-on:

I celebrate the Fourth of July!
And what I celebrate you shall celebrate,
And all together we'll go in strong for a celebration. . . .
Then is the Fourth of July, and I, rising, behold it.
I descend to the pavement. I merge with the
　　crowd, I roar exultant, I am an American citizen.
　　I feel that every man I meet owes me
　　twenty-five cents.

Another parody that ran in the *Saturday Press* was entitled "I Happify Myself," by journalist Richard Grant White:

O my soul!
O your soul, which is no better than my soul,
　　and no worse, but just the same!
O soul in general! Loafe! Proceed through
　　space with a hole in your trousers!
O pendent shirt-flap! O dingy, unwashed, fluttering linen! . . .

By golly, there is nothing in this world so unutterably magnificent as the inexplicable comprehensibility of inexplicableness. . . .

O triangles, O hypotheneuses, O centres, circumferences,
　　diameters, radiuses, arcs, sines,
　　cosines, tangents, parallelograms, and parallelopipedons.
O myself! O yourself.
O my eye!

Clapp even took the extraordinary step of reprinting in the *Saturday Press* bad reviews from other publications. He recognized the value of creating a forum on the pages of his journal, filled with discussion of Whitman, both positive and negative. This created the impression that the controversial poet was being widely and passionately discussed. The greatest danger is to be ignored—modern-minded Clapp knew this lesson oh so well. Whitman would later say, "Henry was right: better to have people stirred against you if they can't be stirred for you—better that than not to stir them at all."

It didn't take long for Clapp's publicity blitz to show results. Sales started to pick up. Whitman's collection was gaining momentum. In July 1860, Thayer & Eldridge went back to press, issuing a second printing of this latest edition of *Leaves of Grass*.

CHAPTER 8

Year of Meteors

THE YEAR 1860 brought great promise for the Bohemians: Whitman published the monumental third edition of *Leaves of Grass*. Clapp's *Saturday Press* was at the height of its power and influence. Ada Clare's first novel, *Asphodel,* was slated to appear in the fall.

In equal measure, the mood in 1860 felt ominous. The year contained the last gasps of peace as America continued to slide toward a drawn-out and horrific bloodletting. The nation's collective anxiety kept building, growing progressively more urgent. As the sense of impending crisis grew, the Bohemians would be affected, some deeply and painfully.

For Adah Menken, 1860 certainly began on a high. It was less than a year since she'd moved from Cincinnati to New York, and already her acting career was starting to take off. Things always happened quickly for Menken. She was also having some luck getting her new poetry, on topics other than Judaism, published in places other than the *Israelite*. To top it off, following a whirlwind romance, she had gotten married for the third time. Her new husband, John Heenan, age twenty-four, was a boxer.

Heenan was scheduled to fight a match in England in the spring of 1860. His opponent was Tom Sayers, the pride of London's Camden Town. It was billed as the first-ever world championship bout. The exact location was yet to be revealed. Caution had to be taken with arrangements for the big match, as boxing was against the law in both the United States and England. The sport was especially punishing in this era; opponents fought gloveless after first treating their hands with elixirs such as walnut brine, the better to harden their bare fists. A round ended when a boxer fell. A match ended when someone couldn't get back up.

Menken's new husband was a big man and knock-down handsome. Given boxing's illegality, he occupied a strange place in society as a kind of netherworld celebrity, a folk hero whose activities were followed avidly by the public at large and the sporting crowd in particular. Between bouts, Heenan made his living as an enforcer for New York's corrupt Tammany political machine. His job was to menace undecided voters, intimidating them into casting their ballots for Tammany-backed ward chiefs and the like. Menken and Heenan had married on a whim, following a night of passion at the Rock Cottage, a kind of no-tell lodge on Bloomingdale Road in upper Manhattan. The lodge's sleazy proprietor had summoned a priest to perform a quickie ceremony. Menken and Heenan had agreed to keep their marriage secret, even from most of their closest friends. Heenan worried that his reputation would suffer if the public learned of his marriage, especially with the championship bout looming. It might make him look soft. At least, that's what he told his new wife.

Menken continued to frequent Pfaff's, but without Heenan in tow. The boxer would have been woefully out of place at Clapp's long table, as a hulking bruiser who favored dandyish dress—striped trousers and a silk top hat. By all accounts, Heenan was an impressive physical specimen, but not an agile wit. On other evenings, however, Menken accompanied her secret husband to his haunts, taverns such as the Old Crib and the Exchange. Menken thrilled at rubbing shoulders with bookies and roughs, people steeped in a world of boxing, cockfights, and heavily wagered battles between huge, ferocious rats. At Manhattan's Sporting Museum, Menken even took boxing lessons and did some sparring in a hidden back room where an illicit boxing ring was set up. This was a shocking activity for a nineteenth-century woman. Like Whitman, Menken valued keeping her life in separate compartments. She craved experience, big experience, and was able to move between the utterly incongruous worlds of Pfaff's and the Old Crib.

On January 4, high noon, Menken stood on a dock in Jersey City, watching as Heenan boarded the steamship *Asia,* bound for Liverpool. There was no question of her going along to England. She had her acting and poetry career to tend to. What's more, a convention existed, then as now, that boxers should abstain from sex while training. "Spirits, porter, gross feeding, stimulants, tobacco, onions, pepper and sexual intercourse must vanish," counsels *Fistiana; or, The Oracle of the Ring,* a boxing manual of the day. The plan was for Heenan to spend a few months in England, preparing for and then fighting his match, before returning to America, more famous than ever, with a nice payout as well. (The winning boxer would receive £400, equivalent to nearly $500,000 in current US dollars.)

As Menken saw Heenan off on that January day, she held yet another secret, one she'd kept even from her new husband. She was pregnant with his child.

Meanwhile, the darkness continued to gather as the North and the South traded harsh words and warned of worse, much worse. Already, America's sectional divide had proved more than empty posturing. There had been the violence in Kansas Territory and John Brown's raid.

A pair of battling books heightened the tension. Above the Mason-Dixon line, sensation attended a fresh publication of Hinton Helper's *The Impending Crisis of the South: How to Meet It.* The book had originally appeared in 1857 to little notice. But now it was an election year. The Republican Party—only six years old, founded explicitly to stem slavery—got behind Helper's book and was in the process of distributing one hundred thousand copies. Helper's book brimmed with incendiary language. He called slaveholders "tyrannical" and "lords of the lash" before delivering such provocations as "The first and most sacred duty of every Southerner, who has the honor and interest of his country at heart, is to declare himself an unqualified and uncompromising abolitionist." What made the book especially controversial: Helper was himself a Southerner, excoriating his own region.

The slave states answered with *The Sunny South*. This book took the form of a series of unsigned letters, celebrating idyllic plantation life, purportedly written by a *Northern* governess who had relocated to Mississippi.

The rhetoric was growing ever more heated. On February 5, 1860, Henry Ward Beecher delivered the "Pinky sermon," one of his most famous turns at the pulpit. Beecher was the minister of Brooklyn's Plymouth Church and brother of Harriet Beecher Stowe. For this particular sermon, he assumed the guise of a slave dealer, but with a twist. Gesticulating wildly, employing the rat-a-tat-tat cadence of an auctioneer, Beecher urged his congregation not to purchase a slave, but rather to buy freedom for one—an actual slave named Sally Diggs, a.k.a. Pinky. The donation basket passed from pew to pew, and more than $900 was raised. The money was used to buy Pinky from her master and set her free.

But the Southern way of life had no shortage of eloquent defenders. William Yancey, most vociferous of the so-called Fire Eaters, crisscrossed the region, delivering impassioned oratory in support of slavery and states' rights. "We want negroes cheap," boomed Yancey, "and we want a sufficiency of them, so as to supply the cotton demand of the whole world."

Once again, some of the most extreme discord occurred in the very halls of Congress, where ideologically opposed Northerners and Southerners met on a daily basis. It was a genuine flash point. Already, there was quite a history of incidents such as the fifty-member melee that broke out on the House floor in 1858 and a particularly ugly episode in 1856 when South Carolina's Preston Brooks confronted Charles Sumner of Massachusetts on the floor of the Senate and proceeded to beat him senseless with a cane. Sumner required a year off to recover, and his faculties would never fully return.

In the early months of 1860, yet another flare-up occurred in Congress. On March 7, Charles Van Wyck of New York was in the midst of delivering a scathing attack on slavery before the House of

Representatives. Suddenly, Mississippi's Reuben Davis rose and cut him off, shouting, "I pronounce the gentleman a liar and a scoundrel. I pronounce the gentleman's assertion false—utterly false."

"My time is short," said Van Wyck, "and I hope not to be interrupted."

"You have no right to utter such foul and false slanders," continued Davis.

The situation quickly spun out of control. Davis challenged Van Wyck to a duel, suggesting that they repair to a location outside the District of Columbia, where the practice remained legal.

"I travel anywhere, and without fear of anyone," rejoined Van Wyck.

The duel never happened. But a feeling of menace, more profound than ever before, settled over Congress. Supposedly, many members started carrying weapons into the chambers. "Every man in both houses is armed with a revolver—some with two—and a bowie-knife," reported Senator James Hammond of South Carolina in a letter of April 19, 1860. This was hyperbole, no doubt. But matters had truly sunk to a frightening new low.

Against this backdrop, the impending Heenan-Sayers prizefight was followed with avid interest. The match was one of the very few things capable of bridging the divisiveness that gripped America. It promised to be savage, a kind of proxy for all of the country's simmering hatred and fury and bloodlust. But it had the advantage of being a sporting event, a mere diversion. What's more, the fight pitted America against Britain, the original enemy.

While in England, Heenan's handlers disguised his identity, furnishing eyeglasses and less flamboyant clothing. He remained constantly on the move, training at a variety of undisclosed locations. Secrecy was paramount. On both sides of the Atlantic, vast sums were being wagered on the outcome. No one wanted the big fight disrupted by authorities. Several American papers dispatched reporters to Britain, among them the *New York Herald* and the *Spirit of the Times,* a sporting sheet. The reporters gathered whatever tidbits could be learned about Heenan, dutifully relaying them to hungry readers back home.

News traveled slowly between England and America, however, due to an unfortunate circumstance. A couple of years earlier, in 1858, the transatlantic telegraph line had gone dead after less than a month of spotty operation, and no one had figured out how to revive it. Now, the only communication between England and America was provided by ships and took about a week. Still, the appetite for news—even delayed news—of the fight preparations was quite simply insatiable. "The sporting fraternity talk of nothing else," stated the *Plattsburgh (NY) Republican*.

For Menken, the situation quickly grew excruciating. It wasn't so much that she was in suspense or worried about her new husband's prospects; rather, she sensed that a golden opportunity was passing her by. All this delicious hype was building, and here she was, saddled with a secret. Menken could contain herself no longer. She approached a couple of New York columnists and revealed that indeed she was the wife of the famous boxer. This fresh subplot in the Heenan saga was picked up by papers across the country. "Commonplace people and commonplace events are out of fashion," announced the *New-York Illustrated News*. "Startling sensations are more the order of the day. That a poetess should marry a prize-fighter seems a contradiction of the laws of 'affinity'—but such a fact has occurred." A bemused Whitman referred to Menken as "Mrs. Heenan."

The marriage revelation gave her career an instant boost, exactly as she must have calculated. Soon she was performing protean comedies such as *Satan in Paris* and *An Unprotected Female* to packed houses. When Menken took curtain calls, audiences chanted her husband's name. By now, Menken was several months along in her pregnancy. She was probably showing, but the ever-resourceful actress, it seems, relied on wraps and scarves and assorted loose-fitting frippery to hide her condition.

Presently, the date of the big fight arrived, April 17. A regulation ring, twenty-four by twenty-four feet, had been set up in an open field right outside London. A huge crowd was gathering. In recent days, people had learned the location through a kind of whispering campaign that moved through London's sporting pubs.

In one corner stood Heenan, six-foot-two and 195 pounds, wearing a red-white-and-blue belt. In the other stood Sayers, his belt emblazoned with a British gold lion. At five-foot-eight, 149 pounds, Sayers was dwarfed by his American opponent. Weight class was no consideration in illegal boxing, though. Sayers was considered an extraordinarily crafty fighter: patient, elusive, always a threat to deliver punches in surprising and creative combinations. As British champion, he had bested plenty of larger men. He possessed an additional potent weapon: desperation. A bricklayer by trade, Sayers had fallen deep into debt and was trying to support a wife and five children in a London slum. He once allowed that he would fight "an elephant for fifty quid."

The match got under way at 7:29 A.M., scheduled for first thing in the morning in the hopes of avoiding detection by London's metropolitan police. During the early rounds, the two boxers circled warily, squinting in the light of the rising sun. Heenan looked to have the advantage. He landed repeated punches, some knocking Sayers down. Other times, Heenan simply picked the smaller man up and hurled him to the ground, ending the round. As he lay there, Sayers always made a point of smiling broadly. It was unsettling.

Round 7 was a turning point, setting the tone for the rest of the match. At the opening bell, Heenan bolted from his stool, came barreling out toward Sayers. The American wanted to end this now. Sayers danced around, ducking and weaving. Suddenly, he lashed out and caught Heenan's left cheek. Heenan's eyes widened in genuine surprise. Now, it was Sayers who menaced Heenan. The Brit landed repeated blows, working and tearing at the gash on Heenan's face with his bare knuckles. Relentlessly, Sayers directed punch after punch at this same spot, and Heenan was lulled into a rhythm, using every parry to protect his left cheek. Then, without warning, Sayers landed a punch square on Heenan's right eye. The eye began to swell shut. Still, Heenan managed to knock Sayers down to end the round. It lasted thirteen minutes, an unusual amount of time for a bare-fisted boxing round.

Vendors worked the crowd, hawking oranges and ginger beer. Petty thieves circulated, pinching spectators' pocket watches. A surprisingly large press corps was on hand, scribbling notes. The British accounts would be especially colorful, featuring passages such as "Tom got a hot 'un on the whistler, which shook his ivories, and turned on a fresh tap." (Translation: Sayers took a punch to the mouth that rattled his teeth and caused him to drool blood.) Even erstwhile Pfaffian Thomas Nast was present, on assignment for the *New-York Illustrated News,* making lightning-quick sketches of the match.

It was during round 9 that the first bobbies showed up. There were only two of them, so they simply stood on the periphery, doing nothing. They were woefully outnumbered. The crowd had now swelled into the thousands. It wasn't composed only of bookies and rowdies and fight aficionados, either. Novelist William Thackeray was on hand, along with assorted professors, clergy, and other pillars of society, some watching the action through monocles. According to a fast-circulating rumor, Lord Palmerston, the prime minister, was present in disguise with orders to convey the results immediately to Queen Victoria.

As the match crossed the one-hour mark, it started to take on the quality of an endurance contest. Heenan had landed a terrific blow to Sayers's right arm. The arm had stiffened and became useless as anything but a shield. The Brit's strategy was clear to everyone present. Heenan's right eye had swollen shut. With his good arm, Sayers stabbed and jabbed, hoping to connect with Heenan's *good* eye. The pair slogged on, passing twenty, then thirty, rounds. Between rounds, the fighters drank hot tea spiked with brandy, trying just to keep going.

Bobbies kept arriving, and eventually they assembled a critical force. They began to press through the crowd, waving their nightsticks. Inside the ring, bedlam broke out. The referee fled and spectators milled about. Sayers staggered and pitched, grotesquely diminished from his earlier fleet-footed self. Heenan—both eyes now puffy, nearly blind—swung wildly, frequently connecting with innocent bystanders. As the bobbies burst into the ring, the two boxers fell in with the throng, set off running across the field, and managed to evade capture. Heenan was checked into a country inn, where he lay low, quite literally, spending two whole days in a darkened room, recovering.

According to the "official" tally, the match went an outrageous forty-two rounds and lasted two hours and twenty minutes. Because it had been broken up by the police, the first-ever world championship bout was declared a draw. Heenan and Sayers split the £400 purse.

Back in America, people awaited results of the April 17 contest, expected sometime the following week. The *Vanderbilt* was the first scheduled steamer out of England following the fight—it would be the bearer of news. Predictably, all kinds of shady operators tried to profit on the time lag, claiming inside knowledge of the outcome. A particularly enterprising con artist printed a fake edition of the *Spirit of the Times,* announcing Heenan the victor of a one-hour bout. The ruse succeeded in bilking some bettors, but most people were sophisticated enough to recognize the edition as fake; it had appeared too soon. On April 28, the *Vanderbilt* chugged into New York Harbor, and at last the results were known.

As she read the *New York Herald*'s vivid, blow-by-blow account of the fight, Menken experienced a rush of mixed emotions. She was thrilled that Heenan had fought so bravely, but disappointed the match had been called a draw. Most of all, she was anxious: the *Herald* article represented the only news she had received about her husband for some time now. She had written to Heenan repeatedly, in care of his English handlers. But he had stopped sending letters in return.

Such an odd, conflicted, confounding time, and not just for Menken, but for everyone. An extraordinarily unusual occurrence on July 20, 1860, only added to this feeling.

The day was sweltering across much of the Eastern Seaboard. Temperatures remained uncomfortably high well into evening. As a consequence, many people remained outside, sat near open windows, or went up on tenement rooftops—just hoping to catch a breeze.

Those who witnessed the event noted that it began at roughly 9:45 P.M. A kind of orb, shrouded in purplish mist, appeared on the horizon. As it started across the night sky, the orb split into two distinct bodies. The lead one was round and bright as a full moon, the trailing one slightly smaller and dimmer. To witnesses, the two bodies seemed to move very slowly and in perfect unison. One onlooker felt that they traveled "a little faster than the usual speed of a horse." It was generally agreed that it took a full minute for the twin orbs to traverse the sky, entering at the northwest horizon, exiting to the southeast. Many reported seeing flaming tails or sparks flying off the astral bodies. One witness suggested that they were "like two chariots of fire."

What transpired that evening was an earth-grazing meteor procession, caused when a meteor dips down into the atmosphere and breaks apart and the pieces continue along the same trajectory. This is an incredibly rare occurrence. Modern astronomers know of only three other instances: in 1783, 1876, and 1913.

The 1860 meteor procession was visible from Boston to Baltimore, seen as far west as Detroit, and was watched by sailors aboard a ship two hundred miles out to sea. It lit up city streets and bathed the countryside in an eerie glow. It was seen by a vast number of Americans— untold thousands—who stared up at the sky with a mix of awe and anxiety.

The *New York Herald* described it as a "most sublime spectacle," adding that "meteors, like comets and eclipses, have been, from the remotest antiquity, regarded as portentous omens." A headline in the *Philadelphia Inquirer* asked, "A Forerunner of Ruin?"

It's quite possible that Whitman saw the meteor procession, perhaps even while walking along Broadway en route to or from Pfaff's. He certainly heard and read all about it. Astronomy was one of his myriad interests; he'd attended countless lectures on the subject. Five years in the future—in a very different time, when a great deal had changed— Whitman would publish a poem, "Year of Meteors (1859–60)." In it, he would look back on this period as a "year all mottled with evil and good—year of forebodings!" Whitman would also make a connection between himself and the strange celestial occurrence of July 20: "As I flit through you hastily, soon to fall and be gone, what is this chant, / What am I myself but one of your meteors?"

And then it happened, this strange, unsettling year's most decisive event: on November 6, Abraham Lincoln was elected the sixteenth president of the United States of America.

He inherited a perilously divided nation. Throughout 1860, as the political situation slid ever further into dysfunction, America's traditional two-party approach had utterly broken down. The presidential contest had featured candidates from four different splinter parties: Republican, Northern Democrat, Southern Democrat, and Constitutional Unionist. Each had a decidedly regional bias. Lincoln won 180 electoral votes (28 above the threshold for victory), but received only 39.9 percent of the popular vote. He didn't carry a single state below the Mason-Dixon line. In fact, ten of those states refused even to place Lincoln on the ballot. In effect, Lincoln was the Northern and Republican president of a United States that was anything but. His victory triggered an immediate secession crisis.

Shortly after the election, Buchanan, the outgoing president, delivered his annual message to Congress. He declared that states had no right to secede from the Union, but he also allowed that the federal government had no constitutional authority to stop them. So deep was the crisis by then that it was unlikely that anybody could have headed it off. But dough-faced Buchanan, with another feeble on-the-one-hand, on-the-other statement, was certainly the wrong man at the wrong time. On December 20, South Carolina's state legislature convened a special session and resolved to leave the Union by a vote of 169–0. In rapid sequence, Mississippi, Florida, Alabama, Georgia, Louisiana, and Texas also announced their intention to leave.

The massive crisis that was brewing had broad fallout, sometimes resulting in very specific and localized consequences. Within weeks of Lincoln's election victory, the *Saturday Press* folded. Even in its brightest fiscal moments, the publication had always been a hair's breadth from ruin. The uncertainty of the national situation, prompting advertisers to be skittish and subscribers to not renew, gave the journal that final, fatal shove. Only a few months earlier, Thayer & Eldridge, Whitman's publisher, had made a small investment in the *SP* with plans eventually to buy it. They intended to keep Clapp on as editor. "*We* can make it *pay* (we think) in a very short time," the two young proprietors had announced with characteristic bravado. They had envisioned a smart combination of their publishing house and the influential journal.

Thayer & Eldridge's small cash infusion wasn't enough to sustain the *SP*. The final issues are filled with pleas for money. "All that is wanted, as we said last week, is a little more capital," wrote Clapp in one. As ever, edgy Clapp became earnest and humorless when begging for money. That he, of all people, couldn't figure out a way to write a sly money solicitation—it's a poignant window into his desperation. Still, as the *SP* wound down, he did manage to publish several appreciations of Booth's acting, a poem by O'Brien, and a "Thoughts and Things" column by Ada Clare. Fittingly, the very last page of the final issue (December 15, 1860) includes "A Portrait," a poem by Whitman.

Clapp took the death of his beloved journal very hard. He upped his drinking, drastically, but there wasn't enough whiskey on earth to drown his pain. This was such a disappointment, such a comedown. His reduced circumstances, as he told Whitman, left him racked by insomnia, caught in "a scrape the horror of which keeps me awake o' nights."

Thayer & Eldridge, so recently profitable, also went bankrupt. As a Northern publisher of radical fare, specializing in the works of abolitionists and Bohemians, it faced the same problems as the *SP*—in extremis. The two partners tried to arrange emergency financing, but credit had seized up and banks weren't lending. "We go by the board tomorrow or the next day," wrote Thayer mournfully in a December 5 letter.

The new edition of *Leaves of Grass* had been on sale for only six months. Momentum had been steadily building. Roughly three thousand copies had sold, and Thayer & Eldridge had gone back to press. But those sales, while highly respectable, weren't sufficient to keep the publisher alive—not in this environment.

The firm's meltdown was also costly to Ada Clare. Only a few months earlier, she had traveled to Boston, as Whitman had, to oversee the production of her novel. Now, *Asphodel* was canceled. The original handwritten manuscript, proofs, plates—every single version of the unpublished book—eventually disappeared. Sadly, the Queen of Bohemia's first novel has been scrubbed from history.

During the bankruptcy, Thayer & Eldridge were forced to sell the plates for the landmark third edition of *Leaves of Grass.* They wound up in the hands of Horace Wentworth, a rival publisher, who turned out to be a highly unscrupulous man. Wentworth demanded that Whitman buy the plates from him, threatening that otherwise he planned to distribute a pirated printing of *Leaves.* Whitman couldn't meet his fee. Over time, Wentworth would sell thousands of copies, many more than the legitimate version had sold. Of course, Whitman didn't see a cent in royalties from these sales. (Supposedly, he managed to collect only $250 before Thayer & Eldridge went bankrupt.) In a crucial way, however, Whitman benefited mightily from his shotgun-wedding association with Wentworth. Following the demise of Thayer & Eldridge, at least someone was still printing *Leaves of Grass.* The pirated version would tend the flame, would help keep the poet's reputation alive through the sad, chaos-filled years that lay ahead.

During his earlier stay in Boston, in a letter to brother Jeff, Whitman had confided an anxiety as he readied *Leaves of Grass* for publication. Perhaps the book would not take off "in a rocket way." This proved true. *Leaves* would be one of those slow-burn classics, achieving its stature with the passage of many years.

That was of no solace to Whitman in December 1860. Once again, his future looked bleak. He had just been slammed with a one-two combo worthy of Tom Sayers. The publisher of *Leaves of Grass* was bankrupt. The *Saturday Press,* tireless champion of his work, was no more.

En route to Washington to assume the presidency, Lincoln made a stopover in New York City. It was then that Whitman got his very first glimpse of the new president. Whitman was riding along Broadway in a stage and got caught in a huge traffic jam. As usual, he was sitting up front, beside the driver and way up high. "I had," Whitman would recall,

" . . . a capital view of it all, and especially of Mr. Lincoln, his look and gait—his perfect composure and coolness—his unusual and uncouth height, his dress of complete black, stovepipe hat push'd back on the head, dark-brown complexion, seam'd and wrinkled yet canny-looking face, black, busy head of hair, disproportionately long neck."

Whitman was especially struck by the quietness of the crowd. There must have been forty thousand people lining Broadway, he estimated, yet it was strangely silent. New Yorkers weren't exactly partial to Lincoln; he had carried only 35 percent of the city's voters in the election. Manhattan papers mostly cast the president-elect as a rube, a backwoods naïf. There was a great deal of skepticism about whether he was up to the momentous challenges that faced him. Lincoln stepped out of his coach. He briefly surveyed the crowd—no smile, no wave—before stepping into the Astor Hotel.

Whitman felt an instant affinity for this tall, awkward man from the West. The poet was forty-one years old now and still living at home with his mother. Brother Jeff had just had a baby daughter, would soon have another. The Brooklyn basement apartment was more crowded than ever. Whitman scrawled an idea for a "Brochure" in one of his notebooks:

> Two characters as
> of a Dialogue
> between A.
> L____n and
> W [illeg.]
> —as in? a dream
> or better?
> Lessons for a
> President elect
> Dialogue between WW.
> and "President elect"

It was another of his schemes, like being a wander-speaker, but blurrier. What else could he do? Whitman had come so tantalizingly close to achieving his dream. He'd actually climbed partway to poetic fame and fortune, only to have it come tumbling down.

As 1860 came to a close, perhaps nobody in the Pfaff's set had fallen further than Menken. The year, which had started for her with such promise, ended in a plunge.

Menken's baby boy—born in June—lived only a few days before succumbing to Saint Anthony's fire, a bacterial infection. Meanwhile, Heenan—who had stopped writing from England—simply refused to see her upon his return to America.

Menken faced the indignity of trying to connect with her estranged husband at a public rally held in his honor. The setting was Jones Wood, a stretch of farmland that ran along Manhattan's East River. The turnout was huge, estimated at fifty thousand by the *New York Daily Tribune*. Even though the championship bout ended in a disappointing draw, Heenan had emerged a bigger celebrity than ever.

As the boxer arrived in a coach, people chanted, "Tiger! Tiger! Tiger!" Menken was stuck on the crowd's edge, pressing toward her husband, along with thousands of others. Heenan stepped out and greeted his adoring public, smartly dressed in a silk shirt and flannel breeches. He raised one arm, waving. Clinging to his other arm was a woman. It was his pretty new English girlfriend, Harriet Martin. In that instant, for Menken, the reason for Heenan's silence became clear—blonde, buxom, and painfully clear.

Menken's prospects kept spiraling down. Her brief moment as a theatrical sensation had ended, and soon the roles began to dry up. Heenan had moved on and the public along with him. Menken was just another struggling actress. She vacated her home at Third Avenue and 14th Street and took a dingy flat in Jersey City. But she continued visiting Manhattan on a regular basis, pounding the pavement, trying to find work. Spying Menken making the rounds, a gossip columnist for the *Charleston Courier* wrote unflatteringly, "Adah, as she walks the street with her hair frizzled over her forehead, and her eyes widely wandering, reminds one of Ophelia in the mad scene of Hamlet."

Late at night, Menken poured her grief into what she called "wild soul poems." She claimed to write these in a kind of fugue state. Menken was highly influenced by Whitman, and idolized him for being "centuries ahead of his contemporaries." In stark imitation of *Leaves of Grass,* many of her works are composed in free verse and contain assorted experimental touches. But while her outpouring of pain and sorrow was genuine, as a poet she lacked that essential something. Menken was no Whitman. "Oh, is this all?" she implores in "Drifts That Bar My Door," one of her poems from this period. "Is there nothing more of life? See how dark and cold my cell. The pictures on the walls are covered with mould. The earth-floor is slimy with my wasting blood."

By December 1860, Menken was reduced to working at the Canterbury, one of Manhattan's notorious concert saloons. "Gives the most varied entertainment in the world," promises a newspaper advertisement for the Canterbury, before listing sundry other features: "$6,000 expended in Mirrors, Mirrors, Mirrors," "the novel feature of revolving chairs," and "crowded nightly with men of real taste and judgment."

The Canterbury trotted out an endless stream of slightly blue acts such as singers of bawdy songs and lecherous magicians. Menken found work there as a racy actress, performing double-entendre-filled skits. At a concert saloon, such entertainments were merely a diversion, though. The real enticement was the waitresses, who worked the saloon floor in their garish makeup and revealing outfits. As long as a customer kept ordering expensive drinks, he was guaranteed the rapt attention of his waitress. If the pair really hit it off, he might inquire about more intimate services, discreetly available.

At the Canterbury, Menken took the stage at regular intervals throughout the evening to perform her suggestive skits. She was a born entertainer; that was what she did and all she knew, in the best of times and the worst. "I can not sew or work as many women," she once confessed. But performing at a concert saloon was drastically less than what she'd hoped for and imagined. In the first months of 1860, she'd managed the briefest taste of sweetness and promise. Then, she'd fallen so far so fast. Even so, the Canterbury's "waitresses" must have been a constant and unsettling reminder that a person can always slide still further. Wherever one is, there are stations below, occupied by countless persons, and below that and that and lower still, endless grisly rungs—terrifying to contemplate.

The evening of December 29, 1860, found Menken sitting alone in her Jersey City flat, regarding her reflection in a cracked vanity mirror. The only light in her small room came from a flickering oil lamp. She stared at herself for a long while. She was wearing her favorite dress, navy satin with white lace cuffs.

Menken was supposed to meet the crowd at Pfaff's. Instead, she started composing a note in blue ink on a piece of lined paper, addressing it "To the Public."

Menken lamented the fact that Heenan had abandoned her, writing that the boxer had "absorbed all of good and beauty, and left me alone, desolate." She asked for forgiveness from God and also asked God to forgive Heenan and everyone else who had wronged her. Then she declared, "Because I am homeless, poor and friendless, and so *unloved*, I leave this world."

Menken peeled off her clothing layer by Victorian layer: navy dress, corset, and assorted undergarments. Near at hand was a vial containing a potent tincture, purchased from an apothecary. She lifted the vial to her lips and took a long draw.

Over at Pfaff's, meanwhile, it seems that a man named Stephen Masset had grown concerned about Menken's failure to show up. Masset was a singer and sometime guest at Clapp's table. A small, obsequious person, he curried Menken's attentions through flattery and endless favors. Masset was aware that Menken had grown extremely depressed of late. So he left Pfaff's and traveled to Jersey City. On arriving at the flat, he found the door unlocked. He pushed inside, where Menken was lying naked on the floor.

Masset threw open the window, letting in a blast of icy late-December air. The actress was still breathing, and gradually came to, though groggy and weak.

CHAPTER 9

Becoming Artemus Ward

BAD LUCK, assorted professional setbacks, a suicide attempt: it had all been piling up for Clapp's set. The past year had been painful, as a hopeful mood gave way to a sense of dark foreboding. Who knew what fresh disasters awaited the Pfaffians, ready to be ushered in with the arrival of a new year? Instead, they got Charlie Brown.

On January 1, 1861, at four in the morning, Brown arrived in New York City by train. He checked into the Western Hotel and caught a few hours of sleep. Upon awaking in the afternoon, Brown walked around the city and was perplexed to find the streets fairly quiet and nearly every business closed. It took him a while to figure out why. It was New Year's Day. But at first opportunity, he made a crucial stop on his itinerary and visited a legendary spot: Pfaff's.

Clapp and the other Bohemians were intrigued by the new arrival. Proprietor Pfaff waited on him personally. Brown's reputation very much preceded him, as author of the wildly popular "Artemus Ward" humor columns, and he promised some relief from all the grim events of recent months. He had just moved from Cleveland to take a job with a magazine in New York City.

Charlie Brown was tall and lanky, a gangle of limbs, stretching out of sleeves, extending below pant cuffs. For that first visit to Pfaff's, one of the Bohemians noticed that he was wearing a broadcloth vest cut way too high. All his clothes were so old-fashioned and provincial. His hair was very straight, very yellow, and very messy, like an untidy pile of hay. But Brown's most distinguishing feature was his nose: massive, beak-like, and entirely throwing off the composition of his face.

During his first night at Clapp's table, Brown was disappointingly quiet, wearing a hangdog expression—in a somber mood maybe. But he did perk up long enough to fold his napkin into a puppet and dance it beside his coffee cup. Everyone laughed. It was what the Bohemians would most remember about Brown's debut evening. While there is nothing remarkable or inherently hilarious about making a napkin puppet, Brown simply had an instinct for humor.

Brown—twenty-six when he arrived at Pfaff's—had grown up in Waterford, Maine, before heading West. In his youth, the town had a population of two hundred and consisted of about forty houses, nestled in the foothills of the White Mountains. He'd had a strict Congregationalist upbringing, very similar to Clapp's. His father, Levi Brown, worked a variety of jobs, including dry goods merchant, farmer, surveyor, and supervisor of a potash plant. But Levi saved his greatest energy for temperance activities. Brown stock had lived in Waterford since the time of the Revolutionary War. He had relatives with names like Abraham, Aram, Moses, Bathsheba, Asaph, and Abijah. Waterford was the kind of New England community Hawthorne had in mind when he wrote about the "gray shadows" of one's forefathers.

From the time he was a small boy, Brown balked at his town's solemn piety. He became a skilled prankster. One time, Brown hid a deck of playing cards in a minister's robe. When the minister performed a baptism in the river, the cards came floating to the surface. Another reliable source of amusement was sending fake letters to local businesses. This was the nineteenth-century equivalent of a prank phone call. He'd write an angry letter, claiming that a harness hadn't been crafted to specifications, or he'd send the town cooper a note containing an unfulfillably large fictitious order for barrels. In 1846, the year Brown turned twelve, the Smithsonian Institution was founded. Something about its high seriousness triggered Brown's sense of the absurd. So he wrote a mock scholarly work entitled "Is Cats to Be Trusted?" and mailed it off to the new museum.

The next year, his father died. His mother soon grew strapped financially and could not afford to continue caring for either Brown or his older brother. The two boys were shipped off to serve as apprentices. Brown worked a series of jobs as a printer's devil at newspapers such as the *Norway (ME) Advertiser* and the *Coos County (NH) Democrat*. It was the same kind of work Whitman had done in his younger days. Some of Brown's employers were borderline Dickensian, treating him as little more than a live-in drudge. He escaped from an unpleasant work situation at the *Skowhegan (ME) Democratic Clarion* by stringing together bed linens and climbing from a second-story window in the dead of night.

But Brown fell into a happier situation with a publication called the *Carpet-Bag*. He was taken on as an apprentice there in 1851, the year the Boston-based magazine was launched. It was one of America's first comic publications, edited by a man with the wonderful name of Benjamin Penhallow Shillaber. Shillaber was a stout, jolly man akin to Mr. Fezziwig in *A Christmas Carol*. "To promote cheerfulness" was the official mandate of the *Carpet-Bag*. The magazine very quickly achieved a national reputation. Soon it was publishing the efforts of talented writers such as George Derby and Mathew Whittier, the poet's younger brother. Because many of the *Carpet-Bag*'s contributors were otherwise serious writers, they often hid their identities behind pen names such as Enoch Fitzwhistle, Peter Snooks, and John P. Squibob. As a printer's devil, Brown's job was to arrange letters in trays, preparing pages of the magazine to be run off on the press. For apprentice Brown, constructing works of comedy word by painstaking word proved an illuminating exercise.

During Brown's *Carpet-Bag* stint, a young man named Samuel Langhorne Clemens published a short item entitled "The Dandy Frightening the Squatter." To this point, Clemens's efforts had appeared exclusively in the *Hannibal (MO) Western Union,* edited by his older brother, Orion Clemens. This then represented his first published piece outside the family venture. It ran in the May 1, 1852, issue of the *Carpet-Bag;* Clemens was then sixteen years old. It's quite likely that Brown typeset Clemens's item, though it wouldn't have particularly stood out. "The Dandy Frightening the Squatter" is very short and failed to garner much attention. The byline was simply initials, S. L. C.

(Clemens and Brown were destined to meet in the future, under vastly different circumstances—different names, too.)

Brown also managed to place his own first published effort in the *Carpet-Bag*. After writing a comic piece he thought suitably promising, Brown recopied it, disguising his handwriting. Then he surreptitiously placed it on Shillaber's desk. The editor acquired it at once. Only after he'd had the pleasure of typesetting his own creation did Brown reveal that he was in fact the author. The piece was about a drunken George Washington, commanding the Continental army at Yorktown. For a pseudonym, Brown chose "Lieutenant Chubb." (*Chubb* was a kind of mashing up of *Charlie* and *Brown* as well as an ironic reference to the gangly author, who was anything but chubby.) Brown went on to write about a half-dozen Lieutenant Chubb items.

In 1853, the *Carpet-Bag* folded. Brown headed West by rail and stage, looking for work. He carried with him the tool of his trade—a compositor's stick—and he took whatever jobs he could find, often lasting a matter of weeks or days. Once, Brown simply walked along the banks of the Sandusky River until he arrived at tiny Tiffin, Ohio, where he got a job at the *Seneca Advertiser*. From there, he moved up to the larger *Toledo Commercial*. In Toledo, Brown once again got the chance to write, this time as a newspaper reporter. Soon, he graduated to one of the most esteemed papers in the West, the *Cleveland Plain Dealer*.

By now, Brown was twenty-three and already a publishing veteran. He was hired as the *Plain Dealer*'s local editor, charged with writing the "City Facts and Fancies" column. Each day, he had to fill his column with reports on arrests, fires, civic board meetings, and the arrival and departures of trains. The job was a monotonous grind. Once, on an especially slow news day, Brown slipped an imaginary letter into his *Plain Dealer* column from a man named "Artemus Ward." It was an instant hit with Cleveland readers. So Brown began producing Ward letters on a regular basis.

The fictional Ward was a traveling entertainer who promised moral betterment to his audiences. Writing as Ward, Brown employed idiosyncratic spellings: "noncents," "puncktooaly," and "Decleration of

Inderpendunse." Many of these fractured spellings were quite expressive, such as "glowrius" (shouldn't the word include *glow*?) or "confisticate" (doesn't seizing property seem like it should involve a *fist*?). While Ward's traveling show was forever going disastrously wrong, he still managed—in a satisfyingly ridiculous and roundabout way—to deliver the moral enlightenment he promised. It was quite a winning comedy formula.

As for the name "Artemus Ward," there are many stories about its origins. The most convincing is probably the simplest: one of Brown's Maine forebears was named Artemas. Brown simply changed the spelling to "Artemus" and then paired this colorful first name with "Ward," a plain-vanilla last name, and—voilà—a character was born.

Each new Artemus Ward letter in the *Plain Dealer* was met with great anticipation. Thanks to the same postal exchange system that had benefited the *Saturday Press*, Brown's comic stylings were soon being reprinted in papers all over the country.

Presently, *Vanity Fair* came calling, signing up Brown to contribute a series of original Artemus Ward letters. *Vanity Fair* (no relation to the modern title) was a short-lived but pioneering humor journal, following on the heels of the failed *Carpet-Bag*. While the *Carpet-Bag* specialized in gentle whimsy, *Vanity Fair* was far edgier. It was more akin to *Punch*, the British magazine. *Vanity Fair* was based in Manhattan and had close ties to Pfaff's; many of the Bohemians were regular contributors, including O'Brien and Ada Clare. From Cleveland, Brown published several Artemus Ward letters in *Vanity Fair*. He was paid $10 per piece, then a small but respectable sum.

J. W. Gray, editor of the *Plain Dealer*, was livid when he learned that his star humor columnist was freelancing. He demanded that Brown publish all future Artemus Ward letters first in the *Plain Dealer*, his employer, after all. Brown's response went something like this: *I'll happily give my entire output to the paper, but you need to give me a raise.* Brown, who was earning a very modest $800 a year, asked for $1,200. Gray refused. So Brown started corresponding with Charles Leland, editor of *Vanity Fair*. Leland offered him a job as an associate editor at a salary of $1,000. The arrangement called on him to contribute

Artemus Ward columns and also to edit pieces by other writers. Brown quit the *Plain Dealer*. When he arrived in Manhattan on January 1, 1861, it was to start this new job.

Brown quickly found his niche in the conversational whirl at Clapp's long table. He possessed a unique brand of humor, which he doled out in small doses, judiciously. Sometimes, he'd sit for long minutes in silence with the most mournful look on his face. (Like so many funny people, Brown was deeply sad at core.) Suddenly, he'd brighten and say something that had the crowd in stitches, before retreating back into silence.

Brown was crafty, very crafty. He was a man of immense ambition as well as a remarkably fast study. For years, he had worked as an itinerant newspaperman, forever wandering into fresh situations, so he knew how to adapt in an instant. "Quiet as he seemed, in three weeks he had found out everything in New York," Leland, the *Vanity Fair* editor, would recall.

Brown also was quick to make friends at Pfaff's. One night, around three, he and William Winter staggered home after a night of hard drinking. They arrived at Brown's rooming house on Great Jones Street. All their rattling roused one of the landlord's servants. Brown asked the man to deliver a message to the landlord.

"It is late, sir," said the servant.

"I know it is late," replied Brown, "but I have a message for him, of the utmost importance. It is urgent, and I am sure he will be glad to receive it. Do you think you could wake him?"

The servant asked what it was.

For some minutes, Brown worked to earn the man's assurances that he would deliver the message with perfect accuracy. Brown seemed so earnest and intent. The servant promised that he would relay every word. Then Brown delivered his message for the landlord: "Tell him, with my very kindest regards, that—*the price of liberty is eternal vigilance.*"

The servant stalked off, shaking his head in puzzled disgust. But the episode really stuck with Winter. It captured something essential about Brown. "He possessed, in an extraordinary degree, the faculty of maintaining a solemn composure of countenance while making comic or ridiculous statements," Winter would recall.

Drunken nights were followed by work-filled days at *Vanity Fair*. Brown's hours were explicitly spelled out; he was allowed to arrive at the magazine's Spruce Street offices at the leisurely hour of ten. He wrote regular Artemus Ward letters. He also edited the work of many of the Bohemians, including Ludlow. To this point, Ludlow had failed to follow up the audacious promise of *The Hasheesh Eater*. Instead, he was making an increasingly precarious living as a freelance writer for magazines and newspapers. Something was clearly holding him back, and his beautiful wife, Rosalie, was growing more resentful by the day. With Brown as editor, Ludlow managed one of his more successful efforts, a serial comic tale for *Vanity Fair* entitled "The Primpenny Family."

Still, Brown quickly came to the conclusion that *Vanity Fair* wasn't a long-term employment prospect. The *Saturday Press* had recently died; the climate that killed it was only growing worse during the first months of 1861. In the likely event that *Vanity Fair* failed, Brown knew he needed a fallback. He decided to work up a comic lecture in the guise of his wildly popular fictional creation, Artemus Ward. Of course, this would require making certain adjustments. There were many aspects of the character that simply wouldn't translate from the written page to a performance. For example, it's not possible verbally to deliver a fractured spelling such as "vishus beest." Yet Brown recognized that there was a way to capitalize on Artemus Ward's renown, while at the same time reimagining the character.

Sometimes, Brown tested his work in progress at Clapp's table. It was extremely well received. "He came with about half his effort, and for three-quarters of an hour the party was, literally, in a roar," recalled J. W. Watson, a sometime Pfaffian.

To play the role of Artemus Ward, Brown also recognized that he needed to alter his appearance. He needed a costume. Ward, as Brown conceived him, would be a kind of send-up of popular lecturers of the day such as John Gough, Wendell Phillips, and even Ralph Waldo

Emerson. These deeply serious men played packed houses, delivering bromides about self-improvement and moral betterment—or at least that was Brown's comic view.

With the help of the Pfaff's crowd, he began to assemble the costume. He sought input from some of the members with theater experience, such as Ada Clare and Winter, who coupled poetry with drama criticism for newspapers. Brown bought a fittingly somber dark suit, a too-fancy bow tie, and a pair of patent-leather slippers. Taking the transformation still further, he visited a coiffeur, who dyed his yellow hair jet black and curled it into a ridiculous frizzy mane.

Brown was preparing to embark on a "lecture tour" the likes of which the country had never seen. Soon, nobody who knew him—neither old friends in Cleveland nor new friends at Pfaff's—would call him Charlie Brown. He was about to become Artemus Ward.

CHAPTER 10

"The Heather Is on Fire"

LATE IN THE EVENING of April 12, 1861, Whitman was walking along Broadway on his way home to Brooklyn. He had just attended a performance of Verdi's opera *A Masked Ball,* at the Academy of Music. Lincoln, ever a devotee of the arts, had attended the same production during his recent visit to the city.

Suddenly, a group of newsboys came tearing up the street toward Whitman. They were hawking extra editions with an intensity way beyond their usual ardor. From their cries, the poet quickly learned the news. Though hardly unexpected, it was shocking just the same.

Whitman bought a paper. He walked to the nearby Metropolitan hotel, planning to read by the light of a gas lamp. Several dozen people had already gathered when he arrived. One of them began to read from a paper out loud. The details started to emerge.

Southern soldiers had fired on Fort Sumter in Charleston Harbor. This was the culmination of a tense standoff that had been going on all through the first months of 1861. Francis Pickens, governor of first-to-secede South Carolina, had provided the crisis's original spark, demanding that the federal government renounce claim to any and all property in his state. That included Sumter. Major Robert Anderson and a garrison of soldiers had then holed up in the fort, maintaining it for the United States. Over time, they began to run low on food and supplies. Anderson and his men soon faced the prospect of being starved out of Sumter.

Throughout its initial weeks, the Lincoln administration had been consumed by this emergency. Finally, the president and his cabinet hit

135

upon a plan: dispatch a fleet of boats to Sumter, bearing only food and provisions (no weapons or ordnance). Lincoln took the additional step of informing Governor Pickens ahead of time. This was a tactical master-stroke, Lincoln's first brilliant move as president. It promised a dilemma for the newly formed Confederacy. If the relief boats were allowed to sail across Charleston Harbor to Sumter unmenaced, it would be a moral victory for the federal government and for the concept of national unity. But if ships carrying food were fired upon, it would be viewed as an act of Southern aggression. Jefferson Davis, president of the fledgling Confederacy, didn't bother waiting for the relief flotilla. He gave the order to take Sumter. The first shots were fired on April 12 at four thirty in the morning. Word reached New York City that evening.

Whitman and the crowd at the Metropolitan listened as the newspaper account was read aloud. Afterward, people stood around for a minute or two, saying little, mostly absorbing the news. "I can almost see them there now, under the lamps at midnight," Whitman wrote many years later. Then this impromptu group of strangers dissolved, slipping back into the city.

Hard to believe: a fractured nation was taking up arms against itself. Now that civil war had broken out, the Pfaff's set would be forced to make sense of a new reality. Some such as Whitman would struggle mightily to find their way. Others would adjust with startling speed. Over time, most of these artists would manage to carve out their own unique places in a nation at war.

To do so would require leaving New York City and the cloistered safety of Pfaff's, though the group's members would return to their favorite haunt whenever they passed back through Manhattan. They would also manage to reconnect in other parts of the country, meeting up in some vivid new settings. The Civil War would have a profound effect on Clapp's circle, pushing its members in unexpected directions. Along the way, they would carry the Bohemianism forged in that underground saloon out across the land.

During the war's very first days, a surprising mood prevailed. There was a curiously festive, almost giddy feeling in the air. For years, the threat of civil war had been hanging over the nation. A string of presidents, most recently "dung-eating" Pierce and "dough-faced" Buchanan, had offered tepid compromises to maintain an uneasy peace. Whitman's 1860 edition of *Leaves of Grass* had been filled with dark presentiments of strife between the states, yet with the arrival of war, it was as though a long pent-up tension had broken.

"The heather is on fire," said a Harvard professor. "I never knew what a popular excitement can be." Thayer, the recently bankrupted publisher, wrote to Whitman from Boston: "My soul swells as I contemplate the mighty issues involved in this contest." The time had come, at last, to put to rest a conflict that had been dogging the nation since its very inception. There was also a sense that this would be a short war. Both sides, North and South, were certain that it would require only a single battle to demonstrate their military—and moral—superiority. William Seward, Lincoln's newly appointed secretary of state, predicted that the war would last sixty days.

New York, especially, became caught up in war fever. This was something that no one would have expected. Because the city maintained a vast network of trade relationships with the South, it had always struck a posture of ambivalence toward the region, bordering on amorality. The business of New York was business. But now that war had been declared, the city's loyalties were instantly clarified: New York was a Northern city staunchly in the Union camp. American flags went up everywhere: raised on rooftops, hanging from tenement windows, flying on carts and coaches. A flag was even added to Manhattan's tallest building, the Trinity Church. It was hoisted to the very tip of the spire, 284 feet up in the air for everyone to see. Shopkeepers did a brisk business in Union-color neckties and portraits of Major Anderson, hero of Sumter. "The excitement caused by recent events . . . is most intense—it is indescribable," noted the *Brooklyn Eagle*. "Every one, old and young, man and boy, and even women and children, are fired with a military enthusiasm such as no one alive has ever before witnessed in this country."

When Lincoln requested seventy-five thousand volunteers for ninety-day terms of service, New York was especially fervent in

answering the call. The city's residents moved quickly to form compa-
nies of soldiers. These tended to mirror Manhattan's polyglot makeup:
The 8th New York Volunteer Regiment, known as Blenker's Rifles,
was composed almost entirely of German immigrants. There were also
regiments consisting mostly of Italians, Poles, and Dutchmen. During
these earliest days, there wasn't yet any kind of standardized dress for
the Union army. Only later, as a mighty war machine cranked up,
would the Union troops come to be identified by signature blue uni-
forms. At the outset, however, the Cameron Highlanders, a regiment
of Scottish immigrants, wore tartan trousers (no kilts, at least) and had
its own bagpipe band. The 55th New York Volunteer Infantry, a French
regiment also known as the Garde de Lafayette, were stylishly outfitted
in red pants, dark-blue frock coats, and caps. Upon being mustered
into service, soldiers outfitted in wildly un-uniform uniforms marched
down Broadway on their way out of town. Huge crowds saw them off,
applauding and tossing flowers. One soldier described Broadway as a
"tempest of cheers, two miles long."

Departing troops marched directly past Pfaff's. Whitman was often
on hand, watching as they filed by in brightly colored formations. Early
in the war, he wrote the following in a notebook: "I have this hour, this
day resolved to inaugurate a sweet, clean-blooded body by ignoring
all drinks but water and pure milk—and all fat meats, late suppers—a
great body—a purged, cleansed, spiritualized invigorated body." There
was a loftiness to this statement, coupled with a vagueness, reminiscent
of his earlier desire to become a professional "wander-speaker." But he
didn't keep to his resolve for long. He continued going to Pfaff's, kept
drinking lager and enjoying late suppers of his favorite beefsteak. He
was becoming shaggier, too, letting his hair and beard grow out. More
than anything, it seems, Whitman's "resolution" was a search for a way
to get caught up in the sweep of events.

Enlisting was out of the question. Now forty-one, he was too old
and certainly lacked a soldier's temperament. "Could there be any-
thing more shocking and incongruous than Whitman killing people?"
a friend once asked. It perfectly sums up the matter.

Most of Whitman's fellow Pfaffians proved similarly unsuited for military duty. Clapp wasn't exactly a joiner. In any case, at age forty-six, he was too old. Ludlow, Winter, the poet Arnold, and others didn't feel compelled to volunteer for assorted reasons, including age, lack of physical hardiness, or a generally unmartial disposition.

O'Brien was an exception, and he enlisted immediately. He'd never shied from a good fight. He was also handy with guns, or at least was more comfortable using one than his fellow Bohemians. One time, he had gotten into a heated discussion in a Manhattan restaurant about whether the story of William Tell shooting an apple off his son's head was truth or myth. Truth, insisted a drunken O'Brien. To prove it, he drew a gun and proceeded to point out as targets—then shoot—various portions of the chandelier.

O'Brien volunteered for the 7th Regiment of the New York Militia, an outfit with a reputation for being filled with dandies. One newspaper called it a "Regiment of Beaux." For O'Brien, it was a perfect fit. He was especially drawn to the pomp of soldiering: "Why, when I am marching down Broadway I do not know whether I am a part of the universe, or whether the universe is a part of me."

Among Clapp's circle, one of the few others who sought military service was Thomas Aldrich, the poet and onetime *Saturday Press* deputy. In fact, Aldrich and O'Brien would ultimately compete for the same position, as an aid to General Frederick Lander. O'Brien would win the post.

While Pfaff's saloon wasn't exactly a wellspring of soldiers, it did produce some war correspondents. As a consequence, *Bohemian*—a term that had proved so versatile for the French—took on an additional meaning in English. At the beginning of the Civil War, *Bohemian* became synonymous with *journalist,* a meaning that would hold for years to come, before fading out of usage. This made sense: war correspondents tended to be scruffy, hard-drinking sorts, the type of people who were associated with Bohemianism in the popular imagination. Only a portion of these so-called Bohemians had actually spent any time at Clapp's table. Poet Edmund Stedman; Edward House, a drama critic for the *New York Tribune;* and Charles Webb, a regular contributor to *Vanity Fair,* along with a handful of others, successfully made the transition from Pfaff's habitué to war correspondent.

Public tastes were changing fast. Now in demand was a steady stream of war news. The *New York Tribune* debuted an evening edition. The *Herald* answered by introducing three separate afternoon editions at 1:30, 3:00, and 5:00. The appetite had greatly diminished for the types of writing favored by Clapp's coterie, such as satire, scathing cultural criticism, and experimental poetry. The *Saturday Press* was no more, and *Vanity Fair* was barely alive. Many of Pfaff's wordsmiths found themselves quickly out of step.

Whitman tried to adapt. During those heady first days, he roughed out a brief poem called "Broadway, 1861." It was—for lack of a better term—a recruiting poem, not in any official capacity, but simply in subject and style. Other poets, also trying to adjust to the new realities, wrote "recruiting poems" at around this time. William Cullen Bryant, for example, offered "Our Country's Call."

Whitman's poem was inspired in part by his brother George. As the most practical Whitman sibling, George was the only one of the six brothers to enlist. Less than a week after Sumter, he signed up for the army. When George's ninety-day service was up, he would reenlist, joining the 51st New York.

Whitman, however, would abandon "Broadway, 1861." He didn't polish it further, didn't try to get it ready for publication. He must have recognized that it was not one of his finest efforts:

> The sights now there
> The splendid flags flying over all the stores
> (The wind sets from the west—the flags are out stiff and broad—you
>   can count every star of the thirty-four—you can count the thirteen
>   stripes.)
> The regiments arriving and departing,
> The Barracks—the soldiers lounging around,
> The recruiting band, preceded by the fifer—
> The ceaseless din

In the future, Whitman would write very different types of war poems, often infusing the subject with an air of ambivalence, even dread. Finding his own distinctive voice for capturing a war would prove difficult. It would require authentic experience, and even then Whitman would forever question whether art—limited, imprecise art—offered an adequate window into something as vast and chaotic as war. Ultimately, he would require something larger than poetry to find his place.

While some writers and artists foundered with the outbreak of the Civil War, others prospered. As quickly became clear, people on the home front had two distinct and utterly contradictory needs. They wanted a constant flow of hard news about the war, with maybe the occasional martial-themed poem thrown into the mix. Otherwise, they desired pure escapism. This created an unexpected division among Clapp's set of Bohemians.

While the scribes mostly struggled at the outset, the actors were quick to thrive. Asia Booth described the Civil War as "the harvest time for theaters." As the sister of Edwin and John Wilkes, she was in a position to know. Looking back on this time, one New Yorker would say, "I remember well, in the first year of our war, when we were profoundly miserable and frightened, what a relief it was to go and see [Edwin] Booth in 'Hamlet.'"

Demand for dramatic fare was so great that in 1861, impresario John Ford opened a theater in an abandoned church in Washington, DC. It burned down the following year. Not wanting to miss the boom, he would race to build a new Ford's Theatre.

For the most part, actors were identified with a particular region, either the North or the South. After war broke out, Edwin began his successful run of *Hamlet* in New York. Brother John was a frequent performer in the Confederate states. But there was a looseness to the North-South rule, at least where actors were concerned. They certainly weren't soldiers; neither were they pillars of the community, such as merchants, doctors, or preachers. On matters other than stagecraft, society didn't tend to take actors very seriously. Their political views were considered inconsequential. This served as a kind of passport. Actors could move more easily between the North and South than most people during the Civil War. Thus, John also performed extensively in the North. In fact, Whitman attended an 1861 performance of *Richard III* in New York City with John playing the lead. Whitman never met Edwin's brother. But the poet later said, "He was a queer fellow: had strange ways: it would take some effort to get used, adjusted, to him: but now and then he would have flashes, passages, I thought, of real genius."

An unanticipated result of this theater bounty was the sudden and spectacular reemergence of a fallen Pfaffian. Less than a year earlier, Adah Isaacs Menken, reduced to performing at the tawdry Canterbury concert saloon, had fallen into near-fatal despair. But one of Menken's defining traits was a capacity for startlingly rapid transformation. With the outbreak of the war, her fortunes revived. In fact, her career took off like one of the 23rd New York Light Artillery's rockets.

The mastermind of Menken's unlikely comeback was Captain John Smith, manager of the Green Street Theatre in Albany. The dramatic vehicle that transported her to glory was *Mazeppa; or, The Wild Horse of Tartary,* a shopworn historical play and repertory staple for decades. Captain Smith, a man with considerable Barnum flair, hoped to breathe new life into this tired tale. Menken was key to his vision.

The play was loosely—very loosely—based on the story of Ivan Mazeppa, a Ukrainian Cossack born in the 1600s. The real Mazeppa led an eventful life, filled with byzantine political intrigue involving such figures as Russia's Peter the Great and Charles XII of Sweden. But it was a single episode, almost certainly apocryphal, that managed to capture the imagination of people beyond the northern latitudes. Supposedly, Ivan Mazeppa and a Polish count were rivals for the affections of the same beautiful woman. To dispense with his adversary, the count arranged for Mazeppa to be stripped naked, lashed to the back of a horse, and sent off into the wilderness to die. Somehow, Mazeppa survived and became a Cossack chieftain.

In 1819, Lord Byron published a lengthy poem, "Mazeppa." He transformed his subject from a Cossack into a Tartar—why worry the details? The poem's central conceit, a bound and bare Mazeppa, strapped to a stallion, hurtling across frigid and punishing terrain, proved an irresistible image for Byron. In his rendering, against all odds, Mazeppa survives his equine ordeal to lead an uprising against the Poles, vanquishing his people's evil oppressors. Mazeppa is a man ruled by overwhelming passions. He's a fighter—a freedom fighter—and a lover, who in the end wins back his lady true.

And so it was that the blurry outlines of the life of an obscure Balkan political figure became fodder for art. Inspired by Byron, Victor Hugo wrote an epic poem of his own about Mazeppa. Both Géricault and Delacroix painted the "Tartar" hero. Franz Liszt composed an especially challenging piano étude devoted to the subject.

In 1831, English playwright Henry Milner did a treatment of Mazeppa. Milner was no Shakespeare; his work is distinguished by slovenly plotlines, cardboard characters, and overwrought dialogue. Nevertheless, he possessed a keen instinct about popular tastes. He was among the first to adapt Mary Shelley's *Frankenstein* for the stage. The immortal line "It's alive!" is actually from Milner's play, not Shelley's novel. With *Mazeppa*, he managed to create an enduring work. The winning formula was spectacle, what today would be called special effects. His *Mazeppa* calls for lush costuming, elaborate set pieces, and epic battle scenes. Many productions even featured a live horse onstage. By 1861, an entire generation of theatergoers had been treated to *Mazeppa*. Over time, it had become safe, reliable fare. The play was—in the truest sense—a warhorse.

Captain Smith, the Albany impresario, planned to change that. Rather than have a man play the lead, he wanted a woman. And why not bind her to a real horse? Traditionally, for the play's climactic scene, the actor playing Mazeppa was replaced by a dummy, which was strapped to a docile dray horse. The horse would trot in circles for a spell, moving against a backdrop painted to look like a wilderness scene. In some productions, the horse even went up a small ramp, suggesting a climb through a treacherous mountain pass. This furnished audiences with a serviceable, but not exactly pulse-quickening, simulation of that wild ride. None of that for Captain Smith; he wanted a gorgeous woman atop a horse.

Menken was the ideal choice—for so many reasons. For starters, there was a robustness to her sensuality; she was no dainty, delicate beauty like her friend Ada Clare. This quality apparently suggested Menken might be convincing in drag, as a Tartar warrior. Once she was stripped down—to a sheer, flesh-colored body stocking—she was certain to command an audience's attention. Menken's fearlessness was also a plus. To play the role would require that she be bound to a horse while lying on her back, spread-eagled, yet somehow manage to hang on. An ingenious rig had been fashioned, making it possible for her to tighten her precarious purchase on the horse's back by tugging on the lashings. This was like a circus trick. Once again, Menken filled the bill, as she could draw on equestrian experience gained while touring Texas with Victor Franconi's Imperial Hippodrome. She was almost uniquely qualified to play the role. As for the whiff of scandal that surrounded Menken—well, that was simply a bonus in the eyes of Captain Smith.

Mazeppa opened on June 7, 1861. To drum up advance publicity, the captain had paraded the production's thoroughbred lead, Belle Beauty, up and down Albany's Main Street. He plastered posters on every available surface. As a result, the Green Street Theatre was "crowded from pit to dome," recalled Smith.

During the opening scenes, Menken comported herself adequately. She engaged in a rousing sword fight, even managed to remember some of her dialogue. Captain Smith was prepared for this: he had placed himself in the production, playing a character that tails Mazeppa. That way, he was able to feed whispered lines to his star. Then came the big scene. At the urging of the Polish count, soldiers ripped off Mazeppa's tunic, revealing the buxom Menken underneath. The audience gasped. In the weak glow of the theater's calcium lights, it was impossible to tell whether or not she was naked. She was lashed to Belle Beauty. Then the horse started up a specially built ramp that wound around and around, rising to a height four stories above the stage. It featured canvas panels with images of rocks and trees and a waterfall—at last, a prop that could proximate a mountain. Up and up climbed Belle Beauty. At the very top, horse and rider exited through an archway.

Following the wild ride, unfortunately, plenty of play remains. *Mazeppa* is a badly paced drama, like everything in the Milner oeuvre. The remaining action includes battles, a wedding, and some kind of Tartar tribal hootenanny; there are mistaken identities, reunited lovers, and endless soliloquies. When the curtain fell opening night, however, the Albany audience remembered only one thing. "It had to be seen to be believed," said one attendee. "Parts of the body of this actress were exposed that God never intended to be seen by any eye other than her mother's."

Captain Smith had a hit. *Mazeppa* enjoyed a six-week sold-out engagement at the Green Street Theatre. Then, beginning in July 1861—right after Bull Run, the Civil War's first major battle—the show went on the road, traveling from Pittsburgh to Cincinnati to Milwaukee. The timing for a successful revival of *Mazeppa* was perfect. The play's battle scenes had a degree of resonance with the new reality of an America at war. But only a degree: the combatants were Tartars and Poles, so there was no risk of audiences being too closely reminded of current events. *Mazeppa* also promised cultural enrichment. In the prudish Victorian era, this provided convenient cover for many playgoers. To attend *Mazeppa* was an edifying experience, a chance to gain useful information about history, pageantry, and the customs of faraway lands. All that, plus you got to see a naked lady.

As *Mazeppa* traveled from town to town, Menken, predictably, never succeeded in fully memorizing her lines. Audiences were treated to a different version every single night. "I was not impressed by her acting though her form spoke loudly," recalled one theatergoer.

Nevertheless, Menken took herself very seriously as an artist. While she offered neither consistency nor much dramatic ability, she brought a rare intensity to the role. No doubt, that helped sell the production. Menken wrote an account of playing *Mazeppa* where she described "resting on the bare back of the leaping, dashing steed, and whirled up the mimic mountains of peril and danger." She added, "I am as wild and as earnest in my dressing-room, and woe to the unlucky creature who displeases me, or opposes me in look or deed! . . . They think I am crazy at night. My attention can never be turned to any subject but the stage as long as the piece lasts. I see and hear nothing else. I feel nothing but the character I represent. To be so intense requires soul."

During a run at Boston's Howard Athenaeum, Menken managed to summon that passion both on- and offstage. "My business here is wonderful, and enthusiasm is on the increase," she wrote to her freshly hired advance man in New York. Yes, *Mazeppa* had become so popular so quickly that already she needed an advance man. She added, "Last night I had to go before the curtain *four times*!"

During her Howard Athenaeum stand, it seems, Menken also had a sexual fling with none other than Artemus Ward, her fellow Pfaffian, née Charlie Brown. The pair "'went it' pretty rapid for a few days here," as she put it. Apparently, they were also spotted together in public. Worried that she and Ward would become grist for the gossip columns, Menken instructed her advance man to deny any reports that they were an item, and certainly any claims that they were altar bound. "It won't do to be married," Menken wrote. That was something she'd already done, thrice. Only recently had she obtained a divorce from Heenan, her absentee boxer husband. What had happened with Ward, she assured her advance man, was only a brief dalliance, nothing more.

But what about Artemus Ward? What was he doing in Boston besides going it rapid with Menken? Turns out that Ward was in the midst of a wildly successful tour of his own. His timing had been exquisite. Not relying solely on writing, diversifying with a stage act, had proved a brilliant move. He'd practiced his material at Clapp's table. He'd refined it based on the frank feedback of the Bohemians. When the Civil War broke out, he was ready. Ward, it's safe to say, was the only member of the Pfaff's set currently creating even more of a sensation than Menken.

Ostensibly, he was delivering a lecture called *The Babes in the Wood*. The posters and notices that went up in advance of his performances simply offered, "Artemus Ward will speak a piece." His act was bizarre, like nothing audiences had ever before witnessed.

To begin each performance, Ward would stand there in silence, allowing the audience to look him over. Many attendees had expected they'd be seeing the "Old Showman" character from the popular "Artemus Ward" letters in the *Plain Dealer* and *Vanity Fair*. Others weren't sure what to expect. But one thing was now clear: the man on stage was so young. Yet he was dressed like a man twice his age: silk cravat, suit and tails, shiny cuff links, a pocket watch on a chain. He had a shockingly large nose and a truly ridiculous coiffed mane of jet-black curls. His expression was mournful.

Ward would maintain his silence for many minutes, providing the audience a long—an uncomfortably long—opportunity to study him. Invariably, people would start to snicker. At this, Ward would dart his eyes nervously, maybe shift from one foot to another. More snickering. Finally, he would announce in a halting voice, "Ladies and gentlemen: When you have finished this . . . unseemly interruption . . . I guess I'll begin my discourse."

The crowd would erupt. This was a tour-de-force opener; it never failed to break the tension. As an attendee at one of his shows recalled, "And the audience, as if feeling that it could not come to the relief of the unhappy man too quickly, and assure him of its entire neighborliness and sympathy, broke out spontaneously with hand-clapping that said plainly enough, 'Welcome, welcome! Be not cast down! We shall laugh at anything you say.'"

Ward would then launch into his act, rarely smiling, never breaking character. He'd begin an anecdote, only to drift off on to some other topic. He'd sputter and weave, unable to quite find his conversational balance, forever trying to recover. Many of his jokes depended on non sequiturs. For example, "I met a man in Oregon who hadn't any teeth—not a tooth in his head." He'd pause for a moment, letting the audience absorb that. Then he'd add, "Yet that man could play on the bass drum better than any man I ever met."

When the audience laughed, Ward would often look flustered. It was as if he wasn't sure what he'd said, or why it was funny. Sometimes, the laughter would appear to cause him to lose his train of thought. A look of reproach might cross his face, as if to say, *I'm struggling here, valiantly trying to make a serious point. Why is everyone laughing?* This only added to the crowd's enjoyment.

Like all the finest humorists, Ward had a gift. Also, like Menken with *Mazeppa,* he benefited from the fact that his work resonated with the times. To wit: his act consisted of a man in a dark suit, who, in a tone of complete seriousness, speaks utter nonsense. At some level, it certainly reminded audiences of all the oratories and lectures and sermons they'd been forced to endure, delivered by assorted pompous moralists. Perhaps, some even caught a hint of the politician in Ward. Politicians—with their distinguished bearings and stentorian voices—could talk a good game. But they'd pitched the nation into war just the same.

Ward was a meticulous artist. While Menken didn't bother to learn her lines, he practiced every "um" and "ah," timed every pause. The impression that his performances were rambling and spontaneous was just that, an impression: he was in complete control. As he moved deeper into a show, audiences grew accustomed to his quirky rhythm. It became possible to trot out highly precise comic bits, dependent on subtleties of timing and delivery.

An example is Ward's penitentiary joke. He would begin by struggling to describe the claustrophobic feeling of traveling inside a very small stagecoach. "Those of you who have been in the penitentiary . . . ," he offered. But then his voice trailed off, and his eyes filled with panic. He realized his error. He'd just suggested that members of his audience had been to jail.

As Ward tried to extricate himself from this awkwardness, the audience could almost see the wheels turning in his mind. He spoke slowly, trying to buy himself time to recover: "and stayed there . . . any length . . . of time . . . " Suddenly, his expression brightened. He added hopefully, " . . . as *visitors.*" He stood up straight, pleased with himself. But then Ward's trademark crestfallen look returned. He recognized his error. Even suggesting that members of his audience had merely visited the penitentiary didn't do the trick. That only meant they had friends and loved ones in jail.

This was bravura material, requiring an intense rapport with an audience. Along with timing and delivery, Ward benefited from some physical attributes, unique to him. He had a highly expressive face, making it possible to communicate emotions to people sitting at quite a distance. He was also easy to hear, blessed with a voice that one attendee called "clear as a bell and peculiarly magnetic; it seemed to grip you." In the days before electronic amplification, the value of a strong speaking voice cannot be overstated. Stage careers—Ada Clare's is an example—could be dashed by a weak one. Even in a packed auditorium, audiences were able to pick up every nuance of Ward's act. There's even speculation that he achieved sonic advantage thanks to his huge nose—perhaps it acted as some kind of amplification device. (While one can endlessly dissect Ward's skills and formula, his magic will always be elusive. Whatever made him so uproariously funny is simply unknowable.)

Ward's show clocked in at exactly one hour. Just as it opened on a high note, it closed on one, too. As the hour mark drew nigh, Ward would reach into his pocket and retrieve his watch. He'd stare at it, an expression of alarm spreading across his face. He had been rambling for many minutes, traveling countless conversational tangents, yet he'd failed to address the subject at hand, "The Babes in the Wood." But what could he say now? What pithy comment about the topic could he offer that might tie things up? There simply wasn't enough time left. After a few more stumbles and false starts, Ward would apologize, promising to give the subject a full airing during his next lecture. Then he'd bid a good night to his delighted audience. The next morning, the critics' columns would be full of praise.

Ward's show was so fresh that no one was even sure what to call it. Newspapers often referred to his act as a "humorous lecture." But it's fair to describe Artemus Ward as America's first stand-up comedian.

Throughout those first months of the Civil War, Ward kept up a relentless schedule. By day, he would travel to his next engagement, often aboard trains packed with soldiers headed for destinations of their own. In the evenings—save for Sundays—he played a succession of towns:

Brooklyn; Newark; New Haven; Hornellsville, New York; Paterson, New Jersey; South Danvers, Massachusetts. But even after he'd completed a show, his day wasn't done. It was his practice to make late-night visits to the offices of the local newspaper in whatever town he happened to be playing.

Over the years, Ward had worked for dozens of papers as everything from a printer's devil to a columnist. Though he was a comedian now, he retained a kind of homing instinct. Every town—no matter how small—usually had at least one newspaper. For a man as itinerant as Ward, it seems, this provided a sense of consistency. Journalists tended to work late, too. There was comfort in being surrounded by the presses and type boxes. Sometimes, after a show, Ward was known to drop by a newspaper unannounced, roll up his sleeves, and help set type.

For a while, the frenetic Ward also continued his association with *Vanity Fair,* contributing an occasional piece from the road. Thanks to his celebrity, he was even promoted to editor. But he'd prove an absurdly absentee editor. The magazine died soon enough, anyway. "Comic copy is what they wanted for *Vanity Fair,*" he quipped. "I wrote some and it killed it."

While traveling the Union North, Ward and Menken often crossed paths. They began to develop an uneasy friendship. It appears that Ward wanted more out of the relationship. But Menken didn't reciprocate the feelings. She and Ward had already had their fling, and her eye was now on other playthings.

While in Racine, Wisconsin, touring for *Mazeppa,* Menken wrote a long letter to Hattie Tyng, a twenty-one-year-old poet who would later publish a popular volume, *Apple-Blossoms.* Menken asked Tyng:

> Do you believe in the deepest and tenderest love between women? Do you believe that women often love each other with as much fervor and excitement as they do men? . . . We find the rarest and most perfect beauty in the affections of one woman for another. . . . The electricity of the one flashes and gleams through the other, to be returned not only in *degree* as between man and women, but in

kind as between precisely similar organizations. And these passions are of the more frequent ocurrence [*sic*] than the world is aware of—generally they are unknown to all but the hearts concerned . . . I have had my passionate attachments among women, which swept like whirlwinds over me, sometimes, alas! scorching me with a furnace-blast, but generally only changing and renewing my capacities for love.

Menken was intense, all right. When she wanted something—or someone—she could really come on strong. Even so, Hattie Tyng looks to have resisted her advances. But this much is certain: for a traveling Bohemian, life on the road offered ample opportunity for adventure.

CHAPTER 11

Whitman to the Front

FOR THOSE BOHEMIANS left behind at Pfaff's, a feeling of stagnation began to seep into that vaulted room beneath the Broadway pavement. The old crowd was thinning, its prospects dimming, the champagne banter growing stale and flat. Once a refuge, the saloon was becoming a trap instead. Whitman would later describe this period in his life as a "quicksand" year.

Already, the Civil War was moving into a terrible new phase. Whatever sense of giddiness once existed had dissipated. Northerners had brimmed with confidence at the outset, certain that the sheer righteousness of their cause guaranteed quick victory. *Yanks talk a good game about preserving the Union and ending slavery*, went the Southern refrain, *but let them get a taste of Confederate gunfire and they'll turn and flee*. Below Mason-Dixon, a popular saying held, "A lady's thimble will hold all the blood that will be shed."

By early 1862, way more than a thimble's worth had been spilled. The death toll had already climbed into the thousands. Bull Run—the war's first big battle—had been a victory for the South, leaving the North shocked and shaken. But the wages of Bull Run were terrible for both sides: 460 Union soldiers and 387 Confederates killed. It was followed by such major early battles as Wilson Creek, which resulted in 535 dead for the two sides combined, and Fort Donelson, with a total death count of 834. Still ahead lay the Civil War's most horrendous battles, which would produce thousands of deaths, tens of thousands wounded or taken prisoner.

Americans were witnessing carnage on a level that dwarfed anything they'd experienced previously. For the War of 1812, the entire tally of US combat deaths was 2,260. During the American Revolution, even major battles such as Yorktown and the two at Saratoga routinely resulted in fewer than 100 deaths among the Colonial forces.

But the Civil War was a novel conflict, waged with efficient new weapons. The soldiers of previous generations had relied on smooth-bore muskets, spraying chunky iron balls with comic inaccuracy. Now, a different kind of gun, featuring a rifled barrel, fired a new type of projectile, the familiar pointed bullet, that rotated in flight like a tiny football—giving it tremendous aerodynamic stability—and could strike a distant target with cruel precision. Even so, many generals from both the North and the South failed to adjust their strategies accordingly. They clung stubbornly to the Napoleonic tactics they'd learned at West Point and other military academies, marching orderly rows of soldiers right into the teeth of enemy fire.

No doubt, all this mayhem seemed particularly deranged to Clapp's set, composed as it was of writers and artists. When Whitman spotted a ragged old woman lurching along Broadway near Pfaff's (just a small urban episode), it was oddly freighted with meaning. In a brief notebook entry, dated January 9, 1862, he described the woman as "either insane or drunk, wretchedly drest, affectedly promenading the sidewalk." This was a poetic scrap, something to tuck away and maybe use later. But it also appears to have struck Whitman as a fitting metaphor: here was this shambling old woman alone on Broadway, the same boulevard where cheering crowds had seen off regiment after regiment of soldiers. Everything had changed, seemingly in an instant. War was revealing its true self: ugly and messy and crazy.

Early in 1862, the crowd at Pfaff's received word from the front concerning one of their own. On February 16, O'Brien had taken part in a military maneuver, a late-night foraging expedition, where he'd joined thirty-five cavalrymen charged with rounding up one hundred head of secessionist cattle. This would provide much-needed food for his hungry regiment. At four in the morning, near Bloomery Gap in what is today West Virginia, O'Brien's detail encountered a much larger force of Confederates. O'Brien broke into a horseback charge, riding directly at the enemy. A Confederate officer yelled, "Halt! Who are you?" O'Brien shouted, "Union soldiers!"

Simultaneously, O'Brien and the officer opened fire. The officer's second shot passed through O'Brien's left shoulder, shattering his scapula bone. The officer then wheeled around on his horse and led his troops in a hasty retreat. O'Brien's charge had been so reckless, it seems, that the Confederates naturally assumed he was part of a large Union force in the area, not simply a band numbering a few dozen cavalrymen. Losing blood fast, O'Brien rode the roughly twenty-five miles to Cumberland, Maryland. There, he was placed in a field hospital under the care of a surgeon. In letters to Pfaff's friends, O'Brien cheerfully described his condition, noting that the injury had rendered his left hand useless, fit for "no higher occupation than to clutch pennies."

On learning the news, Clapp quipped, "Aldrich, I see, has been shot in O'Brien's shoulder." This was a reference to the fact that O'Brien and Aldrich had competed for the same military post.

At least Clapp still retained his razor wit. More than ever, he was left to derive pleasure from cracks delivered at Pfaff's long table—had to make them count—because he didn't have many other outlets. Clapp had been forced to take a straight job, as theater critic for the *New York Leader*. He still got to write the occasional barb, but he no longer enjoyed anything like the latitude he'd had with his own *Saturday Press*. There was certainly no opportunity to rant about Boston or devote an entire column to savaging some esteemed public figure he considered a ponderous windbag.

The *Leader* was turning out to be a kind of island for lost Bohemians. Ada Clare, William Winter, and George Arnold also became frequent contributors. While none of them was granted anything like the freedom of the *SP,* at least the paper paid a few dollars. Whitman also wrote a series of articles for the *Leader*. Struggling as a poet, he turned to journalism once more. He used the pseudonym Velsor Brush. This was a combination of his mother's maiden name (Louisa Van Velsor) and that of his paternal grandmother (Hannah Brush). Such efforts earned him a measly five dollars per week.

Soon there was more news of O'Brien. Following an operation to his shattered shoulder, complications had set in. He developed lockjaw. O'Brien wasted away, dropping from 163 pounds down to 120. On the morning of April 6, he looked to be rallying a bit. He was sitting up on his hospital cot, sipping a glass of sherry. Suddenly, he turned ashen and fell backward, dead. O'Brien, the charter Bohemian, Clapp's very first recruit, was thirty-three.

As further details trickled in, however, a more complicated picture began to emerge. A few days before that late-night cattle-wrangling expedition, an old friend had visited O'Brien in camp. During their entire time together, O'Brien kept singing a line from a song: "Then let me like a soldier die." O'Brien explained that he liked the line, found it oddly comforting. Further, O'Brien told his friend, he had a presentiment that he would be shot before long. The friend emerged from the visit with an uneasy feeling.

Then there was the matter of the letter O'Brien had written from the front, asking Frank Wood to act as his literary executor. Wood was a journalist, playwright, agent—a kind of jack-of-all-trades—and a frequenter of Pfaff's. (He briefly served as Artemus Ward's agent, before Ward outgrew him.) In the letter, O'Brien confided—and Wood now shared this with others in Clapp's circle—"After I'm dead I may turn out a bigger man than when living."

The Bohemian life was draining, filled as it was with constant debauchery, drafty attic rooms, artistic rejection, romantic rejection, and money woes, always money woes. O'Brien may have been more worn down than anyone knew. Perhaps he decided it was easiest to slip out of life and place his trust in the wisdom of the future, hoping posterity would render a generous verdict on his merits as a writer.

O'Brien left behind a mountain of hackwork, but also a few masterful pieces that show just what he could achieve when he gave his best. There's "The Diamond Lens," the fantastical story started shortly after he began frequenting Pfaff's, the one about a man who peers through a microscope lens and spies a tiny, beautiful woman inside a droplet of water. He also wrote a couple of other memorable macabre tales, such as "What Was It?" about an invisible supernatural creature that can be detected only through its interaction with the physical world. There's a particularly chilling scene, where someone throws a blanket over the creature and manages to glean some details about its otherworldly appearance as it kicks and struggles.

In death, O'Brien would indeed cut a larger figure than most writers. Following the Civil War, for decades, his best stories would be reprinted in magazines and included in numerous anthologies. *A Gentleman from Ireland,* the play O'Brien humorously self-reviewed in the *Saturday Press,* would continue to be staged until 1893. As recently as 1923, the noted critic Fred Pattee wrote, "No more electric and versatile genius had ever appeared among American authors." But time itself proved ruthless. With the passage of the years, O'Brien's literary reputation would waste away, growing ever smaller and smaller, until, at last, he was largely forgotten.

As 1862 staggered along, Whitman became increasingly anxious. He and his family in Brooklyn were worried about George. They were able to follow the progress of his regiment through newspaper accounts. What they could glean was alarming. The 51st seemed to be involved in far more than its fair share of combat. Throughout the year, George's regiment saw action in a dizzying succession of major battles: Roanoke Island, New Bern, Cedar Mountain, Chantilly, and South Mountain. George was also at Antietam, where 3,654 men were killed during a few hours of close-range fighting in a Maryland cornfield. That battle remains the single deadliest day in American combat history.

Following each battle, the Whitmans would pore over the lists of in-
jured and dead soldiers that ran in all the major New York papers. The
lists grew longer and longer. Each time they made it through without
encountering George's name, a huge feeling of relief settled over the fam-
ily. They knew that soon they could expect one of George's letters with
details of the battle. Because he lacked Walt's facility with language, also
because he wasn't an especially emotional person, George's letters re-
count bullets whistling past his head and the gruesome demises of some
of his fellow soldiers with surprising nonchalance. Unintentionally, these
homely missives struck the perfect comforting tone for the nervous Whit-
mans back in Brooklyn. Of course, the letters also arrived after a time lag,
depending on the punctuality of the mail service, sometimes lasting days,
sometimes weeks. By then, George had long since moved on to a fresh
battle with new dangers. For all the family knew, they were reading the
last words of a dead man. *Read George's laconic account of the previous bat-
tle. Scan the papers for news of the latest one.* It was an excruciating cycle.

Whitman became increasingly depressed, falling into what he called a
"slough." He actually upped his attendance at Pfaff's, if that was possible.
He began going every single night—excepting Sundays, when the saloon
was closed. Yet even though surrounded by people, Whitman appears
to have been lonely. He hadn't had a serious romantic attachment in
the couple of years since his relationship with Fred Vaughan ended. He
continued to meet men in the other, larger, room at Pfaff's or while
walking through the midnight streets of Manhattan and Brooklyn. As
always, he made notations about who they were (soldier on furlough,
butcher, picture-frame maker), what they looked like (blond or brunette,
mustachioed or clean shaven), what they did (talked maybe, or went for
a stroll), and sometimes he mentioned if they spent the night together.

Thos Gray good looking young Scotchman elegantly dress'd,—does
the tricks, cutting hs finger &c—at Pfaff's . . .

John McNelly night Oct 7 young man, drunk, walk'd up Fulton &
High st. home works in Brooklyn flour mills had been with some
friends return'd from the war

David Wilson—night of Oct. 11, '62, walking up from Middagh—slept
with me—works in blacksmith shop in Navy Yard—lives in Hampden st.
—walks together Sunday afternoon & night—is about 19

Whitman didn't publish a single poem in 1862. Only two years ear-
lier, with the third edition of *Leaves of Grass,* he'd published an entire
cathedral's worth. Strangely, though, a poem credited to Whitman and
entitled "Wounded" did appear during the year. It was published in a
magazine called the *Continental Monthly* and was reprinted a couple of
places, including the *Oneida (NY) Circular*. It's a pretty good approxi-
mation of Whitman's free-verse style. But it wasn't his work. Someone
was trading on his good name.

Not only did Whitman publish no poetry during the year, but he
didn't write much of it, either. One of his few efforts—little more than
a fragment, really—is entitled "The Two Vaults." Whitman scrawled it
in pencil in a notebook:

> The vault at Pfaffs where the drinkers and laughers meet to eat and drink
>   and carouse,
> While on the walk immediately overhead, pass the myriad feet of
>   Broadway
> As the dead in their graves, are underfoot hidden
> And the living pass over them, reckoning not of them,
> Laugh on laughers! Drink on drinkers!
> Bandy the jests! Toss the theme from one to another!
> Beam up—Brighten up bright eyes of beautiful young men!
> Eat what you, having ordered, are pleased to see placed
>   before you—after the work of the day, now, with appetite, eat,
> Drink wine—drink beer—raise your voice.
> Behold! your friend, as he arrives—Welcome him, when, from the upper
>   step, he looks down upon you with cheerful look

The poem continues for another dozen or so lines, growing increas-
ingly fractured. Words are crossed out in numerous places. Then it
ends abruptly, cutting off midline:

The lights beam in the first vault—but the other is
     entirely dark
In the first

Still, where Whitman was headed with the poem is clear enough.
He seems to have been aiming to create an association, per the title, be-
tween two vaults, the first being that celebrated room in Pfaff's saloon
and the second—a burial vault. But the poem would remain unfin-
ished, not discovered until after Whitman's death.

Then comes an evening, sometime late in the autumn of 1862. Whit-
man was at Pfaff's, as ever, sitting at Clapp's long table. Maybe it was
the 250th time—or maybe the 251st—that he'd been to the saloon
that year, sitting and listening, talking a bit, taking bites of beefsteak,
and listening some more. As the hour grew later and looser, George
Arnold—master of effervescent verse, sometimes called "the Poet of
Beer"—stood up at the table and launched into an elaborate verbal
conceit, some kind of mock toast. He droned on, enumerating the
supposed virtues of the Confederacy and the secessionist cause. He
even raised his glass and offered, "Success to the Southern Arms!" As
Arnold jested, Whitman grew increasingly irritated. Finally, he stood
up, face gone crimson, those drowsy eyes now flashing, and started
yelling at Arnold, telling him what an ass he was being and perhaps
was. Arnold reached across the table, grabbed hold of Whitman's
beard, and tugged hard.

Quite a scuffle ensued. Clapp jumped in between the two men,
dropping and breaking one of his precious clay pipes. Herr Pfaff re-
portedly cried out in broken English, "Oh! mine gots, mens, what's
you do for dis?" As Whitman and Arnold tussled, according to one
account, "we all received a beautiful mixture of rum, claret, and coffee
on the knees of our trousers."

Whitman stormed out of Pfaff's.

And then a morning not long afterward: December 16, 1862. The New
York papers were filled with news of a battle that had just been fought

near Fredericksburg, Virginia. It was the largest engagement of the Civil War so far, pitting 114,000 Union troops under General Ambrose Burnside against 72,500 Confederates commanded by Robert E. Lee. Despite superior numbers, the North was defeated. More than 1,000 Union soldiers were killed. Two-thirds met their deaths in the same spot, shot down in front of a low stone wall as wave upon wave tried in vain to take a piece of ground called Marye's Heights. The bodies just kept piling in front of the wall. Mixed with the dead were the wounded and dying; accounts say the air was filled with their howls and moans of suffering. On learning of the defeat, Lincoln reportedly said, "If there is a worse place than Hell, I am in it."

In Brooklyn, the Whitmans anxiously riffled through the *New York Herald*. On page 8, under the heading "Wounded," they came across "First Lieutenant G. W. Whitmore." The last name was different. But the rank of lieutenant was correct, as were the two initials and the wounded soldier's regiment: 51st New York. The account contained no additional information, such as the type or severity of the injury. Still, the Whitmans were certain—sickeningly certain—that this was George.

The family instantly mobilized. Walt made plans to set out for Washington at once. There was a decent possibility that wounded George had been moved from the battlefield to one of the numerous hospitals in and around the capital. Walt rushed to the Brooklyn mayor's office and secured a letter of introduction to a US congressman who represented his district. Through his boss at the Brooklyn Water Works, Jeff obtained a second letter of introduction for Walt, this one to the assistant quartermaster of the Union army. Mother Whitman hurried to the bank and withdrew $50 in savings for her son's journey.

Within hours, Walt was on the Brooklyn ferry, crossing the East River. In Manhattan, he boarded a second ferry and crossed the Hudson River to Jersey City. There, he caught a train to Washington, DC, requiring a switch in Philadelphia. This was the exact route taken by countless soldiers as they were mustered into active duty. On December 16, 1862, it was the route taken by the loved ones of soldiers, legions of them, descending on Washington in the day following the disastrous battle. All along the way, the various modes of transport were heavily crowded, filled with panicked travelers.

In Philadelphia, Whitman was pickpocketed. So he arrived in Washington penniless. The letters of introduction proved worthless, too. Not only were the congressman and assistant quartermaster unavailable, but their offices didn't offer the poet any assistance. Whitman went from hospital to hospital on foot, but he wasn't able to locate George. Neither was he able to gather any information about his brother's condition or whereabouts. "The next two days I spent hunting through the hospitals," Whitman recalled, "walking all day and night, unable to ride, trying to get information, trying to get access to big people, &c—I could not get the least clue to anything."

Fortunately, he managed to connect with Charles Eldridge. With the outbreak of war, the young publisher of *Leaves of Grass* had departed Boston for Washington, where he'd taken a post attending to clerical matters involving the Massachusetts volunteers. He gave Whitman some money. About the incident in Philadelphia, Eldridge would later quip, "Any pickpocket who failed to avail himself of such an opportunity as Walt offered, with his loose baggy trousers, and no suspenders, would have been a disgrace to his profession."

Eldridge also secured a pass that allowed Whitman to take government transport all the way to the front. On Friday, December 19, Whitman arrived at a vast military encampment near Falmouth, Virginia. It was on the west bank of the Rappahannock River, the side opposite Fredericksburg. The Union army had massed here in the days leading up to the battle. In the aftermath, the army was trying to regroup there.

Whitman worked his way among the soldiers, going from campsite to campsite, looking for the 51st New York. On the day he arrived, he was able to find George's regiment and with it George—alive and well. He had been injured, all right, but his wound—though gory—was minor. During the battle, a percussion shell had exploded at his feet, and a piece of shrapnel had torn a hole in his cheek. "You could stick a splint through into the mouth," noted Walt. Following the battle, George had written home to Brooklyn to tell everyone he was fine, but the letter was still in transit when Walt arrived. Actually, George was better than fine: he'd just been promoted. "Remember your galliant Son is a Capting," he wrote to his mother.

Just to be certain, to make sure the family was aware that George was safe, Walt made an arrangement with someone headed to Washington. The man agreed to send a telegram to the Whitmans in Brooklyn.

Walt decided to stay on for a while with George at the front. He ate military rations. He slept in his brother's tent, crowded into its tight confines with three other enlisted men. At night, around the campfire, Whitman enjoyed listening to the soldiers' stories. In one of his ever-ready notebooks, he recorded bits of overheard slang: A "healthy beat" was a reliable soldier, while a "dead beat" was someone full of excuses. New recruits were "$700 men." Crackers were called "army pies," and "wash" was the name for coffee. Pour some whiskey into coffee, and it became "western milk."

The flippant terms belied a far-harsher reality. Months of hard fighting had decimated George's regiment; its number had dwindled from eleven hundred to two hundred. One soldier told him he had spent fifty hours lying wounded on a battlefield, unable to even lift his head. He was one of the lucky ones.

Whitman looked on as a burial detail crossed the Rappahannock under a white flag of truce. They returned to the Falmouth side, bearing bodies of their dead comrades. The detail made quick work of its grim task. There was little ceremony, only a few muttered words as the bodies were piled into unmarked graves. "Death is nothing here," noted an amazed Whitman. He sketched out a few lines:

Sight at daybreak (in camp in front of the hospital tent) on a
    stretcher, three dead men lying, each with a blanket spread over
    him—I lift up one
and look at the young man's face, calm and yellow. 'tis strange!
(Young man: I think this face, of yours the face of my dead Christ!)

This would become the basis for "A Sight in Camp in the Daybreak Gray and Dim." But first, he would need to rework and re-rework it, polishing it into a finished poem.

Brother George was busy with soldiering duties, leaving Walt to spend a great deal of time alone. He didn't mind. "Both in and out of the game and watching and wondering at it," goes a line in Whitman's "Song of Myself." That had always been his approach at Clapp's table (*both in and out of the game*), and so it was at Falmouth. This was a new world—a world at war—with its own sights and sounds and rules and mysteries, all for the gleaning. There was something eerie, Whitman found, about the sound of a donkey braying on the edge of camp at midnight. He took the time to watch an observation balloon as it rose slowly up into the air. "A beautiful object to me—a graceful, pear-shaped thing," he noted. Then he continued watching as the balloon came slowly back down, even walked over and examined it as it lay on the ground.

Whitman was particularly drawn to the makeshift field hospitals. He spent hours visiting them. Often they were nothing more than large tents, crowded with wounded soldiers. Some of the soldiers were awaiting transport to hospitals in Washington and other points North. Many were simply too badly injured to be moved. There were no cots or even mattresses. The wounded lay on blankets spread on the ground, with a layer of pine needles or maybe some hemlock twigs as their only cushion. Not only was the ground hard, but it was bitter cold in the winter of '62. "I do not see that I do much good to these wounded and dying," Whitman wrote, "but I cannot leave them."

The worst cases were confined to Lacy House, a stone mansion on a hill overlooking the Rappahannock. Out front was a horrifying sight: piles of amputated arms and legs. Inside utter pandemonium reigned: surgeons wielding saws, soldiers screaming, soldiers dying, every minute, it seemed. Still, Whitman visited repeatedly. He found that merely by talking to the soldiers, he could provide them some peace in this hellish place.

On Christmas Day 1862, Whitman went off by himself for a time. He sat on a pine log in the middle of a deserted camp. It was high ground, and he could see two or more miles in every direction. Nearby, he watched as an interminable train of army supply wagons lumbered past, each one drawn by a six-mule team. In the distance, he could see "regiments, brigades, and divisions" spread out "at every point of the compass." These were engaged in various military drills. In the crisp air, he could hear bugle calls and the clatter of sabers. As a cavalry unit passed close by, he could feel the earth shake from the horses' hooves. After being sealed away in Pfaff's saloon, hermetically almost, during the first part of the war, it was as if his senses suddenly awakened. He was taking it in, just taking it all in.

After nine days at the front, Walt bid farewell to George and traveled back to Washington. He intended to remain there for a few days. While visiting his brother's camp, Whitman had learned that two soldiers from Brooklyn were laid up at a hospital in the capital. He intended to visit them and carry news of their conditions back to their families.

Then Whitman had a change of plans. A new year had broken, 1863, and with it the promise of shaking free of the "quicksand." Whitman now glimpsed a way to find his own place in the vastness of a war.

CHAPTER 12

Bohemia Goes West

FITZ HUGH LUDLOW—the fresh-faced, high-strung, word-crazed drug aficionado—also found a route to salvation. Like fellow Pfaffians Menken and Ward—Whitman, too, it now appeared—he discovered a way to make sense of his life during wartime. Early in 1863, an incredible and unexpected opportunity came his way. The painter Albert Bierstadt invited Ludlow to accompany him on a journey across the continent.

For Bierstadt, the trip presented a chance to sketch various scenes and gather fresh inspiration. The artist planned to return to New York versed in the wonders of the West and ready to make new paintings that would further bolster his already considerable fame. Ludlow was charged with chronicling the journey in a series of newspaper articles, designed to build up interest in Bierstadt's work. But Ludlow certainly saw the potential for major personal glory in the undertaking. Crossing the continent was still a rare feat. It was sure to provide the grist—at long last—for a worthy follow-up to *The Hasheesh Eater*.

For some time now, Ludlow had been in a slough of his own. The very first time he visited Pfaff's, it had been as an established literary force, an enfant terrible who "held the town in his slender right hand," according to one account. The intervening years had been a steady and relentless slide. Lately, he'd found that he could no longer earn a living, even a meager one, solely as a writer, and he had taken a position with the New York City Customs House. The job was pure drudgery, his salary a paltry three dollars per day. He was writing an occasional piece on a freelance basis, but his work was drying up.

Ludlow was now twenty-six years old. Recently, a brief newspaper item had run, listing some notable personages who had attended a gala event. Ludlow, spotted at the edge of the crowd, was mentioned in passing. In the item, he was cast as a curiosity and a has-been: "With his beautiful wife at his side, Fitz Hugh Ludlow, the author of the 'Hasheesh Eater,' a work of unrivaled eloquence and genius; his dark eyes have a somewhat remote and dreamy expression as if he were still haunted by the remembrance of its perilous glooms and glories."

Even *The Hasheesh Eater* had run its course. Following publication, the book rapidly went through four printings. But the most recent edition sold poorly, and it was no longer available.

This was certainly not the life envisioned by Rosalie, that notably "beautiful wife." Money was so tight that the couple had recently moved into a smaller apartment at an undesirable Manhattan address. The tension between them had grown unbearable. "Fitz did not come back til late. Rose nervous," notes a diary entry by his sister Helen Ludlow, hinting at strife between the couple. Another entry reads, "Rose frightened and good cause—I went over to see about it—Oh Shame!— What will the end be[?]"

Ludlow and his sister were especially close. As it happens, she was one of the few people aware of a deeper, more unsettling cause of marital discord. Flailing as a writer, Ludlow had developed a taste for something far stronger and far more dangerous than hashish. He was using opium.

During his teenage drug forays at that Poughkeepsie apothecary shop, Ludlow had dabbled with opium (he'd tried almost everything). But it simply hadn't spoken to him. As a narcotic, opium promised only numbness. Hallucinogenic hashish lit up his senses. Once he arrived in New York, however, his drug predilections reversed. The pressures of the literary life made escape the desired outcome. Where he'd been expansive about his hash reveries, he was furtive about his opium use. Probably, he was ashamed to be in the grip of a drug that he'd dismissed in his book for offering no adventure, no romance. According to Helen, her brother took opium simply "to goad wearied nerves."

Most likely, he was ingesting the drug in its laudanum form. Laudanum is a tincture, consisting of opium powder dissolved in alcohol. During the nineteenth century, it was widely used as a patent remedy to treat a variety of conditions: headaches, arthritis, anxiety, severe menstrual cramps—and also widely abused. Laudanum was swallowed like cough syrup. Fatal overdoses were shockingly common.

In the evening, on the sly, Ludlow indulged his growing narcotic habit. By day, he worked his deadening job, poring over the manifests of ships docked in New York Harbor and adding up the value of their cargoes to determine how much duty was owed the city. During the Civil War, the Customs House became a kind of holding tank for frustrated litterateurs. After losing out to O'Brien on the military post, Aldrich had taken a job there, too. Ludlow and Aldrich—a pair of polymathic functionaries—whiled away their workdays with various diversions, such as a contest to see who could do the best and quickest translation of an Italian poem. One of their efforts has been preserved on a page of Customs House letterhead:

> Stanza of Italian poetry:
> *Dall uno del mio cuore*
> *Lorse mia sol prece*
> *Che l'idol mio ammiuri*
> *Che io l'ammiori, e muoria*

> Aldrich's translation:
> *Out from the depths of my heart*
> *Has arisen this single cry*
> *Let me behold my beloved*
> *Let me behold her & die*

> Ludlow's translation:
> *From the bottom of my heart*
> *There broke one single cry*
> *Let me look on my idol*
> *Look on him & die!*

Then came this great opportunity, courtesy of one of America's most celebrated painters. Albert Bierstadt was born in Germany and came to America while still an infant. Growing up in Massachusetts, he showed prodigious talent. In 1859, Bierstadt had made his first trip out West, setting out from his home in New Bedford. He got as far as a stretch of the Rocky Mountains in what would today be Wyoming. But the trip furnished the raw studies and inspiration for a series of landscapes. With these paintings, Bierstadt achieved his professional breakthrough.

Eager to capitalize, Bierstadt moved to Manhattan and set up shop in the famous Tenth Street Studio Building. At the time, the building featured such notables as John LaFarge, Worthington Whittredge, and Frederic Church. Bierstadt—a self-promoter extraordinaire—filled his studio with curios gathered during that 1859 western expedition. Prospective buyers were conducted through a space that resembled a theatrical set, generously strewn with arrows, feathers, moccasins, and deerskins. Bierstadt regaled visitors with tales of nearly starving to death in the wilderness (in reality, he hadn't even come close) and encounters with hostile Indians (more hyperbole). A newspaper reporter described Bierstadt's studio as looking like "the depot of a fur trader."

With the advent of the Civil War, certain painters—other than those who enlisted, of course—were surprised to find that their prospects actually improved. This was especially true in large Northern cities, home to manufacturing firms that were churning out munitions, uniforms, blankets, everything necessary to support a massive war effort. The owners of some of these businesses got rich; a portion of them, in turn, used their newfound wealth to purchase paintings, and a boom that nobody could have anticipated was soon under way. The *Boston Transcript* reported that a "golden shower" was falling on New York City's artists. No one was better positioned to benefit than Bierstadt.

Bierstadt was a master at what were then known as "great pictures," dramatic paintings executed on vast canvasses, requiring a command of lighting effects and an eye for composition. Bierstadt's choice of subject matter also helped. Landscapes were his specialty: idyllic, inspiring, and most of all *peaceful*—perfect in a time of war. Like Adah Menken and Artemus Ward, Bierstadt had lit upon a successful formula, creating work that resonated just enough with grim current events, while at the same time offering a needed diversion. As an added attraction, his images were of the West. The United States, that grand experiment, was less than one hundred years old, and already it had fractured. Blood had been spilled, sullying the landscape of the East. But the West represented fresh territory, a place where what was true and best about the American spirit could one day take hold again.

Bierstadt's paintings were like dispatches from a promised land. By 1863, he was reaping the rewards due a top-tier artist. He was able actually to charge admission—as high as twenty-five cents per person—for members of the public to view his work. A man had recently arranged to do an engraving of what was to this point Bierstadt's most famous painting, *The Rocky Mountains, Lander's Peak*. The engraving would make it possible for Bierstadt to sell reproductions of the work, a lot of them, providing a further revenue stream. He'd also just received an offer to buy the original *Lander's Peak* for $10,000, a vast sum at the time. But he boldly turned down the offer, certain that he could get even more money for it in the future.

Bierstadt was only thirty-three years old. He was a neatly groomed man with a trim beard and a bearing that exuded, in equal measure, both aloofness and confidence. His gaze, while extremely direct, was curiously unpenetrating, seeming to look *past* rather than *through* a person. In New York artistic circles, there were whispers that Bierstadt was poised to eclipse Frederic Church as *the* preeminent landscape painter. Several years had passed since Church had achieved his last major triumph, *Heart of the Andes*. Moreover, that was a *South* American rather than a native subject. The time was right, Bierstadt sensed, to take a second western journey, and this time he intended to travel beyond the Rockies, all the way to the Pacific Coast.

It might seem strange that Bierstadt chose to hitch his star to Ludlow's broke-down wagon. But Bierstadt had his reasons, some of them evident, some perhaps secrets that he was keeping to himself. One thing was certain: he didn't want to serve as his own chronicler again. During that first journey in 1859, he'd sent a series of letters from points West that were published in the *New Bedford (MA) Mercury*. He recognized that he wasn't much of a writer. This time around, Bierstadt was intent on doing everything in a more polished and professional manner. Though Ludlow was currently foundering, he was still seen as a brilliant writer.

The faith Bierstadt placed in him was immediately rewarded, as Ludlow arranged to publish his travel dispatches in a major publication, the *New York Post*. This guaranteed that the articles would draw a great deal of attention to both the painter and the writer. It appears that Edwin Booth played a role in brokering the partnership of Ludlow and Bierstadt. Booth—still in the grip of severe alcoholism at this time—remained close to Ludlow. He was also a good friend of Bierstadt and a frequent guest at receptions held at the Tenth Street Studio. "How I would rejoice if I could take the trip that Ludlow is to start on," commented Booth.

Bierstadt and Ludlow set off in May 1863. The eastern half of the transcontinental journey was the easy leg, so Ludlow's wife, Rosalie, came along. They covered this ground quickly, by rail, recognizing that there was little novelty in documenting the wonders of Ohio or Illinois. Even so, Bierstadt managed to convince the presidents of several railroad companies to provide free passage. In exchange, Bierstadt promised that Ludlow would make favorable mention of their companies in his *Post* dispatches. The railroad presidents were anxious to promote the idea that trains remained a safe way to travel, even with a war raging. They were also pleased to tout the fact that the rails reached right to the West's doorstep. One day soon, they hoped to offer service across the continent.

Ludlow and Bierstadt planned to travel for roughly six months. Along their entire itinerary, they intended to stick to territory that was either decisively Union or where the war was a distant abstraction— with the lone exception of Missouri. That was the only place that held the possibility of war-related dangers. Missouri, like Maryland, was a border state that was forced to contend with fiercely divided loyalties among its citizens. During the Civil War, Missouri sent thousands of soldiers to both sides, Union and Confederate. In St. Louis, Ludlow overheard some secessionist grumblings, but that was about the extent of it.

Rosalie's cousin was president of the Platte Country Railroad. So she was able to arrange more free train passage, from St. Joseph, Missouri, to Atchison, Kansas—the end of the line. Here, Rosalie bid her farewells and split off from the expedition. It had taken only a matter of days for Ludlow and Bierstadt to arrive at this jumping-off point, and the real adventure was about to begin.

The first big event of the trip was a buffalo hunt. Ludlow and Bierstadt rendezvoused with a party of experienced hunters and traveled to a promising spot on the border of Kansas and Nebraska Territory. Soon, the first buffalo were spotted. Through field glasses, Ludlow could make out maybe eight brown dots scattered in the distance. He was underwhelmed; for his first sighting, buffalo reminded him of nothing so much as New England dairy cows.

The party camped for the night on the banks of the Republican River. They dined on antelope steak, which Ludlow found delicious. The next morning, he arose to a very different situation. Viewed through field glasses, a vast stretch of the surrounding plains had turned a kind of deep chocolate brown, now thick with buffalo.

While Bierstadt hung back in camp, executing landscape studies, Ludlow joined in the hunt. Everyone was on horseback, and the plan was to use a kind of divide-and-conquer maneuver on the buffalo. The hunters intended to ride directly at different points along the flank of the herd, spooking the animals. By sparking multiple stampedes, going in all different directions, the cohesion of this massive buffalo herd would be broken, and individuals could be separated and picked off. It was a daring maneuver, reckless even, and one for which greenhorn Ludlow was in no way prepared. While Ludlow possessed many talents, riding on horseback directly at a solid wall of buffalo was not one of them. It didn't take long before he made a mistake, and all at once, he was in the line of a stampede. Terrified, he was confronted by what he estimated to be a mile-wide column of "angry faces, a rolling surf of wind-blown hair," with eyes that were like "a row of quivering lanterns, burning reddish-brown."

He whirled his horse around and set off running ahead of the buffalo. He could hear their hooves thundering and feared he was about to be "wiped out like a grease-spot." In front of him, a low butte rose above the plains. Wisely, Ludlow rode up onto it. The herd simply split, like a river reaching a boulder, and passed to either side. In his saddle, on the crest of the butte, Ludlow was treated to an incredible sight that he described as a "great oscillating patch of hair and hide." A full five minutes elapsed as the buffalo rampaged past. "I was safe," Ludlow would recall. "I had such a view of buffaloes as I never could have expected, never would enjoy again."

By and by, one of the hunters shot a buffalo in such a way that it was gravely wounded, yet remained upright. For this, Bierstadt was summoned. The artist jumped into a little one-horse buggy that had been brought along on the hunt for just such an occasion and set out bouncing across the plains. On arriving at the site, Bierstadt set up in a hurry. He planted a large blue umbrella and sat beneath it on a camp stool. Resting his color box on his knees, palette in hand, he began a series of lightning-quick oil-paint studies of the wounded buffalo.

Periodically, Ludlow and the hunters edged their horses toward the hulking beast, causing it to turn in various directions for Bierstadt's benefit. This went on for a half hour. Finally, it was time to put the creature out of its misery. Ludlow and the hunters all took aim and fired in unison. The bullet-riddled buffalo made one final charge: "He rushed forward at his persecutors with all the *elan* of his first charges; but strength failed him half way. Ten feet from where we stood, he tumbled to his knees, made heroic effort to rise again, and came up on one leg; but the death-tremor possessed the other, and with a great panting groan, in which all of brute power and beauty went forth at once, he fell prone on the trampled turf."

After the hunt, Ludlow and Bierstadt continued westward, now traveling by overland stage. They relied on the familiar Concord wagon, little more than a box on wheels, painted red, laden with mail for stops along the way. It was designed to seat six comfortably, but drivers were never inclined to turn away passengers. The pace was arduous, about four miles an hour.

Ludlow and Bierstadt traveled mostly at night; the painter required daylight to work. So the overland stage was also the overnight stage. Sleep was quite a challenge, though, while forced to remain upright and squeezed in tight on a hard wooden bench, jostling over rutted, uneven ground.

Using clothing and blankets, Ludlow fashioned a kind of halter that suspended him above his fellow passengers. In this way, he was able to assume a normal horizontal sleeping position, though he swung a bit with each bump of the stage. He described himself as an "Overland Mazeppa." The contraption quickly proved as uncomfortable as it was ridiculous, and he abandoned it. Soon, Ludlow fell instead into a pattern of foregoing sleep at night and sitting up front beside the drivers: "This was a place where legs were stretchable and faculties wide awake." Drivers had to remain alert through the long night, and Ludlow kept them company with what must have been a unique brand of jittery, insomniacal banter. During the day, often at one of the godforsaken way stations where the stages stopped, Ludlow would slip off, lie down, and try to catch a short nap.

Sleep became an obsession, and Ludlow filled his diary with references to it—or, rather, the lack of it. Very little about this hardship made it into the *Post* dispatches, however. Promotion-happy Bierstadt had once again cut a deal: free passage via overland stage all the way to California in exchange for a plug or two by Ludlow.

Eastern Colorado Territory looked no different from western Nebraska Territory. The landscape remained unrelievedly flat, the plains stretching endlessly in all directions, broken occasionally by a cottonwood tree or a lonely gravestone marking the final resting place of some unfortunate pioneer. But one day, just as dawn was breaking, a driver pointed into the distance and announced to Ludlow, "There are the Rocky Mountains."

Ludlow was puzzled. Looking in the direction the driver indicated, the writer saw absolutely nothing. It was simply more of the same: flat land, vast sky, puffs of cloud on the horizon. But then he realized that the mountains *were* the sky, what he had mistaken for clouds—their snowcaps. Ludlow burst into tears. Perhaps it was sleep deprivation, but he was seized by an overwhelming sense of wonder: "Nature has dipped her pencil in the faintest solution of ultra-marine, and drawn it once across the western sky, with a hand as tender as Love's."

Using boomtown Denver as a base, Ludlow and Bierstadt made repeated day trips into the Rockies. Up close, Ludlow was able to get a sense of scale and could see how truly hulking and massive these mountains were. They dwarfed anything he'd seen back East in the Catskills or Adirondacks.

For one Rockies foray, Ludlow and Bierstadt traveled to a location that offered an unusually striking view across a valley to a snow-peaked mountain in the distance. Ludlow estimated its elevation as "considerably" above fifteen thousand feet, making it taller than Mont Blanc, the mightiest Alp. Bierstadt said he required about fifteen minutes to do a study.

While he painted, a storm began to gather, and an incredible natural drama—of light and shadow—began to play out. Thunderclouds, rolling in over the mountain, were shredded into indigo ribbons by ridges of rock. Shafts of sunlight stretched through the broken clouds, to the valley floor below. There, the calm, mirrored surface of a lake alternately reflected the black clouds and blue sky above. As Bierstadt worked, Ludlow meditated on the primordial quality of this scene. No one in human history, he was sure, had ever climbed very far up the face of the mountain that stood before them. The crisp air around them seemed virginal, as though it were "quite unbreathed before." The mountain, this incredible mountain that they'd been contemplating, didn't even have a name. Bierstadt christened it "Mount Rosalie" in honor of Ludlow's wife, who had split off from the expedition back in Atchison.

The painter was finding no shortage of worthy subjects. Ludlow was also finding success with his *Post* dispatches. The newspaper splashed them across its front page under the title "Letters from Sundown." By the time the Colorado installments appeared, Ludlow had already graduated from a byline that was merely his initials—F. H. L.—to his full name. Though the *Post* was written for a general audience, Ludlow's editors allowed him a few of his trademark two-bit words, including "enfilading" (directing a volley of gunfire) and "rotatory" (steady alternating movements, such as a horse's legs). In one dispatch, he even described Bierstadt as "our Parrhasius," a reference to an ancient Greek painter. Of course, Ludlow also fulfilled his free-travel obligations, making a few laudatory comments about railroads and stagecoaches.

All the while, he was planning something so much more ambitious. Even as he wrote the *Post* dispatches, Ludlow stowed away his finest thoughts in a diary. This is where he recorded his most acute and erudite observations, drawing on his vast knowledge of art, history, mythology, and religions of the world, past and present. To protect the diary, to keep it from getting wet, he even fashioned a little pocket for it made out of India rubber cloth.

Ludlow was trying to absorb everything. With extreme diligence, he attempted to identify the plants and wildlife he encountered. Whenever possible, he collected specimens to bring back. For example, he caught a number of horned lizards and placed them in a bucket. But a fellow stage passenger released them as a practical joke.

Relying on James Dana's landmark *System of Mineralogy* as a guidebook, Ludlow also made various geological observations. He described a rock formation near Monument Creek in Colorado as follows: "The conglomerate of the latter was an irregular mixture of fragments from all the hypogene rocks of the range, including quartzose pebbles, pure crystals of silex, various crystalline sandstones, gneiss, solitary hornblende and feldspar, nodular iron-stones, rude agates, and gun-flint; the whole loosely cemented in a matrix composed of clay, lime (most likely from the decomposition of gypsum), and red oxide of iron."

The West was a massive subject. Ludlow planned to meet its challenge by writing a big, important book that would silence all doubters, securing his reputation once and for all.

Ludlow and Bierstadt crossed the Continental Divide at Bridgers Pass and then began a slow climb down out of the Rockies. As they moved

into Utah Territory, Ludlow noticed that the mood in the stagecoach
changed palpably, with his fellow passengers growing tense and wary.
They had entered Mormon country, a region that inspired both cu-
riosity and fear in travelers, due to the strange customs of its inhabi-
tants. By now, New York City seemed incredibly distant. As one of the
passengers remarked, they were now traveling through a separate and
distinct kingdom.

It was the middle of the night, per usual, when they arrived in Salt
Lake City. The coach rolled through the streets of the sleeping town,
which seemed orderly to an unusual degree, featuring row upon row
of little adobe houses. In the moonlight, Ludlow could see that each
house had a neat square of lawn and a small garden. An incongruous
lushness held sway here, so different from the harsh western landscapes
he'd experienced. "To understand the exquisite beauty of simple green
grass," Ludlow wrote, "you must travel through eight hundred miles of
sage-brush and *grama*."

Visitors quickly drew notice in Salt Lake City in 1863, particularly
distinguished ones from back East. The next day, Ludlow and Bierstadt
received invitations to meet both Brigham Young and Porter Rock-
well. According to Mormon tradition, it was Young who had received
a divine communiqué instructing him to found Salt Lake City in this
isolated desert valley. Porter Rockwell was the official protector of the
Church of Latter-day Saints against its enemies. Rumor held that he
had killed as many as a hundred men, and he was known by the un-
nerving sobriquet "the Destroying Angel." (Rockwell had not been
convicted of a single murder; then again, Utah territorial courts were
considered suspect by outsiders.)

Rockwell delivered his invitation personally, explaining that he lived
in a house at the western edge of Salt Lake City. No visitor left town
without stopping for a meal. Rockwell hoped Ludlow and Bierstadt
would avail themselves of his hospitality.

Ludlow set about exploring Salt Lake City—more of a town, really.
Only sixteen years had passed since Young had begun the original set-
tlement with 148 Mormon pioneers. The population had since grown
to roughly 10,000. Construction was still under way on a massive

temple the church had planned and would be for many years to come. Ludlow learned that the town received water via an irrigation system that carried snowmelt from the surrounding mountains across the desert floor. Canals ran down every street, and in front of every house a tributary branched off, flowing onto the property. That accounted for those orderly squares of lawn.

It wasn't long before Ludlow witnessed another distinguishing feature of Utah Territory: polygamy. He hadn't been sure how he'd feel about the institution. As author of *The Hasheesh Eater,* he had certainly documented some unusual practices. At Pfaff's, he'd witnessed behaviors that were considerably outside the norm. Nevertheless, he found that he was appalled. While eating a meal, he was deeply embarrassed to discover that two women he'd taken for sisters were actually sister wives: "Yet I, a cosmopolite, a man of the world, liberal to other people's habits and opinions to a degree which has often subjected me to censure among strictarians in the Eastern States, blushed to my very temples, and had to retire into the privacy of my tipped milk-bowl to screen the struggle by which I restored my moral equipoise."

Rumor held that Young had as many as seventy wives and had pledged his devotion to hundreds of others who would join him in heaven. Ludlow simply could not fathom how multiple wives could be satisfied with the scraps of love provided by a single husband. *That* was the beauty of plural marriage, he was repeatedly assured. Tamping down one's baser emotions such as bitterness and jealousy represented a "triumph o' grace." Still, he remained suspicious. Perhaps these women had figured out a way to bury their dissatisfactions deep, but he was sure something was amiss. "Heavens! What strange unsexing operation must their souls have gone through to keep them from frenzy—murder—suicide?"

The audience with Brigham Young took place during a formal ball held at the capacious opera house. Ludlow joined the Mormon leader on a theater balcony, where he was looking out over roughly three thousand of the faithful. Young was sixty-three, but to Ludlow he looked like a man in his forties. He was portly and dressed in a black suit. What most struck Ludlow, on first impression, was that he was in the presence of an autocrat the equal of Napoleon. The transformation from arid valley to lush greenery had been achieved through sheer force of will—*Young's* will. It also occurred to Ludlow that he was in the company of a man who was likely as rich as a Rothschild.

For Ludlow, making conversation with Young proved extremely difficult. There was something distant and abstracted about his manner, a kind of "Scriptural dignity"—as Ludlow put it—to his speaking style. Topic after conversational topic simply died in the air between them. But Young finally warmed to the subject of the Civil War. "Your Union's gone forever," he said with evident glee, adding, "When your country has become a desolation, we, the saints whom you cast out, will forget all your sins against us, and give you a home."

It was a refrain that Ludlow heard throughout his time in Salt Lake City. Here, the distant Civil War was commonly viewed as an act of divine retribution. Northerners and Southerners were bound to fight until every last soldier lay dead. Only widows would be left behind. The widows would then make their way out to Utah Territory, providing a massive influx of fresh brides for the saints. To many of the Mormons encountered by Ludlow, there was an indelible logic to the Civil War, as if it were directed by the hand of God, their God, and destined to unfold like a prophecy.

Young took his leave and went down onto the floor of the ballroom. Presently, Ludlow spotted him dancing. The writer was amused to note that Young was doing a style of two-step that had fallen out of fashion years earlier in the East.

A highlight of the Utah visit was the Great Salt Lake. While Bierstadt worked, Ludlow waded out into the water. He was fascinated by the buoyancy he achieved, and he appreciated the lake's brininess as well. It gave him a "pleasant pungent sense of being in a pickle, such as a self-conscious gherkin might experience." For what must have been an hour, he simply floated lazily on his back. When at last he turned over, he was shocked to learn that he'd drifted into water that was less than a foot deep.

Pfaff's saloon was at 647 Broadway in New York City. It was in the basement of the Coleman House hotel (second building above the cross street, Bleecker, in this photo from the 1860s).

During the 1850s and 1860s, America's first Bohemians met at Pfaff's saloon. Henry Clapp Jr., leader of this remarkably talented collection of artists, always sat at the head of a long table in a specially set-aside vaulted room. Clapp (pictured left with his trademark pipe) had lived in Paris and is responsible for importing Bohemia to America.

Fitz-James O'Brien (above, left), a talented but dissolute writer, was the charter member of the Pfaff's circle. Elegant, quick-witted Ada Clare was dubbed Queen of Bohemia.

This 1854 photo provides an idea of what Whitman looked like when he first started going to Pfaff's.

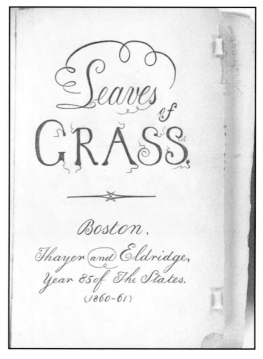

Whitman frontispiece from the 1860 edition of Leaves of Grass. *Time among the Bohemians inspired him to write fresh poems and explore bold new themes.*

Whitman at Pfaff's: This 1895 illustration was based on decades' old memories. Thus, details of the saloon and Whitman are from an 1890s perspective.

Adah Isaacs Menken, nineteenth-century sex symbol and one of the most colorful members of the Pfaff's set. Onstage, she gained notoriety as the Naked Lady, thanks to her role in the risqué equestrian drama Mazeppa. *Offstage, her busy love life provoked equal controversy.*

Mazeppa

Fitz Hugh Ludlow, author of The Hasheesh Eater, *was a psychedelic pioneer.*

Ludlow's wife, Rosalie, and his friend, the painter Albert Bierstadt.

During the 1860s, no term even existed for what Artemus Ward did. People often called his performances "comic lectures." But this Pfaff's regular is more accurately seen as America's first stand-up.

President Abraham Lincoln was a huge fan of Artemus Ward. Young Mark Twain made fast friends with the comedian when they met out West.

The year 1860 was ominous: On April 17, a bare-fisted match between John Heenan and Tom Sayers lasted forty-two rounds. The night of July 20 featured a meteor procession that lit up the sky over Manhattan for a full minute. This is an extremely rare cosmic event; modern astronomers know of only four such occurrences. Whitman and his fellow Pfaff's Bohemians took it as an evil omen.

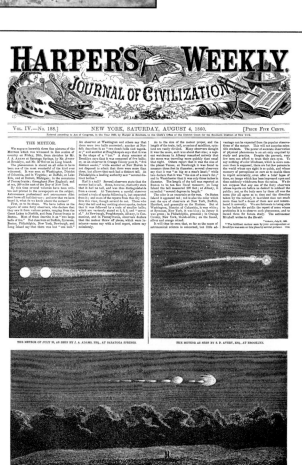

Less than a year later,
America descended into civil
war. The Pfaff's set scattered
but continued to reconnect
in new settings. Whitman
moved to Washington,
DC, where he ministered
to wounded soldiers in
places such as the Armory
Square Hospital (above).
In Washington, he also met
Peter Doyle, the love of his
life (left).

Edwin Booth—tortured, a drunk, but spectacularly gifted—was part of the Bohemian artists' circle. Two of his brothers were also actors. The three appeared together onstage only once for a performance of Shakespeare's Julius Caesar. *Afterward, Edwin and John Wilkes Booth got into a heated political argument. John Wilkes stormed off, and the rest is history.*

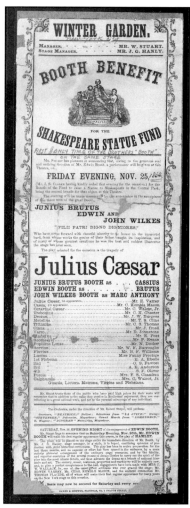

The brothers Booth (left to right): John Wilkes as Marc Antony, Edwin as Brutus, and Junius Jr. as Cassius.

Whitman lived on: While many of the Pfaff's set—including Artemus Ward, Adah Menken, and Fitz Hugh Ludlow—died young, often under tragic circumstances, Whitman carried on into old age, becoming the Good Gray Poet.

Emerging from the lake, Ludlow's hair and beard were thickly caked with salt—his *long* hair and *full* beard. He had neither shaved nor visited a barber on the trip. He'd turned into a "Nazarene," as he put it.

Then it was time to get back on the road. On departing Salt Lake City, Ludlow and Bierstadt dropped by the Destroying Angel's house, as promised, for a visit and a home-cooked meal. Did they really have a choice? Ludlow began the visit feeling considerable trepidation. He studied Rockwell warily, noting his muscled arms, thick neck, and "mastiff head." The man seemed designed specifically for violence, nothing else. But Ludlow noticed that one element of Rockwell's appearance was extremely dissonant: his long black hair, streaked with gray, was twisted into a large bun that he held in place with a comb, like a woman. No other Mormon Ludlow had encountered wore their hair in this fashion. Joseph Smith—Young's predecessor and the founder of Mormonism—had prophesied that, like Sampson, no one could harm Rockwell as long as he didn't cut his hair.

As the meal progressed, Ludlow was able to relax. Rockwell's two wives worked in harmony, bringing out plates of food. Rockwell grew downright genial, telling jokes and long, involved stories. At last, they took their leave of him without incident. Wisely, Ludlow chose not to include an account of his nervous dinner or any other incriminating details about Mormonism in his *Post* dispatches. Those articles ran while he was traveling, and he feared he might get hunted down and fall victim to swift western justice. Ludlow later described Rockwell as the "kindest hearted and most obliging murderer I ever knew."

On July 17, 1863, Ludlow and Bierstadt arrived in San Francisco. Though they had successfully crossed the continent, their trip was far from over. Using San Francisco as a base, they made a series of excursions. The pair traveled to a spot that offered an unparalleled view of Mount Shasta, rising above the plains, and up the coast to Portland, Oregon. Without question, however, the most striking scenery they encountered on their entire trip was during a visit to Yosemite. This natural wonder, Ludlow later wrote, "out-Bendemered Bendemere, out-valleyed the valley of Rasselas, surpassed the Alps in its waterfalls, and the Himmal'yeh in its precipices." (More Ludlow erudition: Bendemere is a reference to a folk song about an idyllic landscape, the Valley of Rasselas supposedly an earthly paradise in ancient Abyssinia.)

Very few non–Native Americans had ever set foot in Yosemite, which remained supremely wild and isolated in this era. Bierstadt did studies of all the various features that would become the valley's icons, such as El Capitan, Half Dome, and Bridalveil Fall. In fact, Bierstadt's paintings would play a major role in familiarizing people with these features, thereby turning them into attractions.

Ludlow fell into his amateur-scientist role, making geological observations and collecting specimens of flora and fauna. While riding through a mountain meadow, he was enchanted to find himself surrounded by butterflies, all colors and varieties—the place fairly swarmed with them. Seized by sudden inspiration, he set about trying to catch some on horseback. According to Ludlow, this was how butterfly collecting was done in royal courts during the Middle Ages. He galloped around the meadow, brandishing a long-handled net like a lance. It all seemed very romantic. But the butterflies stayed well ahead of his horse. Mostly, he managed to annoy his mount by repeatedly swinging the net in front of its eyes.

Ludlow and Bierstadt pitched their tents on the banks of the frigid Merced River. The painter dubbed it "Camp Rosalie." This was the second time in the course of the trip that he'd named something after his travel companion's wife. He explained to Ludlow that he was paying tribute to "a dear absent friend."

Suspicious, though. It was definitely rather suspicious.

By making San Francisco their base, Ludlow and Bierstadt were able to spend considerable time there between side trips. Ludlow got to know the city extremely well. Only fifteen years had passed since San Francisco was handed over by Mexico as part of the Treaty of Guadalupe Hidalgo. Because of its fortunate location, it had quickly grown into a gateway to the West. People arrived from everywhere: they sailed into its harbor from Asia and Latin America and came in from the East by wagon or on foot if necessary. As a consequence, the city, while relatively small—its population of roughly one hundred thousand was less than Cincinnati or Baltimore—possessed a wildly polyglot character. It reminded Ludlow of Manhattan. Here, too, he detected "that magnificent nonchalance and minding of each separate citizen's business which so pre-eminently gives New York the unmistakeable urban stamp."

In San Francisco, everything was possible and available. Ludlow even managed to fall in with a group of local artists. As it happened, the members fashioned themselves after Clapp's New York circle of Bohemians. They frequented the bar at the Occidental Hotel, where they quipped and quaffed, trying gamely to reproduce one of those legendary Pfaff's nights. They even had their own equivalent to the *Saturday Press,* a weekly paper called the *Golden Era,* published at 543 Clay Street. The *Golden Era*'s editor, Colonel Joe Lawrence, like Clapp, was described by one contemporary as an "inveterate pipe-smoker."

Out in the wilds of California, at a time when both the *SP* and *Vanity Fair* had recently failed, Lawrence was managing to keep his publication alive—just barely—by sticking to a truly bizarre formula. Half of the *Golden Era* was devoted to useful information for prospectors and other gritty frontier sorts—or at least those who could read and were willing to pay five dollars for a year's subscription. There were news items about mining claims, homely recipes for dishes like baked beans, and some of the most casually graphic obituaries imaginable: "James A. Rogers, blew his brains out, September 2 nd. Cause: discouraged." The other half of the *Golden Era* featured the literary efforts of the West Coast Bohemians. This group possessed some serious talent, along with some genuine eccentricity—and plenty of blurring between the two categories.

The undeniable star was Bret Harte, then a relatively unknown writer. Harte was at the very beginning of a distinguished career, during which he would receive international acclaim for his depictions of miners and other hard-living California types. As a frequent contributor to the *Golden Era,* he wrote under several pseudonyms, including

"Bohemian." During Ludlow's visit, Harte's novella *M'Liss* was running in serial form in the paper. It would be one of the standouts of Harte's classic collection, *The Luck of the Roaring Camp, and Other Tales.*

Joaquin Miller, meanwhile, had just arrived in San Francisco, down from Oregon for an extended visit. Among the *Golden Era* set, he filled the Adah Menken role. To anyone who'd listen, Miller spun out various episodes from his life story, skillfully blending verifiable details with outrageous falsehoods. Supposedly, he'd worked as a mining camp cook, a drover, and a rider for the Pony Express. He'd been both a judge and a horse thief, as well as a participant in William Walker's famous expedition to Nicaragua. All this, and he was barely thirty. Or was he in his forties? Miller had as many birth dates as he had careers. In the course of his adventures, he claimed, he'd also endured his share of Indian attacks, one time receiving a serious leg injury. But it was duly noted that sometimes he limped with his right leg, sometimes his left.

As the self-styled "Byron of the Rockies," Miller—like Menken—had aspirations to be taken seriously as a poet. Unfortunately, he was hampered by atrocious spelling, a tin ear for meter, and a penchant for making quease-inducing artistic choices. He once attempted to rhyme "Goethe" and "teeth." Thanks to his colorful persona, however, Miller was destined to achieve tremendous popular success in the years to come, even as he was savaged by critics. In fact, generations of nineteenth-century schoolkids would be forced to recite his purplish "Columbus"—a shoddy poem by any reasonable standard.

Yet another pillar of this Left Coast Bohemia was Charles Warren Stoddard. Stoddard had just turned twenty and had recently moved to San Francisco from New York City. As an aspiring poet, he was profoundly influenced by the third edition of *Leaves of Grass.* For Stoddard, the work suggested dazzling new possibilities of subject and form. The young poet was experimenting with free verse and publishing his efforts in the *Golden Era* under the pseudonym "Pip Pepperpod." Stoddard was especially affected by Whitman's "Calamus" poems, which he would always credit with helping him to realize his sexual orientation.

In the years ahead, Stoddard would publish poetry, fiction, and memoirs, assembling a body of work distinguished for its time by an unusually relaxed and open attitude toward homosexuality. "I am what I was when I was born," he once said. Among Stoddard's works are *South-Sea Idylls* (an erotically charged travelogue published in 1873) and *For the Pleasure of His Company* (a 1903 novel).

These upstart Bohemians were thrilled to spend time with Ludlow. As a real-life representative of Pfaff's, as a writer who had tasted success in the fierce eastern literary scene, Ludlow *was* what they aspired *to be*. Encountering such deference must have pleased Ludlow greatly, and he was generous in doling out advice and praise. He urged Stoddard to drop the ridiculous nom de plume "Pip Pepperpod." (The writer followed his suggestion.) And he praised Harte for his "luscious richness of imagery" and "noble strength of original thought," adding that major magazines back East would surely "welcome him with enthusiasm." (Only a few years later, in 1871, the *Atlantic* would extend a contract to Harte, $10,000 for a dozen stories, the most it had ever paid a writer.)

Ludlow also managed to confound the expectations of the San Francisco Bohemians. Naturally, they had assumed that the author of *The Hasheesh Eater* would be world-weary and jaded. Instead, they were treated to this slight and bookish young man, spouting big words and brimming with exotic enthusiasms. They nicknamed Ludlow "the Hasheesh Infant." The group was particularly bemused by Ludlow's lengthy impromptu discourses on Darwin and the theory of evolution. It was less than three years since *On the Origin of Species* had been published. For the California circle, these were odd new ideas, courtesy of an odd new friend.

Whenever talented writers visited San Francisco, *Golden Era* editor Lawrence had a policy: "We purchased their pens and pencils before they had been [here] an hour." In short order, Ludlow was contributing to the paper. Apparently, 1863 was a busy year for Lawrence, for he was also courting another promising out-of-towner: Mark Twain.

Twain, in the midst of a several-month visit to San Francisco, was down from Virginia City, Nevada, where he worked for a highly regarded newspaper called the *Daily Territorial Enterprise*. He was rail thin with gray eyes and curly red hair. Only twenty-seven, Twain had lived an itinerant life, had already experienced entire other careers: as a blacksmith's apprentice, grocery store clerk, and riverboat pilot.

He'd spent the first months of the Civil War back home in Missouri. There, he was one of a group of young men rounded up by a zealous Union army recruiter, but he escaped and took up with the Confederacy instead. He joined a tiny militia, maybe fifteen strong, called the Marion Rangers. It was an exercise, Twain would recall, in "sham soldiership." Mostly, the outfit sneaked around the backwoods, trying to stay ahead of the Union troops moving through Missouri. "I knew more about retreating than the man that invented retreating," he later joked.

Eventually, he simply wandered away from the Marion Rangers ("deserting" is too official sounding) and headed out West. Twain had only recently adopted his pen name. Thanks to his knack for sly, subversive humor, he was starting to develop a regional reputation, though he was a complete unknown back East. During Twain's visit to San Francisco, Lawrence offered him a full-time staff job on the *Golden Era*. He wasn't ready to leave Nevada Territory, but agreed to contribute some pieces on a freelance basis. One issue of the *Golden Era* features both Twain's "How to Cure a Cold" and Ludlow's "On Marrying Men."

Of Twain, Ludlow commented, "He makes me laugh more than any Californian." (Never mind that he was actually a Nevadan at present.) For his part, Twain included the following in a letter to his mother: "And if Fitz Hugh Ludlow (author of The Hasheesh Eater) comes your way, treat him well."

Ludlow deserves credit for being an easterner early to take note of Twain. Other Pfaffians were destined to forge deeper, more meaningful connections with him.

The time came for Ludlow and Bierstadt to return home. Back East, Alexander Gardner was feeding the public's insatiable hunger for

Civil War news with his groundbreaking photographs of battlefields strewn with dead soldiers. The images, some of which were exhibited at Mathew Brady's Broadway studio, offered intimate, privileged flashes from the front, and they left viewers stunned. This, then, was war in all its horror and brutality. Bierstadt, armed with a huge variety of oil studies, was now prepared to answer an opposite need, equally pressing, with peaceful images of prairies and mountains and waterfalls. And Ludlow, diary filled with vivid observations, was ready to paint his own portrait of the West—to deliver in words Eden itself.

The pair had traveled by land all the way to California. For their return trip, they opted for a faster route. They took a steamer down the Pacific Coast and then crossed the isthmus through Panama, before steaming up the Atlantic Coast to New York City.

Before they left, however, Ludlow chose to make one last excursion, alone. During his final week in San Francisco, he paid a visit to Chinatown, slipping down the narrow streets, past butchers and apothecaries, past restaurants with their paper lanterns and barbershops marked by their characteristic signs, featuring four little red knobs, until he arrived at a hong.

A hong is an opium den. A typical one in nineteenth-century San Francisco consisted of a single dimly lit room, tight-packed with patrons, some on the floor, some reclining on bunks. The air would be thick with opium smoke, which has a pleasant, inviting aroma, akin to roasted nuts. On arrival, a visitor would be furnished with a small box made of horn, containing a dollop of black opium paste. It was necessary to break off a little portion. Then, using a piece of wire, one skewered the bit of paste and held it over the open flame of a lamp. When the paste began to smoke, it was transferred to a pipe consisting of a stone bowl, about the size of a thimble, attached to a long bamboo stem. Inhale. Hold breath. Exhale. Smoking opium is so much more potent than taking it in tincture form.

Having traveled across the continent, Ludlow now slipped into a haze.

CHAPTER 13

The Soldiers' Missionary

ON JANUARY 2, 1863, while visiting Campbell Hospital in Washington, DC, Whitman stopped at bed 49 to pass a few minutes with a complete stranger. John Holmes, a twenty-one-year-old private from a Massachusetts regiment, was laid up with a severe stomach ailment and bronchitis. Since arriving two weeks earlier, Holmes had received no medical care whatsoever. Holmes was glassy-eyed and listless; he had pretty much given up hope. Whitman summoned a doctor and insisted that the ailing soldier be given attention. He also gave Holmes a few coins to buy a glass of milk from a woman who was circulating the ward selling goods. At this kindness, the young man burst into tears.

The episode crystallized something for Whitman. Originally, he'd planned only to visit the two soldiers from his brother's regiment before returning home. But he found himself deeply drawn to hospital work, as he had been at the front. There was such a vast, heart-rending need. He decided to stay on indefinitely. While Ludlow wended his way across the continent—visiting American states and other states of consciousness—Whitman would remain in the Union capital, ministering to wounded soldiers. He would keep up with his Pfaff's circle from a distance—both his circles, actually, the Bohemian artists and the gay men who gathered in the saloon's other, larger, room. "I cannot give up my Hospitals yet," wrote Whitman in a letter to his family back in Brooklyn. "I never before had my feeling so thoroughly and (so far) permanently absorbed, to the very roots, as by these huge swarms of dear, wounded, sick, dying boys."

Whitman settled into Washington at a time when it was little more than a provincial backwater. The hallowed notion of states' rights—the very notion that had sparked the war—had kept the city in a state of arrested development. A federation of states didn't require a glittering capital, and throughout its history the city had dutifully reflected this by remaining humble and low-rise. Official buildings had been kept to a minimum: the Capitol, White House, Treasury, and a smattering of others. Construction had stalled on the Washington Monument, and it remained a mere stump, rising 156 feet, a third of its eventual height. Even major thoroughfares such as Pennsylvania Avenue were mostly unpaved, swirling with dust in the summer heat, mired in mud when it rained. The seat of government was a small, odoriferous town, built on reclaimed swampland, home to roaming hordes of feral pigs that rooted through garbage.

For $7 a month, Whitman found a little room at 394 L Street, the first of several shabby rentals he'd take in Washington. Such accommodations, which Whitman described as appropriate to "a sort of German or Parisian student life," suited the poet, now forty-three, just fine. Charles Eldridge came through once again, this time with a job. Eldridge—the publisher of *Leaves of Grass,* who earlier helped Whitman get to the front to find his brother—worked for an army paymaster. He got Whitman employment in the same department, as a copyist. It was an incredibly undemanding post, requiring Whitman to spend two or three hours a day duplicating documents such as vouchers and reports. That left Whitman with ample free time to make the rounds of hospitals.

As of 1863, Washington had around thirty-five hospitals, tending to about twelve thousand soldiers at any given time. This meant the infirm population was one-fifth of the city's peacetime population. To deal with this influx, Washington had been forced to add hospitals at a breakneck speed, starting from a single hospital at the outbreak of the war. While a few true hospitals had been built such as Campbell and Armory Square, many were temporary facilities: churches, schools, and warehouses called into service. One such makeshift hospital was created by joining together the neighboring houses of Stephen Douglas and John Breckinridge, rival candidates who had split the Democratic Party in the 1860 election. Even the US Patent Office building was converted into a hospital. Arrayed around glass cases that exhibited patented American inventions were cots filled with the sick and wounded, groaning in pain.

Some of the worst casualties received treatment in Washington, often soldiers transferred from the front. Many were gunshot victims. The new pointed bullets were made of soft, low-grade lead that blunted on impact, mangling limbs and shattering bones. Amputation was often seen as the wisest course. The hospitals were overflowing with soldiers either awaiting amputation, recovering from rush-job battlefield amputations, or facing the prospect of having the procedure performed again—higher on the stump—because it was botched the first time. They were also full of the chronically ill, soldiers suffering from lingering conditions such as malaria, tetanus, and diarrhea. In fact, forty-five thousand Union soldiers succumbed to diarrhea, the leading cause of Civil War death by disease. Whitman would later say, "That whole damned war business is about nine hundred and ninety nine parts diarrhea to one part glory."

Plenty of soldiers also fell victim to the hospitals themselves. In a pre-antiseptic era, the conditions were shockingly unsanitary. Doctors used their own saliva to wet stitching thread. Nurses dabbed wounds with sponges that, following the previous operation, had been cleaned in simple tap water. There were constant outbreaks of dreaded conditions such as gangrene, erysipelas (a severe bacterial skin infection), and pyemia (back then, the medical term for blood poisoning). Historian George Worthington Adams would observe that "the Civil War was fought in the very last years of the medical middle ages."

Amid so much chaos, any help was welcome in Washington's hospitals. All kinds of people, with all sorts of motives, roamed through the wards. Mothers of soldiers parked themselves cot side and gave their sons the kind of attention the overtaxed medical staffs were unable to provide. Freelance nurses circulated, unaffiliated with the hospitals or any organized aid society. Clara Barton, who would found the Red Cross after the war, fell into this category. (At Falmouth, Barton had been working at Lacy House, the temporary hospital that treated severe injuries, when Whitman visited. Strangely, despite being at the front at the same time, despite both serving in the Washington hospitals, Whitman and Barton appear never to have met.) There were also plenty of unsavory characters slinking about. Petty thieves pilfered items. Scam artists talked woozy soldiers into adding them to their wills, signing away their remaining earthly possessions.

In this lax environment, Whitman had great latitude to carve out his own role. Initially, he acted as a representative for the Christian Commission, an outfit that distributed supplies and religious literature. Such officialdom held no appeal for Whitman, though, and the connection quickly ended. He preferred to work solo. Whitman came up with his own singular role, best expressed by the legend scrawled on the inside cover of one of his notebooks from this time: "Walt Whitman, Soldiers' Missionary."

He wasn't a nurse, nor did he provide medical care in any traditional sense. Rather, he did a lot of what might be called advocacy, though that's too formal of a term. He appealed to the overwhelmed hospital staffers, trying to get them to focus their fragmented attentions on the neediest wounded soldiers. Thanks to Whitman's intervention, Private Holmes—the man who had cried at the kindness of a glass of milk—recovered, returned to his unit, and served out the war. He would always credit the poet with saving his life.

Whitman also spent a great deal of time simply keeping the sick and wounded company, sitting at their bedsides. If a soldier wanted to make diverting small talk, or relive battlefield glory, or unburden himself of a pent-up anxiety, or, overcome by pangs of homesickness, if he wanted to talk about his folks—Whitman was there. "Agonies are one of my changes of garments," he wrote in the poem "Song of Myself": "I do not ask the wounded person how he feels . . . I myself become the wounded person."

These are prescient lines given that they first appeared nearly a decade earlier in the 1855 edition of *Leaves of Grass*. In the wartime hospitals, a poet's empathy became Whitman's great gift. Often he simply listened to the soldiers. Whitman was always most comfortable in that role, as he'd shown at Pfaff's. But he adjusted his methods as needed. If a soldier was quiet, Whitman might do the talking, trying to draw the man out. Sometimes Whitman would read to a soldier, or even sing. Still other times, Whitman would sense that a patient was desperate for quiet, just some peace and quiet. He might sit beside this wounded soul for hours, lending silent support. Once, the poet passed an entire evening at the bedside of Charles Cutter, 1st Massachusetts heavy artillery, fanning him while he dozed in the stifling ward. The hospitals could be such terrifyingly anonymous places, especially for a man or boy—some were no more than boys, truly—who was injured or sick and far from home. Through his mere presence, Whitman gave these soldiers hope, something that was critically lacking. As he put it, "I supply the patients with a medicine which all [the hospitals'] drugs & bottles & powders are helpless to yield."

Every day, before setting off to make his rounds, Whitman ate a large, hearty meal and took a long, hot bath. This became his routine. His goal was to radiate good cheer and robust health. As a devotee of concepts such as phrenology and animal magnetism, Whitman held mystical ideas about health and one's ability to project it onto others. To this point in his life, Whitman had never suffered any kind of serious illness. It was a point of great personal pride. In the absence of medical training, he viewed health as one of his primary attributes, a blessing that was his to bestow. In a letter to his mother, he noted, "I fancy the reason I am able to do some good in the hospitals, among the poor languishing & wounded boys, is that I am so large and well—indeed like a great wild buffalo, with much hair."

Whitman fell into the habit of distributing various items to the soldiers. His notebooks are filled with their modest requests:

David S. Giles, co. F. 28th N.J.V.bed 52 W. 6— . . . wants an apple

Hiram Scholis—bed 3—Ward E.—26th N. York—wants some pickles—a bottle of pickles.

Henry D. Boardman co. B 27th Conn Vol. . . . Bed 25 . . . wants a
rice pudding milky & not very sweet.

Whenever Whitman set out for the hospitals, he would bring a
leather haversack, slung over his shoulder, stuffed with items. He an-
swered a huge variety of requests, delivering peaches, preserves, biscuits,
licorice, oysters, tea, horehound candy, and raspberry syrup for sooth-
ing aching throats. He also provided toothpicks, combs, underwear and
socks, pencils and paper, and books to read. Of course, all of this cost
money. Whitman was earning about $15 per week at his new govern-
ment job in the paymaster's office. Nearly half this pay was devoted to
goods for the wounded soldiers. So he started soliciting donations from
friends back in Brooklyn and elsewhere. Small amounts trickled in: $2
here, $3 there. Every bit helped.

A few months into his hospital service, Whitman bought a cheap
wine-colored suit. He wore it every day, the trousers tucked into heavy
leather boots. He hadn't shaved since leaving Brooklyn. The total ef-
fect—reddish suit, bushy beard, the haversack—was like a Bohemian
Santa Claus. One day, he showed up at Carver Hospital with ice cream
and dished it out to the patients. "Many of the men had to be fed,
several of them I saw cannot probably live, yet they quite enjoyed it,"
he noted, adding, "I gave everybody some—quite a number western
country boys had never tasted ice cream before."

Whitman also filled requests for items such as brandy and playing
cards. The soldiers appreciated the fact that he wasn't a moralist. Along
with worried mothers and freelance nurses, a constant stream of preach-
ers poured through the hospitals. Many provided great spiritual solace.
Nevertheless, soldiers often objected to the sheer volume of preachers;
so many visited that the little cot-side shelves reserved for one's few be-
longings were often piled high with tracts and testaments. "A wounded
soldier don't like to be reminded of his God more than twenty times a
day," recalled Colonel Richard Hinton. "Walt Whitman didn't bring
any tracts or Bibles; he didn't ask if you loved the Lord, and didn't
seem to care whether you did or not." Instead, at Hinton's request,

"this old heathen came and gave me a pipe and tobacco . . . about the most joyous moment of my life."

Whitman got to know certain soldiers quite well. Often he was present at their bedsides, sitting in vigil, as they exited this world. His notebooks, filled with the soldiers' wants (oranges, a handkerchief), are also filled with details about their deaths (typhus, pyemia)—both equally humble. Lorenzo Strong, 9th US Cavalry, was hit by a piece of shrapnel and had to have his right leg amputated. He died from complications. Oscar Cunningham, 82nd Regiment Ohio Infantry, arrived at Armory Square hospital, a big, hulking man, but Whitman had seen him waste to a skeleton by the time he died of a stomach ailment. John Elliott, 2nd Pennsylvania Cavalry, shot in the leg and weakened by infection, was administered chloroform for an operation and never came to. "Poor young man," Whitman wrote to his mother, "he suffered much, very *very* much. . . . Not a soul here he knew or cared about, except me." Whitman added, "To see such things & not be able to help them is awful—I feel almost ashamed of being so well & whole."

After soldiers died, Whitman often took it upon himself to write letters to their parents. The official notifications sent by the government were brief and matter-of-fact. The poet wanted to mark the soldier's passing in a more fitting manner.

When Erastus Haskell died of typhoid fever, Whitman sent a letter to his parents in Breesport, New York. "I thought it would be soothing to you to have a few words about the last days of your son," Whitman began. He indicated that the dying soldier's wish had been to send his love to his parents, brothers, and sisters. He described Erastus as "a quiet young man, behaved always correct & decent, said little." And Whitman also commented on a fife that lay on Erastus's bed stand. He had promised to play for Whitman, had he recovered his health. "He is one of the thousands of our unknown American young men in the ranks about whom there is no record or fame, no fuss made about their dying so unknown, but I find in them the real precious & royal ones of this land." He closed by assuring the Haskell family that although they were strangers, although they were unlikely ever to meet, he, Whitman, also sent them his love.

Whitman was overflowing with emotion. Surrounded by death, he'd become more fully alive, receptive to all this raw feeling coursing through him. He was like a crucible for poetry. He talked to Eldridge about bringing out a fresh collection of his work. Never mind that Eldridge was a failed publisher, in no position to help. Never mind that Whitman had no other publishing prospects. He'd been at this point before. Whitman started planning a new collection anyway, focused on his Civil War experiences, everything from watching soldiers on Broadway in 1861 to the visit with brother George at the front to his current role, ministering to the wounded in Washington. After three editions of *Leaves of Grass,* he envisioned it as his first work outside of that franchise. The subject matter seemed to demand its own stand-alone volume.

Some of Whitman's finest new poems would grow out of his hospital service. There's "The Wound-Dresser," a lovely poem, and also a source of confusion for future generations. (Whitman wasn't a nurse and wasn't charged with dressing wounds. But he was certainly capable of inhabiting the persona of someone who was and did.) There's also "Come Up from the Fields, Father," where the poet imagines a couple who lives on a farm, receiving a letter such as he'd sent to the Haskells, with news of their son:

> Open the envelope quickly,
> O this is not our son's writing, yet his name is sign'd,
> O a strange hand writes for our dear son, O stricken mother's soul!

For now, Whitman was mostly gathering ideas. He was making notations, trying to capture feelings and observations in the moment. Per his usual methods, he would need to live with this material for a while, painstakingly spinning it into poetry.

Following a hospital visit, Whitman's habit was to go for a long walk. Time was, he'd promenaded Broadway. He'd cased Washington Street during his earlier stay in Boston. Now it was DC that he explored on foot. A favorite destination was the Capitol, currently under renovation. Scaffolding surrounded the unfinished dome. Blocks of granite and architectural flotsam—lintels and pilasters—were scattered about the grounds, giving the appearance of a Greek ruin. It was possible to walk into the building at any hour. He enjoyed wandering the maze of hallways, hearing the click of his boot heels on the marble floor.

Hours after he'd left a hospital, sometimes Whitman would start trembling uncontrollably, recalling the horrors he'd seen earlier. By then, he might have meandered to some distant corner of Washington.

One night he ambled right onto the lawn of the White House. He remained for quite a while. "To-night took a long look at the President's House," he noted. "The white portico—the palace-like, tall, round columns, spotless as snow—the walls also—the tender and soft moonlight, flooding the pale marble, and making peculiar faint languishing shades."

Standing on the White House lawn at midnight seemed perfectly natural to Whitman. After all, he saw Lincoln nearly every single day. Sometimes, while Whitman was walking to a hospital, the president hurried past, surrounded by advisers. Or he would see Lincoln in a carriage, en route to the country house where he often slept during warm weather. Mary Todd might be beside him. Once, Whitman saw Lincoln's young son, Tad, riding alongside the carriage on a pony.

In the poet's eyes, Lincoln was the "Redeemer President," a living symbol of union. Ever since Whitman had watched him move through that hostile crowd in New York, he'd felt a special bond. "I see the President often," Whitman noted. "I think better of him than many do. He has conscience & homely shrewdness—conceals an enormous tenacity under his mild, gawky western manner." Following another spotting, Whitman wrote, "He has a face like a hoosier Michael Angelo, so awful ugly it becomes beautiful, with its strange mouth, its deep cut, criss-cross lines, and its doughnut complexion."

Lincoln, for his part, was almost certainly aware of *Leaves of Grass*. Around 1857, William Herndon, his law partner, purchased a copy of the work, likely the second edition. This is extraordinary, when one considers how few were sold. Nevertheless, one wound up in the possession of a lawyer in Springfield, Illinois. Just as Whitman was an artist with a rare grasp of politics, Lincoln was a politician with an unusual relish for the arts. It's quite possible that Lincoln read the work.

Now, only a few years later, Whitman saw him constantly. One time, Whitman looked out the window of one of his rented rooms (this one at 456 Sixth Street) right when Lincoln pulled up in a carriage. Whitman lived in a garret, but it also happened that Salmon Chase, the treasury secretary, lived in a mansion across the street, steeped in every luxury and attended by a gaggle of servants. Presently, Secretary Chase emerged from his home. He walked up to Lincoln's carriage, and the two men conversed for about fifteen minutes.

There was such a curious sense of enclosure to wartime Washington. Enemy cannon fire was constantly heard from nearby Virginia battlefields; General Lee threatened to descend on the city at any moment. That, combined with the capital's small size, fostered the illusion of an intimate village—the treasury secretary across the street, the president just down the way. Whitman saw Lincoln so often that he began to notice variations in his appearance and demeanor. "I had a good view of the president last evening," Whitman wrote to his mother, "—he looks more careworn even than usual—his face with deep cut lines, seams, & his *complexion gray*, through very dark skin, a curious looking man, very sad." Whitman saw Lincoln so often that it must have seemed almost real when he pronounced, "I love the President personally."

But it wasn't. There was a genuine connection on Whitman's part, for he observed the president minutely. It's possible that one existed for Lincoln, too, as he may have read *Leaves of Grass*. But the two never met.

Whitman was lonely. Though surrounded by people, he was finding, as he often did, that it was difficult to forge meaningful connections. At the hospitals, he'd come to realize, only two outcomes were possible. Soldiers got better and rejoined their units. Or they died. Either way, they moved on, leaving him behind. Whitman continued to pine for romantic love.

When a soldier named Tom Sawyer rejoined the 11th Massachusetts Volunteers, Whitman pursued him with a series of mooning letters. "If you should come safe out of this war," the poet wrote, "we should come together again in some place where we could make our living, and be true comrades and never be separated while life lasts." In another missive, he wrote, "Not a day passes, nor a night but I think of you."

Whitman had made Sawyer a parting gift of a shirt, underwear, and socks. He was hurt when Sawyer returned to the front without bothering to pick them up: "It would have been a satisfaction to me if you had accepted them." Whitman wondered whether the intensity of his feelings had left the soldier bewildered: "I suppose my letters sound strange & unusual to you as it is, but as I am only expressing the truth in them, I do not trouble myself on that account." As time went on, Whitman despaired of ever hearing back from Sawyer: "I do not know why you do not write to me. Do you wish to shake me off?"

Sawyer, evidently, was spooked by this onslaught of needy epistles. He wasn't exactly a wordsmith, either, being—per Whitman's usual preferences—something of a raw, uneducated young man. After many months, Sawyer wrote Whitman a brief note: "I hardly know what to say to you in this letter for it is my first one to you. . . . I hope you will forgive me and in the future I will do better and I hope we may meet again in this world."

Granted, Sawyer held out the possibility of seeing one another again. But what comes through most clearly is his hesitancy. Whitman knew enough about matters of the heart to recognize that this wasn't going to work out.

Each morning, when Whitman awakened in his cramped garret room, he would fire up some coals in a little sheet-iron stove. He would riffle around the pine box that served as his cupboard, withdrawing a parcel of tea leaves, a paper bag full of brown sugar, and the assorted other fixings for the heartiest breakfast possible on a pauper's dime.

To make toast, Whitman used a pointed stick to hold pieces of bread over coals in the stove. He used a jackknife to spread butter. As he prepared breakfast, he enjoyed singing to himself. One of his favorite

songs, "The Greatest Pain," was based on a seventeenth-century poem
by Abraham Cowley and contains the following verse:

> A mighty pain to love it is
> And yet a pain that love to miss
> But of all pains, the greatest pain
> It is to love, but love in vain!

Besides skittish Tom Sawyer and wounded soldiers in the hospitals,
Whitman's only other source of social connection in Washington was
a literary salon. It was organized by William Douglas O'Connor, a
fellow Thayer & Eldridge author, who had published a novel called
Harrington. The group numbered about a dozen. Many of them, like
Whitman, were transplants to wartime Washington, doing menial jobs
in government departments. Eldridge was a regular. Others included
Arnold Johnson, an assistant to Senator Sumner of Massachusetts;
Frank Baker, a medical historian at the Smithsonian; and J. J. Piatt, a
poet from Ohio.

O'Connor's wife once described the group as a "stimulating mental
society," filled with "fun and good-natured banter." Literature was a
frequent topic of discussion, as were abolitionism, foreign relations,
the Mormon question, and the matter of which dictionary was more
authoritative, Webster or Worcester. Another favorite activity was play-
ing the game Twenty Questions. For one round, the correct answer was
the white beard of Gideon Welles, secretary of the navy. But there was
something so prescribed about the group's conversational topics and its
parlor games. Even the timing—the get-togethers were held on Sunday
evenings—smacked of formality.

Clearly, O'Connor's straightlaced salon was no Pfaff's.

Whitman hungered for news of his subterranean haunt. "I happened
in there the other night, and the place smelt as atrociously as ever,"
wrote John Swinton in an 1863 letter to Whitman. Swinton was a *New
York Times* editor and peripheral member of Clapp's circle. He com-
mended Whitman for his work in Washington, adding, "It must be

even more refreshing than to sit by Pfaff's privy and eat sweet-breads and drink coffee, and listen to the intolerable wit of the crack-brains." Swinton also mentioned that "Pfaff looked as of yore." The saloon's proprietor, it seems, was still his rotund, cheerful self. Otherwise, there wasn't much to report.

The old crowd was thinning out. O'Brien was dead, Ludlow traveling. Ward and Menken dropped by Pfaff's when they were in New York. Each was touring ceaselessly, so their visits were becoming more and more infrequent.

Left behind were Clapp and Clare. In the depths of war, one can only imagine the kind of Bohemian irregulars and misfits who now joined them at that long table. One can only imagine how curdled Clapp's quips had grown, as the King of Bohemia was forced each night to reign beside Queen Clare, whom he desired, who respected his keen intellect—yet who would have nothing to do with him sexually. He must have been a terror. By now, Whitman was drifting away from Clapp. The *Saturday Press* was defunct, and his onetime champion could do nothing to advance his poetry.

From Washington, Whitman also corresponded with some of the men he knew from the other portion of Pfaff's saloon. To Hugo Fritsch, he reminisced about "our meetings together, our drinks & groups so friendly, our suppers with Fred & Charley Russell &c. off by ourselves at some table, at Pfaff's off the other end." In another letter, addressed jointly to Fred Gray and Nathaniel Bloom, he wrote, "My darling, dearest boys, if I could be with you this hour, long enough to take only just three mild hot rums." (Hot rums? Two rooms. In the vaulted one, at Clapp's table, his drink was lager, but he appears to have enjoyed different drinks in that other, larger, room.)

Whitman had been so ready to escape Pfaff's. Having done so, as often happens, nostalgia quickly set in. "I was always between two loves at that time," he said many years later. "I wanted to be in New York, I had to be in Washington." Whitman recognized how badly the wounded soldiers needed him. They had become his priority, their care a calling—one that was higher right now than poetry, higher right now than anything else in his life.

Whitman was in Washington for some of the major battles of the Civil War. He was there during Chancellorsville and Gettysburg and Wilderness and Spotsylvania. In notebook entries and letters home, however, he didn't tend to refer to these engagements by name. Over time, it seems, he grew to see the fighting as simple carnage—all guts, no glory. Whitman got so that he could gauge the severity of a distant battle by the level of activity in the Washington hospitals. After major clashes, the doctors and nurses rushed to free up cots, releasing patients who looked to have gotten better, even those who showed the first vague hints of wellness. A strange tension would then settle over the hospitals, everyone waiting.

Then, the deluge. Wounded soldiers flooded into Washington. Whitman made his rounds. He filled his notebooks with fresh nota-tions, listing soldiers' names, companies, hospital wards, and cot num-bers. But all too often, in the turmoil and frenzy, they were reduced to that—notations. A notation would get better. Or a notation would die. "I feel lately as though I must have some intermission," he pleaded.

But the wounded kept coming, wave upon wave. "O mother," he wrote in one letter, "to think that we are to have here soon what I have seen so many times, the awful loads & trains & boat loads of poor bloody & pale & wounded young men again." In another, he cataloged the horrors of his recent days. He concluded, "Mother, I will try to write more cheerfully next time—but I see so much."

Under terrible stress, Whitman's own health began to suffer. Prior to the war, he proudly claimed, the only ailment he'd ever experienced was a bout of sunstroke, something he attributed to an ill-advised hat-less stroll following a haircut. But now he started to develop various mysterious maladies. He had dizzy spells and terrible ringing head-aches. By day, he was oversensitive to light, and at night he lay awake, tossing and sweating. His symptoms hadn't coalesced into any defin-able syndrome or condition. Yet Whitman would never be the same.

In his poetry, Whitman had passionately defended the Union. Now, he had compromised his precious health, aiding the soldiers. It was a willing sacrifice. So many others were giving so much more.

CHAPTER 14

Twain They Shall Meet

THE SUMMER OF 1863 found Adah Menken and Artemus Ward continuing to tour, relentlessly. A great opportunity was about to come their way. Soon they would be plying their respective entertainments—the equine drama *Mazeppa* and comedy routine *The Babes in the Wood*—in some of the most dramatic settings imaginable, surrounded by some truly memorable characters. Menken and Ward were about to travel out West.

During the brief time they'd been performing their acts, both had grown incredibly popular. Menken played sold-out houses everywhere she went. Though no reliable box-office figures exist, Menken was easily outearning most of the day's foremost actors such as Edwin Forrest and James Murdoch, her co-star for that dubious performance of *Macbeth* in Nashville. She was trouncing such top-draw novelty acts as Bihin the Belgian Giant, Dora Dawson the Double-Voiced Singer, and Charles Signor Bliss, a so-called antipodean walker who could stride upside down across ceilings. "My business is still *immense*," she boasted.

By now, Menken had pretty well blanketed the Union—save for recent-entry Kansas and distant California. She had even slipped down into the border state of Maryland to play a theater in Baltimore. Though Maryland had not seceded, sentiment in Baltimore tilted toward the Confederacy. So Menken requested that her dressing room be painted Confederate gray. Around the edge of the room's mirror, she slipped photos of Jefferson Davis and generals such as Braxton Bragg.

Menken could be savvy—and shameless—about courting the public. Perhaps, too, someone as boundary defying as Menken (born in the South, living in the North, probably biracial, casually bisexual) simply didn't wish to be hemmed in by considerations such as Union and Confederate. Regardless, the ploy worked, stirring up great excitement. "It is really true that we must turn people away," she wrote to one of her handlers (by now, she required an entire retinue of them). "Tonight is the 13th of 'Mazeppa' and the house last night was *crowded*. . . . Such a run of a piece was never known in Baltimore." Better yet, her brief secesh dalliance didn't have any adverse professional consequences. Menken quickly resumed her successful touring through the Northern states. (Audiences weren't flocking to *Mazeppa* for her political views.)

Ward was an even bigger deal. He was proving to be one of the few entertainers capable of outshining Menken. Not only was he the darling of critics, playing sold-out houses everywhere he went, but he even had a best seller to promote, *Artemus Ward, His Book*.

Carleton, a New York publishing house, had rushed the title into production to capitalize on the success of *The Babes in the Wood*. Of course, Ward's stand-up routine didn't really translate onto the page. It was highly dependent on facial expressions and perfectly wrought pauses. The publisher's solution was to collect a series of reprinted columns from the *Plain Dealer*. In other words, the book featured the newspaper "Artemus Ward" rather than the stage creation, a distinctly different personality, and a source of possible confusion for buyers.

No one seemed to notice or care. Ward's routine was hilarious, and so were his old newspaper columns. *Artemus Ward, His Book* sold an incredible forty thousand copies in the six months following its May 1862 release date. The only title that outpaced it was the English translation of Victor Hugo's latest epic, *Les misérables*.

Ward even found an admirer of his humor in the president of the United States. On September 22, 1862, five days after the battle of Antietam, Lincoln summoned his cabinet to the White House. All seven members were present, including War Secretary Edwin Stanton, Treasury Secretary Salmon Chase, and Secretary of State William Seward. None of them knew the reason they had been called together, only that it must concern some vital matter.

To open the meeting, Lincoln picked up a copy of *Artemus Ward, His Book* and began reading aloud. The cabinet members were puzzled. "With the fearful strain that is upon me night and day, if I did not laugh I should die, and you need this medicine as much as I do," Lincoln explained. He made halting progress through a brief chapter entitled "High-Handed Outrage at Utica," stopping frequently to let out hearty guffaws.

Lincoln then put down the book and retrieved a single sheet of paper. It had been lying on a nearby table, pinned beneath his stovepipe hat. Once again, the president read aloud to his cabinet, but now his tone was considerably more sober. This was Lincoln's first presentation of a hallowed document, the Emancipation Proclamation. The *New York Herald* was wonderstruck: "Upon somewhat the same principle that Alexander the Great read the *Iliad* before beginning a battle, the President now reads a chapter of Artemas [*sic*] Ward's book to his Cabinet before beginning business."

Artemus and Adah: While their brief fling in Boston was now a distant memory, they remained a pair of sorts. Ward turned twenty-nine in 1863; Menken was twenty-eight—or so she claimed. At the height of the Civil War, these fellow Pfaffians had emerged as two of the most popular acts in the Union states. Success built on success, and soon they attracted the attention of Tom Maguire, a powerful and accomplished western theater impresario. Maguire had gone to California in the gold rush year of 1849, escaping New York City, where he'd spent a shiftless youth as a stage driver, saloon keep, and low-level Tammany thug. Ready for a fresh start, he arrived West already in possession of a critical insight: chasing gold was not the way to go. He didn't even bother staking a claim. The real riches lay in serving the needs of the miners by selling them pickaxes and tent cloth and one-dollar eggs.

Maguire became a purveyor of entertainment to the miners—that was his particular racket—and he made a fast fortune. By 1863, he owned roughly a dozen theaters in western locales such as San Francisco, Sacramento, and Virginia City, Nevada. His entertainment empire was bringing in millions of dollars per year.

A tall man, well over six feet, Maguire had a full head of prematurely white hair—*prematurely* because he was believed to be in his midforties (his birth date is unknown). He favored silk top hats and finely tailored suits. His fingernails were always buffed, his hair neatly slicked with pomade, his mustache waxed to a perfect taper. He rounded out his impeccable look with diamonds—a lot of them. A diamond stickpin held his scarf in place; his fingers sparkled with big, gaudy diamond rings.

That he'd achieved such wealth is doubly impressive when one considers another fact about Maguire: he was illiterate. When he staged a production, he couldn't read a word of the script. But he had keen instincts for the kind of theatrical talent that would fill his houses. It was necessary to pick the right acts. Simply getting one to travel out West was expensive and logistically complicated. Maguire even brought in some performers from as far away as England.

A winning formula, he'd found, was to offer sensationalistic fare with a measure of sophistication. So many different types of people had moved out West, and audience tastes ranged from opera high to burlesque low. At his San Francisco theaters, increasingly, Maguire was finding that he needed to cater to cultivated urbanites, the kind of audience one might find back East in New York or Philadelphia. But he also owned theaters in the kind of frontier outposts that San Francisco had been a decade earlier. The inhabitants of such places dreamed big dreams of quick-strike riches—and in their leisure hours, they craved similarly outsize entertainment.

Maguire, certain that Menken and Ward were perfect, began pursuing both entertainers. He didn't want them to perform together or even on the same bill. Rather, savvy Maguire wanted each to travel his theatrical circuit independently. News had carried way out West of the man who made Lincoln laugh and the woman who did the notorious horseback act. Even out here, many people were familiar with these daring and original artists; some even knew the name for their ilk: Bohemians. Maguire smelled opportunity and recognized that Menken and Ward were the kind of acts that could cut across his diverse audience. One notable East Coast Bohemian artist would drum up interest in the other, and the diamonds would come raining down.

"They seem crazy to have me out there," wrote Menken to one of her handlers, a reference to ongoing negotiations with Maguire. Ultimately, she received extraordinarily generous terms. For a western tour, Maguire agreed to pay Menken a reported $500 per week, plus one-third of the nightly gross receipts and half the take from Friday nights and matinees.

Around the same time, Ward received a telegram from Maguire, inquiring about his availability. (Because Maguire was illiterate, an associate wrote it on his behalf.) While passing through New York City, Ward dropped by Pfaff's and showed the telegram to Clapp. "What will you take for forty nights in California?" it read. "Brandy and soda" was Clapp's suggestion for a humorous response.

What's truly funny: Ward sent a return telegram bearing that message.

It proved a fantastic opener for a business negotiation. *Brandy and soda:* Ward came across as so confident and relaxed. No doubt, it made Maguire that much more resolute about landing the comedian. The terms of Ward's deal are not known, but one can bet that they were also extremely generous.

Ward and Menken were getting everything they had ever desired. Like all Bohemians—the vanguard French and otherwise—the two had always hungered for glory. Why bother with a burdensome artist's life unless that's the goal? It's what they had wanted and had struggled for. But now, Menken and Ward would find it increasingly difficult to accommodate.

Just as the first days of the Civil War felt giddy, not as anyone would have expected, fame—once achieved—didn't feel as one might have imagined. Ward, a funny man with a cold current of melancholy, would increasingly lose himself in drink. Menken, underneath it all, simply remained a mess. She once described herself as "dumb and cold when I should be all grace and gratitude." She regularly signed her letters "Infelix," Latin for "the unhappy."

Menken departed for the West first, sailing out of New York Harbor aboard the *Northern Light* on July 13, 1863. She brought eight trunks of clothing along with her fourth husband, Robert Newell. (Despite her resolve to avoid the altar, she had made yet another trip.)

Newell was a writer who had lately found success under the pseudonym "Orpheus C. Kerr." It was a play on "office seeker." His humorous pieces skewered the corrupt political patronage system that was rapidly taking over in wartime. Newell was a delicate man with a trim little mustache, a surprising follow-up to prizefighter Heenan. With her latest mate, Menken seems to have been trying to pivot from brawn to brains. But the contrast left Newell insecure. Only four days into the marriage, he had locked his wife in the bedroom of their Jersey City flat to keep her from venturing out into the world—source of a potentially limitless supply of Menken suitors. She climbed out the window. It was not an auspicious start. Now, nearly a year into her latest troubled marriage, Menken sailed through the Golden Gate.

Mazeppa debuted at Maguire's Opera House in San Francisco on August 24, 1863. For the new production, everything had been pushed up to an even greater level of sensationalism. Maguire was full of ideas. When Menken was stripped down, it was no longer to sheer pink tights. Instead, at Maguire's suggestion, she donned a wrap, a kind of mini toga, which exposed ample bare leg. When she was strapped to a horse, it was no Belle Beauty (the horse from those first performances in Albany). It was a scraping, snorting California mustang. Before the production began, Menken had to devote a couple weeks to rehearsing with this beast.

Tickets were fifty cents for general admission. Paying twice that amount entitled one to the luxury of a reserved seat, then an unusual arrangement. Plenty proved willing to hand over a dollar to see Menken, though. The smart set could talk of nothing besides the "Frenzy of Frisco." Menken's run made such an impression that a parody *Mazeppa* later ran at the Bella Union, a seedy melodeon house. It featured a performer called Big Bertha, who was stripped down and strapped to the back of a donkey.

Menken played about a month's worth of sold-out shows in San Francisco. She demanded only a single break, for Yom Kippur, the traditional Jewish Day of Atonement. Maguire's Opera House was darkened on that date. And then it was time for Menken to move on to other Maguire theaters in other towns—most colorfully, Virginia City.

As her stagecoach wound through the Sierra Nevada range into Virginia City, Menken was greeted by a remarkable sight. Even on its outskirts, playbills for *Mazeppa* were plastered on the rocks and trees, and in the city proper they were everywhere: on walls, in windows, stuck to fences and street lanterns and pieces of mining equipment. Maguire had arranged for twelve hundred playbills to be posted. He'd also distributed a number of *cartes de visite* photos of a scantily clad Menken. Maguire knew his audience. In Virginia City, the ratio was seventeen men to every woman. It didn't take much to stir this population. "Feminine laundry, hanging on a line, filled them with mad longing," according to an old account of the town.

Menken had wowed the sophisticates in San Francisco, but this promised to be an altogether different experience. Virginia City was only a few years old, founded during the silver rush that broke in 1859, exactly a decade after the gold rush. At the outset, a handful of prospectors had gathered here, living in tents, working claims with colorful names like "Gouge-Eye" and "Wake-Up-Jake." They'd chosen their spot well, smack on the Comstock Lode, site of the richest silver strike in US history. Now an entire city (population twelve thousand) had sprouted, halfway up the side of Sun Mountain. It had grown so quickly and haphazardly that it consisted of just four long streets, running in parallel across the face of the mountain. They were named simply, and in descending order: A, B, C, and D Streets. No one had even bothered to create connecting streets. To get from B to A, say, one had to climb a steep path.

Virginia City wasn't merely situated on Sun Mountain; the mountain was also the repository of those rich silver deposits. Beneath the city, there existed a parallel one, a vast honeycomb of mining shafts and tunnels and dimly lit galleries. The commotion was incredible. According to another old account, this one in *Harper's New Monthly Magazine,* "Steam-engines are puffing off their steam; smoke-stacks are blackening the air with their thick volumes of smoke; quartz-batteries are battering; hammers are hammering; subterranean blasts are bursting . . . picks and crow-bars are picking and crashing." The mining companies worked Sun Mountain so hard, they'd created such gaping underground hollows, it seemed, that residents frequently wondered if Virginia City would simply collapse back into the earth from whence it came.

The miners worked around the clock in shifts. These were hard-luck characters, men who had traveled out West hoping to get rich, some of them deserters from the Union army, some from the Confederate army. When their own schemes failed, they were forced to take jobs in the mines. They toiled so that others—the wealthy mine supervisors and claim holders up on A Street—could realize their dreams. Climbing from D to C to B to A Streets may have been physically grueling. Even more difficult was attaining the wealth necessary to move up the mountain to a better, higher, address. Few made it. In their off hours—whether it be 5:00 P.M. or A.M.—the miners frequented saloons such as the Sawdust Corner. They pounded back forty-rod, a type of strong, cheap whiskey that took its name from the distance a person could supposedly walk, after drinking a shot, before keeling over.

During his recent trip across the continent, Ludlow had passed through Virginia City. Despite his colossal vocabulary, he found that the place beggared description. The best he could manage was "feverish." Virginia City—feverish western boomtown—was situated in a feverish western boom territory. Only a few years before, this entire region had been part of the vast Utah Territory. After the Comstock discovery, however, a large chunk of Utah was split away, separating silver country from the troublesome Mormon lands to the east. This breakaway piece became the Nevada Territory.

Menken's visit occurred during the very brief window before—in record time—Nevada made the transition from territory to statehood. Millions of dollars' worth of silver were being extracted annually. Absorbing Nevada into the *United States* promised to secure a source of funding for the *Union* war effort. Lincoln—bypassing the usual constitutional requirements—would simply proclaim Nevada a state.

Everything was new and raw and wild and exaggerated. Even Maguire's Opera House in Virginia City had been open for only a few months. Fittingly, on its very first night, two miners in the audience got into a heated dispute. One pulled a gun and started firing. Audience members scattered, crouching behind seats and lying on the floor.

The theater featured a massive stage, far larger than its San Francisco counterpart. There was a double tier of box seats, done up in scarlet brocade and fronted by velvet-lined railings. The curtain, embroidered with a scene of Lake Tahoe from a Sierra summit, was the work of an Italian artist. Off from the main auditorium were all kinds of side attractions—a long mahogany bar, a billiards parlor, gambling tables—representing further moneymaking opportunities for Maguire.

Opening night for *Mazeppa*—March 7, 1864—didn't feature any gunplay. But there was plenty of excitement. Throughout Menken's performance, the stage periodically shook and the footlights flickered, the result of subterranean mining detonations.

Two of the city's most notable residents were on hand. In the best box in the house sat Julia Bulette, wealthy owner of the most popular brothel in town. In the press pew sat Mark Twain, audacious cub reporter for Virginia City's *Daily Territorial Enterprise*. The paper was considered among the finest west of the *Chicago Tribune*. Its stories were frequently picked up by other publications, sometimes from as far away as London. The Nevada silver rush was a major current event, producing a steady stream of important news. The paper employed a talented team of reporters who covered mining innovations, labor unrest, and impossibly convoluted claim disputes with vast sums at stake. Thrown into the editorial mix were humorous pieces and hoaxes, a specialty of western papers of this era. Very often, these were the work of young Twain.

Twain was no fan of Menken. His recent stay in San Francisco had coincided with her run of *Mazeppa,* and he'd caught a performance. In a review for the *Territorial Enterprise,* Twain had taken Menken to task for being graceless and frenetic: "She pitches headforemost at the atmosphere like a battering-ram; she works her arms, and her legs, and her whole body like a dancing-jack." Even the much-ballyhooed strip-down scene failed to move him. It left Menken wearing a "superfluous rag" that reminded him of an item "indispensable to infants of tender age." To Twain's unsparing eye, Menken's new mini toga looked like a diaper.

Now, as he watched *Mazeppa* again, Twain was busy crafting fresh barbs. He planned to really tear into the actress. Before he got the chance, however, Joseph Goodman, editor of the *Territorial Enterprise,* stepped in and wrote a positive review. A second savaging by the same reporter for the same paper would have been overkill.

While Menken played Virginia City, Ada Clare arrived in San Francisco, her young son, Aubrey, in tow. The Queen of Bohemia had flown Pfaff's at last. King Clapp was left to his solitary reign.

Clare had decided to move to San Francisco after securing a promise of steady writing assignments from Joe Lawrence, the pipe-smoking *Golden Era* editor with the aggressive recruiting style: "We purchased their pens and pencils before they had been here an hour." Lawrence was thrilled. This was an opportunity to offer an established and sophisticated female writer to his readership. In an editor's note, Lawrence crowed that he'd signed up "Ada Clare, the beautiful, accomplished, talented, and brilliant young *feuilletoniste.*" Clare jumped at the chance to have the kind of freedom she had once enjoyed with the *Saturday Press.*

For the *Era,* Clare would write columns contrasting women's clothing fashions in New York versus San Francisco and praising a local outfit called Robinson's Gym Classes for offering instruction to women as well as men. In one column, "The Man's Sphere of Influence," Clare humorously inverted nineteenth-century gender roles, imagining a world where it was men who stayed home. For this particular piece, Clare wrote in the guise of a cranky social conservative, lamenting that times were changing and not for the better: "I noticed one thing that grieved and annoyed me. That is, seeing so many gentlemen out without any body to take care of them, expressing their opinions without asking any lady's leave, and enjoying the music without begging any lady's pardon."

Before embarking on her new job as a *Golden Era* columnist, however, a trip to Virginia City beckoned. Clare and Menken had stayed in touch through letters. Menken invited her to come to Virginia City for a visit. Clare arranged for someone in San Francisco to look after Aubrey while she was gone. After all, Virginia City was no place for a child. That, too, would become a future *Golden Era* column: the challenges working women face when trying to line up reliable child care. As always, Clare was way ahead of her time.

Clare arrived in Virginia City as Menken mania was reaching full crazy bloom. A group of men stood outside the International Hotel where Menken was staying and serenaded her. The town fire company presented her with a red morocco leather belt that had a silver buckle featuring their insignia. When she visited the hot springs near the Ophir Mine to boil an egg, an entire crowd tagged along.

The locals were agog. Throw in the fact that this fetching woman could hold her own among men—well, it was enough to make one fall off Sun Mountain. At the Sazerac saloon, Menken stood on the bar and demonstrated some of her boxing moves. At a casino, she managed to impress the hard cases at the faro tables by maintaining the same blasé expression whether she was winning or losing. "She smoked and rode astride, and gambled with a freedom that was delightful to the men on the Comstock," an old-timer would recall.

When they'd first met at Pfaff's, Menken and Clare had been equals. Now, Menken was a famous actress, soaking up adulation. Clare must have felt like she was playing second fiddle. Then again, fourth husband Newell hadn't even been granted a fiddle. For the entire trip out West, he'd skulked along the margins of his wife's big life, ignored.

One Sunday afternoon, Menken arranged a small social gathering at her room in the International Hotel. She invited three people: Clare, Twain, and a *Territorial Enterprise* reporter who wrote under the name Dan DeQuille.

Twain had earlier trashed her in a review. Menken was anxious to correct his impression and confident that she could accomplish this in person, with her ample charms. DeQuille was also an important man to cultivate. He was the *Territorial Enterprise*'s star reporter, while Twain was but a promising young talent on the rise. In fact, asked at this time to bet on which of the two writers was most likely to go on to great renown, a smart westerner's money would have been on De-Quille. Also present for this event were an indeterminate number of dogs, apparently strays that Menken had taken in during her visit.

Menken began by announcing that she would like to write a novel. Perhaps she would take a hiatus from acting and live for a while in Virginia City. It was a picturesque setting and might inspire her writing. Clare entertained the idea enthusiastically. The two reporters didn't say much.

This seems to have rattled Menken. The reporters—and the approval they could lend to her desire to be taken seriously as an artist—were the very reason for this little get-together. Menken summoned a waiter and requested that more food and liquor be brought to her room.

Meanwhile, the dogs were growing unruly. The two women began soaking sugar cubes in champagne and then feeding these spiked treats to the dogs. They hoped it would calm the creatures down.

Menken suggested singing a song. Twain demurred, saying he knew only one. Menken pressed him to sing it. So Twain broke into a creaky rendition of a song that included the lyrics, "There was an old horse and his name was Jerusalem." Soon, everyone joined in. It was easier than talking. "Menken was no nightingale," recalled DeQuille. "Clare was a sort of wren, and I was a screech-owl."

The minutes ticked by. Menken kept calling for more food and drink. No one was eating much. But the drinks were welcome. Every time the waiter opened the door, husband Newell peered in from the hallway where he'd been banished.

Soon, everyone was drunk, dogs included. A particularly frisky one started rolling around under the table, bothering Twain. He attempted to kick the dog. But he missed and connected squarely with one of Menken's shapely legs.

Menken limped over to a couch and sat there grimacing and groaning. Twain muttered a few halfhearted apologies. Then he gave up, retreating into sullen silence. The party broke up shortly afterward. The first and only meeting between Menken and Twain had not been a success.

Meanwhile, Ward was also out West, working Maguire's theater circuit. On only one occasion were he and Menken in the same place at the same time. They had a brief overlap in San Francisco. Menken threw a party for Ward where a number of *Golden Era* writers were also present.

For Ward, the most successful part of his western swing—certainly the most exciting—was also Virginia City. He played there right before Menken's run of *Mazeppa*. "He struck the Comstock just at the height of the first great boom and found a condition of things congenial in every way to his feverish and fitful state of feeling," recalled *Territorial Enterprise* editor Goodman. "He was as if strung on wires, vibrating to every impulse of its tumultuous life."

Maguire's Opera House was packed for opening night of *The Babes in the Wood*. As was his practice, Ward used his hangdog antics to win the audience's sympathy. With this quickly accomplished, he owned them, and they were ready to follow him anywhere, even through his act's strange twists and eddies. This debut performance, however, was slightly marred by a curious event. Throughout the opening portion of his routine, whenever the crowd's laughter began to die down after a particular joke, a solitary laugh would rise up, a braying "haw, haw, haw."

It was Twain. Of course, Ward did not know the man. They had never met. Ward only knew that someone in the darkened auditorium was laughing loudly and out of phase with the rest of the audience. To the finely attuned comedian, this strange behavior read as heckling. When it continued, Ward shot an acid comment in the direction of the culprit: "Has it been watered today?"

That shut Twain up. What Ward didn't realize was that the delayed laughter had not been meant as heckling—far from it. According to a fellow *Territorial Enterprise* reporter who sat beside Twain at the show, the young writer was studying Ward's act with incredible focus and intensity. First, he was processing Ward's peerless technique. Humor is serious business. Then, a few beats later, he was letting himself enjoy the jokes. Twain would say, "The man who is capable of listening to 'Babes in the Wood' from beginning to end without laughing either inwardly or outwardly must have done murder, or at least meditated it at some time during his life."

Soon enough, Ward and Twain had occasion to put the incident behind them. Ward always made a practice of dropping by a town's newspaper after his show. In Virginia City, it didn't take long for Ward to find his way to the *Territorial Enterprise*'s C Street offices, where he met the crew. Twain took the opportunity to explain away the lone-laugher episode.

The two had much in common. Twain was twenty-eight, a year younger than Ward. Both lost their fathers the same year, 1847, where-upon each had become wildly peripatetic. Of course, Ward was in Boston working for the *Carpet-Bag* when it published "The Dandy Frightening the Squatter." It's almost certain that he typeset the piece.

Now, the pair had finally met. What they shared most was a kind of glorious detachment, an ability to view their fellow humans from enough distance so as to see the folly and absurdity of their ways. Much later, Twain would say that he admired Ward's "inimitable way of pausing and hesitating, of gliding in a moment from seriousness to humor without appearing to be conscious of so doing. . . . There was more in his pauses than his words."

Ward and Twain became fast friends. During the day, Ward had nothing else to do, so he accompanied Twain on his reportorial rounds. He even joined him for a trip down into a silver mine. Every night, following his show, Ward would drop by the newspaper offices. He'd help put the paper to bed. Then Ward, Twain, and the other journalists would hit the town.

One night, Ward played a prank on Twain. The *Territorial Enterprise* crowd had gathered at the International Hotel's restaurant, and as usual everyone was getting well lubricated. Earlier, Ward had conferred with Twain's colleagues, enlisting their participation in the joke.

Ward waited for an opportune moment. He cleared his throat, made sure Twain was listening, and then offered up a splendidly incoherent bit of rigmarole. It went something like this in DeQuille's recollection: "Ah,—speaking of genius appears to me to be a sort of luminous quality of the mind, allied to a warm and inflammable constitution, which is inherent in the man, and supersedes in him whatever constitutional tendency he may possess, to permit himself to be influenced by such things as do not coincide with his preconceived notions and established convictions to the contrary." Ward paused. "Does not my definition hit the nail squarely on the head?"

All around the table, there were nods of assent. Well, save for Twain. Ward looked down the table and fixed his gaze on Twain, arching his eyebrows.

"I don't know that I exactly understand you," admitted Twain. "Somehow I—I didn't fully grasp your meaning."

"No?" said Artemus. "Why that is very singular. However, I will try and express my idea more clearly."

The others at the table all harrumphed, as if they could not believe how thick Twain was being.

Then, Ward offered a new rendition of his "definition," even more convoluted and inscrutable than the last. The others all nodded sagely. When Ward had finished, however, Twain was forced to admit to being even more confused.

So Ward tried yet another formulation. He was a model of patience this time, delivering each nonsense phrase in a clear and careful voice. "For Gods sake!" cried Twain. "If you go at that again you'll drive me mad!"

The table exploded in laughter. Twain realized he'd been had. Ward's entire spiel was gibberish, he now saw, with the others only pretending it made sense.

Ward was a prankster who could outprank Twain; Twain had nothing but admiration. He recognized there was so much he could learn from Ward. Even though Twain was only a year younger, the difference between the two was stark. Twain was a promising humorist, just starting to build a regional reputation. Ward—pioneering comic, best-selling author, favorite of Lincoln—was an established celebrity. Ward was extremely encouraging to Twain. He urged him to continue writing humor pieces and assuaged the young writer's fears that he was destined, as Twain put it, for a "sage-brush obscurity." Importantly, Ward promised to help Twain in any way he could. If Twain would send him some fresh items, Ward promised, he would bring them to the attention of editors that he knew back East.

Ward packed a lot of living into his stay in Virginia City. Near the end of his visit, the *Territorial Enterprise* crew had another of its late-night revels, this one at Chaurmond's, the town's fancy French restaurant. Ward began the proceedings by raising his glass and proposing a toast. "I give you Upper Canada," he announced.

Puzzled silence, as everyone tried to figure out what Ward was getting at.

"Why?" someone finally asked.

"Because I don't want it myself."

The table cracked up. Soon the others joined in, and the jokes began to fly. Ward, Twain, DeQuille, and the rest were in fine form. They indulged themselves mightily, gulping down exotic French wines and spirits and enjoying all the delicacies they could eat. When the waiter brought the bill, it came to $237, a then astronomical sum.

Ward snatched the bill and made a few joking comments about how *low* the total was. He proceeded to pick up the entire tab. That really brightened the mood.

As the night drew on, the party worked its way down the mountainside, hitting progressively more tawdry establishments. Emerging from one, they were stunned to encounter blinding light. The sun was rising. It was hard to believe that they'd been at this for so many hours. They rubbed their eyes and staggered along D Street.

Suddenly, Ward broke away from the group and clambered up onto the roof of a miner's shack. "I can't walk on the earth," he shouted. "I feel like walking on the skies."

Twain climbed up and joined him. Then Ward leaped across to a new roof. Twain followed. As dawn broke over the Sierra Nevada, the pair just kept leaping, Ward and Twain, roof to roof.

CHAPTER 15

"O heart! heart! heart!"

ON JUNE 22, 1864, Whitman left Washington and returned home to Brooklyn. Doctors' orders: he'd been told to rest. He was instructed to stay away from the military hospitals until he regained his health.

Whitman planned to remain in Brooklyn for only a couple of weeks. Little could he have imagined that, as the Civil War raged on, while his fellow Bohemians were off on assorted adventures, he'd spend the next six months living on Portland Avenue, crammed into the basement with his mother and brothers—plus one of their wives and two children. Whitman had known periods when he retreated from the world. He'd had his share of sloughs. But this would be among the quietest times in Whitman's life.

After everything he'd experienced in the hospitals, Whitman was more broken in body and spirit than he even realized. It's fitting, too, that he came home during the summer of 1864, right in the middle of the Civil War's bloodiest year. It featured the most major battles, one per week on average. Both sides suffered grievously. In 1864, the conflict spread into the Deep South, heaping misery onto the citizens of the Confederacy. Also during that single year, half of the total Union war casualties occurred. On June 3, at Cold Harbor, Virginia, seven thousand Union soldiers were killed, wounded, or captured in a stretch of eight horrifying minutes.

By now, the giddy optimism of April 1861 was like a distant dream, replaced by the stuff of nightmares. Thurlow Weed, one of the era's most accomplished political power brokers, summed it up: "The People are wild for Peace."

Upon returning to Brooklyn, Whitman didn't leave the apartment for three weeks. The bewildering set of symptoms—headaches, dizziness, sleeplessness, sensitivity to light—first experienced in Washington, left him incapacitated. According to the doctors, he had inhaled too much hospital effluvia, absorbing a dangerous level of toxins into his system. It seems likely that he was suffering from high blood pressure, a condition that would have grave consequences for his health in the future. Because certain symptoms—photosensitivity, for instance—aren't consistent with hypertension, probably he was contending with other maladies as well. One candidate is post-traumatic stress syndrome, a condition that wasn't understood in this era.

Gradually, Whitman began to improve. Over a period of weeks, then months, he regained a semblance of his former health. But he would never again be the lean, fit man who first showed up at Pfaff's. Over time, he'd grown stocky, overweight even, the result of too much beefsteak and butter. Everything was taking its toll—though he was only forty-five years old. The poet, renowned for celebrating the body, would never again achieve easy harmony with his own. "It is my first appearance in the character of a man not entirely well," he lamented.

Whitman got in the habit of going to bed early, before ten o'clock. He passed a great deal of time at Coney Island beach, alone, wading in the water, something he found soothing. For the most part, Whitman avoided Manhattan, and he appears to have entirely steered clear of certain old haunts such as Pfaff's. He knew the saloon wasn't exactly conducive to improved health. Something else was going on, too. While in Washington, he'd waxed nostalgic about Pfaff's saloon. Now, it was tantalizingly close, only a ferry ride away. But the carnage Whitman had witnessed had changed him. Parts of his former life struck him now as "tame & indeed unreal."

As his health grew gradually better, Whitman longed to return to hospital duty in Washington. Unfortunately, spending so much time away from the city had resulted in the loss of his clerkship, and he had been forced to give up his attic rental. Whitman wrote to friends such as William O'Connor, trying to enlist their aid in obtaining a new government post.

During this hushed stretch, there's one other matter he focused on, intensely. He polished up his collection of wartime poems. It was to be called *Drum-Taps,* and Whitman was determined to find a publisher. "I intend to move heaven & earth," he announced. The poet described the work as "unprecedentedly sad, (as these days are, are they not?)—but it also has the blast of the trumpet, & the drum pounds & whirrs in it, & then an undertone of sweetest comradeship & human love, threading its steady thread inside the chaos, & heard at every lull & interstice thereof—truly also it has clear notes of faith & triumph."

He evidently had great hopes for this new volume.

While Whitman fought through a lull, Edwin Booth was making preparations for an extraordinary theatrical performance. The actor had been asked to do a benefit, with all the proceeds going toward a statue of Shakespeare for New York's Central Park. Both the play and the resulting statute—the Bard, in marble, permanent—were intended as reminders of the timelessness of art and grace, even in this, the war's bleakest year.

Edwin came up with a novel idea for the benefit: what if he, John, and Junius Jr., the Booth brothers who were professional actors, were to appear onstage together for a single night? It would be the first time the three had ever performed together. It was sure to cause a stir. The Shakespeare play Edwin selected was *Julius Caesar,* a work that features three substantial male roles.

Edwin gave himself the part of the tortured soul Brutus, who obsesses over Caesar's growing ambition and the possibility that he might emerge as a tyrant. He loves Caesar, but loves the Roman republic more. It's Brutus who delivers "the most unkindest cut of all" in Shakespeare's famous words, pulling Caesar close, then stabbing him with a dagger.

Edwin was now thirty-one years old. He prepared for the benefit at a time when he was finally beginning to harness his considerable acting potential. Until very recently, he'd remained an inconsistent performer due to his drinking. "We have seldom seen Shakespeare so murdered," chided the *New York Herald* after he staggered through an

1863 performance of *Richard III*. Shortly afterward, Edwin had decided to battle his condition and had stopped drinking cold turkey.

Since then, he'd been getting along with the aid of cigarettes and copious amounts of black coffee. But he'd also discovered that focus and sobriety were really benefiting his craft, driving him to new heights as a tragedian. The past year had been Edwin's most successful, critically. At last, he was starting to justify all the ink Clapp had once expended in the *Saturday Press*, worrying about the actor's career and potential and choices.

John, twenty-six years old now, was to play Mark Antony, the silver-tongued, double-crossing Roman statesman. It was inspired casting. Throughout the war, despite his avowed loyalty to the Confederacy, John had performed in such cities as Albany, Boston, Chicago, Cleveland, Hartford, New Haven, and Providence. The actor, whose stated goal was *to be loved by the Southern people above all,* rarely left the North. He seems to have appreciated the superior roads, better-organized theatrical circuit, greater attendance, and larger paydays available to someone touring through the Union states.

Mostly, John confined his expressions of dissent to baiting his fellow actors. His views were generally not taken very seriously, though he was arrested in St. Louis for making a treasonous statement that he "wished the President and the whole damned government would go to hell." He was quickly released, after paying a fine and taking an oath of loyalty to the Union. Throughout the war, John had used an address in Philadelphia as his official residence. He also owned a piece of property at 115 Commonwealth Avenue in Boston, that most Union of Union cities, the very stronghold of abolitionism. Presumably, he planned to build a home there, or at least entertained the notion in certain frames of mind.

John remained an erratic performer, though, unlike Edwin, this wasn't rooted in alcoholism, but stemmed instead from lack of discipline, odd mannerisms, and a propensity to ad-lib. One reviewer commented on his "weird and startling elocutionary effects." Another asked, "In what does he fail? Principally, in knowledge of himself—of his resources, how to husband and how to use them." Lincoln had recently seen John in *The Marble Heart.* The actor trudged through the play, giving a listless performance. That was the only time Lincoln ever saw John in a play. By contrast, after Lincoln saw brother Edwin in *Richelieu,* he returned for six more performances.

Rounding out the leads was Junius Jr., at forty-two the eldest theatrical Booth brother. He was the namesake of the clan's brilliant but unhinged father, the man Edwin had devoted his youth to shepherding from venue to venue. But mild June (as he was known) was nothing like mad Junius. For many years now, he had been working in California. In fact, he had recently starred opposite Adah Menken, playing the evil Polish count in Tom Maguire's San Francisco production of *Mazeppa.* For *Julius Caesar,* June was to play Cassius, he of the "lean and hungry look."

The cast was set, a date chosen, and posters went up all over Manhattan announcing an evening "made memorable by the appearance of the three sons of the great Booth." On November 25, 1864, the brothers performed their benefit at the Winter Garden Theatre on Broadway, near Pfaff's. Ticket prices were astronomical for those days, as high as $5 for orchestra seats. The desire to witness this historic performance filled the theater to its two-thousand capacity—it was for a good cause besides.

At the conclusion of act 1, the Booth brothers came out and took bows in unison. Cries of "Bravo!" rained down upon them. Mother Booth and sister Asia looked on proudly. Then, the production resumed and continued to roughly the middle of the second act, when there was a bizarre interruption. Bells started clanging, and some kind of commotion seemed to be happening, though nobody in the Winter Garden could see anything. A rumor moved quickly through the audience: *The theater was on fire!* One after another, people stood up, preparing to bolt.

The play halted, as Edwin conferred with the theater manager. Then Edwin walked to the edge of the stage and calmly explained the situation. There had been a fire, all right. But it was next door, at the La Farge House, a luxury hotel. And it had been very small, had already been put out. The crowd settled down, and without further incident the Booths managed to finish *Julius Caesar*. It was a critical and financial success, raising $4,000 for the Shakespeare statue to be sculpted by the brilliant J. Q. A. Ward.

On the second morning following the performance, the brothers met for breakfast at Edwin's home at 28 East 19th Street. The big story in all the papers was the fire that had broken out during the play—or, rather, *fires*. As it turned out, a group of Confederate officers had set a whole series of them at the La Farge and eleven other hotels as well as the Hudson River docks and a lumberyard. They had hoped that overwhelmed fire companies would be able to respond only to select conflagrations, leaving others to burn out of control. New York City would soon be ablaze. All the fires were quickly discovered, however, and all were extinguished with ease. As plots go, the execution was supremely feeble. (One perpetrator paid with his life—captured, tried, and hung—while the other seven managed to get away.)

The day's news sparked a heated discussion between Edwin and John. Wisely, the two brothers, born in the border state of Maryland, tried to avoid political discussions, though it was proving increasingly difficult. Only a couple weeks earlier, Edwin had voted for the first time in his life, casting his ballot for Lincoln. John had reacted with utter contempt, saying that Edwin would rue his vote when Lincoln turned America into a monarchy and crowned himself king.

Due to the fires that had broken out during *Caesar*—and the fact that this was splashed across all the papers—calm between the brothers was now impossible. Edwin lamented that the war's havoc had made its way to New York City. The fires were warranted, John rejoined, an attempt to pay back recent Northern atrocities such as Sherman torching Atlanta. June looked on in pained silence, trapped between his squabbling brothers.

John kept swearing his allegiance to the Confederacy, declaring his hopes that the South would prevail. Edwin upheld the superiority of the Northern cause and reminded his brother that were New York City to fall under siege, it would be disastrous to the Booth family. By now, the opportunity for sitting down to breakfast together was long past.

The two brothers were standing and shouting. Edwin really let loose, calling John a "rank secessionist" and saying that he'd grown weary of his "treasonable language." Then he demanded that John leave his home at once.

John stormed off into the Manhattan morning.

In January 1865, Whitman's hushed and homebound period came to an end. The worst symptoms of his illness—the headaches and dizziness—diminished, and he was feeling much better. He returned to Washington and started a new job as a clerk, lowest grade, in the Interior Department's Office of Indian Affairs. It paid a modest salary ($1,200 per year). He moved into a garret room at 468 M Street.

"I take things very easy," he wrote to brother Jeff back in Brooklyn, "—the rule is to come at 9 and go at 4—but I don't come at 9, and only stay till 4 when I want." The casual schedule allowed Whitman to resume his service in the hospitals. But he was careful not to push himself too hard. "Jeff, you need not be afraid about my overdoing the matter," he continued. "I shall go regularly enough, but shall be on my guard against trouble."

The Washington to which Whitman returned felt different from the one he'd known but a few months earlier. The flow of wounded into the hospitals—always such a reliable bellwether—was slowing down a bit. There was a strange feeling in the air, palpable, a kind of anticipation. It seemed impossible, but perhaps the war was finally about to end. Whitman resumed his routine of taking long walks following the hospital visits. "The western star, Venus, in earlier hours of the evening, has never been so large, so clear," he would write. "It seems as if it told something, as if it held rapport indulgent with humanity, with us Americans."

Even the sky looked different. And why should it be otherwise? During the early months of 1865, not long after Whitman returned to Washington, something else also happened in the poet's life.

His name was Peter Doyle. He worked as a conductor on one of the large horse-drawn omnibuses—with seats enough to accommodate roughly twenty people—that traversed the capital streets. The two first met, during an evening downpour, when Whitman boarded Doyle's car at a stop along Pennsylvania Avenue. "Walt had his blanket—it was thrown round his shoulders—he seemed like an old sea-captain," in Doyle's recollection. "He was the only passenger, it was a lonely night, so I thought I would go in and talk with him. Something in me made me do it and something in him drew me that way. He used to say there was something in me had the same effect on him. Anyway, I went into the car. We were familiar at once—I put my hand on his knee—we understood."

Whitman remained on the omnibus that first night, traveling past his stop, staying in that empty car with Doyle all the way to the end of the line. The poet's description is concise: "Love, love, love!"

Doyle was twenty-one years old and handsome, with blue eyes, wavy light-brown hair, and a mustache. At five-foot-eight, he was shorter than Whitman and slimmer. He had an easy smile and was quick to laughter, but his expressions were never entirely free of a certain sad aspect.

Doyle had been born in Ireland and as an eight-year-old immigrated to America. His family split up and made the trip over time on two separate voyages. Ultimately, part of the family—Doyle, his parents, and three brothers—settled in Alexandria, Virginia. Two sisters remained behind in Ireland and appear never to have joined the others. Doyle's father took a job as a blacksmith. But work grew scarce after the Panic of '57, and, searching for brighter prospects, the family moved to Richmond. Doyle's only formal education was courtesy of a church Sunday school. He could barely read or write. Even as a child, he worked various jobs such as cooper's apprentice to help support the family.

Two weeks into the Civil War, Doyle enlisted as a Confederate soldier, drawn by the promise of steady pay. He joined the Richmond Fayette Light Artillery and was involved in a number of major engagements before being wounded at Antietam. George Whitman also fought at Antietam, though he was across the battle lines from Doyle, on the Union side of that blood-sotted Maryland cornfield.

Doyle was laid up in a Richmond hospital for several months. During that time, he petitioned to be discharged from military service.

This was granted on the condition that Doyle promise not to give aid to the enemy. Not a problem: he didn't have any stake in this conflict. Union, Confederate—they were mere abstractions to him.

In a statement, sworn and notarized, Doyle indicated that he was going to return to Ireland. But then he decided instead to move to Washington, DC, planning to reconnect with some family who now lived there. While heading north, as Doyle attempted to cross Federal lines, he was detained by Union troops. For three weeks, he was confined to the Old Capitol Prison. On agreeing to pledge loyalty to the Union—once again, no problem—he was released on May 11, 1863. He moved in with a brother who lived at 62 M Street, South. When Whitman met Doyle, he was holding down two jobs. Days he spent as a smith's assistant at the Washington Navy Yard, evenings as an omnibus conductor. He was simply a young man of Irish descent struggling to make ends meet. Or, as Whitman once described him, a "hearty full-blooded everyday divinely generous working man."

Now, the poet had a companion for his ambitious rambles. "We went plodding along the road, Walt always whistling or singing," Doyle recalled. Other times, Whitman would join Doyle on the omnibus and ride with him back and forth along the route. When Doyle's shift was done, they liked to have dinner together at a place near the end of the line, the Union Hotel and Tavern in Georgetown. Doyle worked a long day; by this point, he was often exhausted. Sometimes he'd put his head down on the table and take a nap. Whitman would sit there, not waking him until closing time.

Whitman and Doyle went long stretches without exchanging a solitary word. "It was the most taciturn mutual admiration society I ever attended," a stranger who saw them together would recall. But they had the kind of relationship in which they savored small moments, little shared intimacies. One time, the two men bought a watermelon at a market and sat down in front to eat it. Whitman took out a pocketknife and cut it in half. Some people walking past snickered at the sight of two grown men gorging on watermelon. "They can have the laugh—we have the melon," Whitman told Doyle. Years later, both men would vividly remember this tiny episode.

During that magical spring of 1865, Whitman continued to catch sight of Lincoln, constantly. In the course of a single day—March 4, Inauguration Day—the poet managed several different sightings as the busy president moved to and fro through the capital. For the first, Whitman noted that Lincoln "look'd very much worn and tired; the lines, indeed, of vast responsibilities, intricate questions, and demands of life and death, cut deeper than ever upon his dark brown face." Later, Whitman attended a public reception at the White House. He was standing out front on the lawn when a surge of people—"country people, some very funny," he noted—began pressing their way into the presidential residence. Whitman was carried along by the crowd directly into the White House. Tradition holds that Lincoln shook five thousand hands at this reception. Whitman stood off to the side, observing: "I saw Mr. Lincoln, drest all in black, with white gloves, and a claw-hammer coat, receiving, as in duty bound, shaking hands, looking very disconsolate, and as if he would give anything to be somewhere else." ("Claw-hammer coat" is an old term for a tailcoat.)

Whitman also attended the inaugural speech itself. The poet was on hand as the president, preparing for his second term, intoned those immortal words: "With malice toward none; with charity for all; with firmness in the right, as God gives us to see the right, let us strive on to finish the work we are in; to bind up the nation's wounds." It's possible that Peter Doyle accompanied Whitman to this event. What is certain, however, is that lurking in the crowd on this historic occasion was a strange and angry young actor named John Wilkes Booth.

Now things begin to move very fast, becoming as frantic as they were hushed before, as Whitman's life and big events of his time coil like twin vines.

The day after Lincoln's inauguration, Whitman's mother wrote to him with incredible news: George had come home from the war! Whitman requested a furlough from his new clerical post and was soon back in Brooklyn once more, this time to see his brother. "His preservation and return alive seem a miracle," reflected Whitman. In the

course of his soldiering career, George had—according to Walt's calcu-
lations—traveled twenty thousand miles across eighteen states, fighting
in twenty-one major engagements, and serving under Generals Burn-
side, McClellan, McDowell, Meade, Pope, Hooker, Sherman, and
Grant. He'd also been captured in battle. For the past four months,
George had been held in a series of Confederate prisons, including,
most recently, a facility in Danville, Virginia. Though he'd been able
to write several of his laconic letters while in captivity ("I am in tip top
health and Spirits, and am as tough as a mule," he stated in one), the
Whitmans had been sick with anxiety. Then, just like that, he was free.
He was home. He'd lost a great deal of weight, but seemed otherwise
healthy and whole.

Walt enjoyed a warm reunion with George. He even recounted his
brother's heroics in a kind of local-boy-makes-good story that ran in
the *Brooklyn Daily Union.*

While on furlough, Whitman also began making arrangements for
the publication of his *Drum-Taps* collection. By now, he had concluded
that he would simply have to publish it himself. The war had proved
a lean time for poetry; the market was nearly nonexistent. In 1862, for
example, the entire publishing industry in the Northern states, such as
it was, brought out a total of eighteen books of poetry, according to
one count. The following year, the number rose to twenty-one.

Whitman was no stranger to self-publishing. It was the route he'd
taken with the first two editions of *Leaves of Grass.* Whitman hired a
printer to do a five-hundred-copy run of his new collection. Funds
were limited, so his plan was to squeeze as many poems as possible
into a slim seventy-two-page book. To pay the $254 first installment,
he appears to have used some savings from his new job and also to
have borrowed money. Among the poems slated for the volume were
several based on his visit to George at the front, including "A Sight in
Camp in the Daybreak Gray and Dim." There were poems drawn from
his hospital experience such as "The Wound-Dresser" and "Come Up
from the Fields, Father," as well as "Year of Meteors (1859–60)," about
that strange celestial event, what had come to seem like an augur of the
Civil War.

Whitman was still tinkering with the printer's proofs, as was his habit, when Lee surrendered to Grant at Appomattox Courthouse on April 9, 1865. It was a "propitious" day, in Whitman's recollection, when four years' worth of "woe and failure and disorder" suddenly lifted. He couldn't believe it. The Civil War had ended, and the inviolable union—something of near-mystical significance to Whitman, a subject visited in so many of his poems—had been restored. Back home in Brooklyn, what he noticed most, what seemed to mark this great occasion, were the lilacs. They were now in full, glorious bloom, their scent filling the air.

The elation was short-lived. Only six days later, Whitman awakened to the terrible news. Lincoln had been assassinated. In the Whitman household, the family read through every newspaper and extra edition they could lay their hands on. His mother made breakfast, then lunch, but nobody ate a thing. Portland Avenue was still, so still; the only sound was the tolling of church bells.

In the afternoon, Whitman took a ferry across to Manhattan. It was a Saturday, ordinarily a workday, but all the businesses had already closed. The streets and sidewalks were virtually abandoned. Whitman made his way to Broadway. As he so often had, he took out a notebook and began to record his impressions. He reported that he saw "no pleasure vehicles, & hardly a cart—only the rumbling base [sic] of the heavy Broadway stages incessantly rolling." Among the few people out and about, he noted that their faces showed a "strange mixture of horror, fury, tenderness, & stirring wonder brewing."

As Whitman walked, the day grew overcast. Thunderheads began to roll in over Manhattan. "Lincoln's death—black, black, black," he wrote, "—as you look toward the sky—long broad black like great serpents slowly undulating in every direction." Then the heavens opened up, and it started to pour.

From the moment the news broke, Whitman and the world knew who had shot the president. Even the morning editions of papers screamed the name: John Wilkes Booth. Only over time, however, did the specific details begin to emerge. Later, too, Whitman would be privileged to hear a firsthand account of this event.

Booth, it seems, had spent considerable time in and around Washington during the first months of 1865, hatching schemes as leader of a small, ragtag group of Confederate sympathizers. It included an unemployed malcontent, an apparent psychotic (other than Booth), and an imbecile, for lack of a better term. If anything, this set of conspirators was even more hapless than the group behind the Manhattan hotel fires. As the spring progressed, as it looked increasingly likely that the war was drawing to a close, their schemes became ever more desperate and harebrained. They entertained a variety of ideas: perhaps they would kidnap Lincoln, or kill him, maybe even kill some other Union leaders as well.

On the morning of April 14, Booth went to Ford's Theatre to pick up his mail. He had mail privileges there, although owner John Ford had grown tired of the actor's provoking comments about the Confederate cause. It was during this visit that Booth learned that Lincoln and General Grant were expected at the theater that very evening. The two men and their wives would be attending a performance of *Our American Cousin,* a farce about a Vermont naïf who travels to Britain to claim an inheritance.

Booth dashed off to make preparations. In an instant, it seems, the scheme was adjusted to take advantage of this new information. Booth now could kill both Lincoln and Grant. His sidekicks would take care of Andrew Johnson and Seward. In a single night's coordinated effort, the group could assassinate the president, his top general, the vice president, and the secretary of state.

At 8:00 P.M., as the curtain rose for *Our American Cousin,* Booth and his fellow conspirators remained huddled in a room at a nearby boardinghouse, working out the details of their individual assignments.

Lincoln was late to the theater, held up by various state obligations. He left the White House at 8:15 P.M. in his black frock coat and a silk hat. Mary Todd, head covered in a coal-scuttle bonnet, wore a coat of black velvet edged in ermine over a black-and-white-striped gown.

There had been a change of plans about who would accompany the first couple. Julia Grant detested Mary Todd, so the general and his wife had backed out at the last minute, pleading another engagement. Instead, the Lincolns' carriage swung by to pick up Henry Rathbone, a young army major, and Clara Harris, his fiancée.

The party arrived at Ford's Theatre at 8:35. As they entered the presidential box, situated in the balcony, stage left, word began to travel through the theater: Lincoln was here. The play halted, and the orchestra struck up "Hail to the Chief." Lincoln acknowledged the crowd with a bow. Then he sat down in a rocking chair, provided especially for his comfort. Mary Todd sat beside him in a chair. Nearby, on a small couch, sat Major Rathbone and his fiancée. Lincoln loved the theater, enjoying everything from Shakespeare tragedies to light drawing-room comedies that allowed him "to take a laugh," as he put it. He'd even seen a performance of *Our American Cousin* the previous year.

By now, the conspirators had set off on their various errands. Booth sat alone at the Star Saloon, next door to Ford's Theatre. He was wearing a dark suit, slouch hat, and high riding boots with spurs. He tossed back a whiskey. Then he left the bar and made a short walk down the street. John Buckingham, the Ford's ticket taker, had placed his large frame in the theater's front door, blocking off entry. Grasping Buckingham's hand lightly with two fingers, Booth requested that he be let into the theater for free. The ticket taker let him go.

The actor knew Ford's Theatre well. Over the years, he'd performed here many times; only a month earlier, in fact, he'd been in a production of *The Apostate,* playing the villain Pescara. Booth climbed the stairs to the balcony and then made his way down a sloping side aisle. For the evening, a single DC police officer had been assigned to guard Lincoln. He had abandoned his post, going next door for a drink at the Star Saloon. Nobody was monitoring the door that provided access into the presidential box.

Booth opened that door. He stepped into a short passageway, about ten feet in length, which led to a second door. Beyond it was the presidential box. (Neither door had a working lock.)

Booth walked to the end of the passageway and stood there. The second door had a peephole, making it possible for him to look into the box. Not only was he familiar with Ford's Theatre, but he was also well acquainted with *Our American Cousin*. The play was nearing a point, Booth knew, where one of its biggest laugh lines would be delivered. That would be his cue. Booth peered through the peephole. And waited. Onstage, an actor said, "Well, I guess I know enough to turn you inside out, old gal—you sockdologizing old man-trap!" The audience burst into laughter.

Booth opened the door. He leveled his pistol. He shot Lincoln in the back of the head.

To audience members who heard it, the single-shot derringer's report was a muffled pop, like someone bursting a paper bag. Lincoln slumped forward in the rocking chair, his chin falling onto his chest. For the handful of theatergoers who turned around, a haze of bluish smoke could be seen in the presidential box. Something was going on, but in the moment it seemed so fast moving and chaotic; many figured it was simply part of the play. Booth lunged through the box, making for the railing. When Rathbone blocked his way, the actor drew a dagger and slashed the major's arm.

Booth climbed over the railing, preparing to drop onto the stage. But one of his spurs got fouled in the red-white-and-blue bunting that was draped along the front of the box. This caused him to fall awkwardly. When he landed, twelve feet below, he fractured his fibula, right above the left ankle. Booth straightened from a crouch, stood there unsteadily, gazing out over the audience and waving the bloody dagger. "Sic semper tyrannis," he shouted.

Then he staggered off the stage. "Stop that man!" yelled Major Rathbone. Booth pushed through the theater's back door and into an alley, where a getaway horse waited. Back inside, a sustained unearthly shriek rose above the pandemonium. Mary Todd.

Meanwhile, Booth's fellow conspirators had fanned out across the capital. One, posing as a physician's courier delivering medicine, managed to get inside the Seward residence, whereupon he burst into the secretary of state's bedroom and stabbed him, though not fatally. The man charged with killing the vice president lurked outside Johnson's house for some minutes before, losing his nerve, he repaired to a saloon and drank himself into oblivion. Due to a change of plans, General Grant was safely away from the theater that night.

Sic semper tyrannis. Thus always to tyrants. It's what Marcus Brutus, the historical figure, supposedly uttered when he stabbed Julius Caesar, though Shakespeare didn't use the line in his play.

During the recent benefit, Edwin had handed himself the role of Brutus. Now, his younger brother had stolen the part. Real life and the stage, ancient history and the present: they all bled together for John until it was impossible for him to tell them apart. He was the son of the Mad Tragedian, truly—took the insanity beyond the beyond. But here's one thing John Wilkes Booth appears to have understood with clarity. He seems to have grasped, intuitively, that the bar for spectacular mayhem is so much lower than the bar for great art.

He was late to move on his plot—waiting, in a ludicrous twist, until after the war had ended—and the conspirators failed to dispatch three of their four intended victims. But the fourth was president of the United States.

One week later, on April 22, Whitman returned to Washington, where he resumed his job as a clerk. Already, he was having grave doubts about *Drum-Taps*. It was intended as a Civil War collection, yet it lacked the necessary poems about Lincoln and the assassination. In an instant, his new collection had been rendered obsolete. Even though five hundred copies of *Drum-Taps* had already been printed, Whitman decided to put the project on hold. He elected to wait and not to offer the book for sale just yet.

On a piece of paper, Whitman began a long list: "Melancholy . . . heavy-hearted . . . eloquent silence . . . pain of mind . . . cast down . . . affliction." These are words and phrases related to grief and mourning. Making this list represented, for Whitman, the first raw step in crafting poetry about Lincoln's death. He had devoted the past several years to compiling a set of poems about the war. But that didn't matter. Time and effort be damned. The collection would be woefully incomplete, he recognized, without a fitting tribute to the fallen president. As a gift, Whitman gave his new love the printer's proof of the withheld edition of *Drum-Taps,* all marked up in pencil.

Doyle had something precious for Whitman in return. During Whitman's recent trip home to Brooklyn, Doyle, who remained in Washington, had learned that the president would be attending a play. He grew intrigued with what sounded like an exciting event. On the night of April 14, 1865, Doyle attended *Our American Cousin* at Ford's Theatre. "I heard the pistol shot. . . . It was sort of muffled," he would recall. "I saw Booth on the cushion of the box, saw him jump over, saw him catch his foot, which turned, saw him fall on the stage."

Doyle had been there. He'd seen and heard it all. He would share his account with Whitman, helping the poet to achieve a sense of presence at Lincoln's assassination, making it possible for Whitman to cast his deep, empathetic understanding into one of history's most momentous events.

CHAPTER 16

A Brief Revival

THE FUNERAL TRAIN bearing Lincoln's body moved slowly through Philadelphia and New York and Cleveland and Indianapolis, traveling 1,662 miles. It followed virtually the same route taken to the capital after the victorious 1860 election, now in reverse, carrying the president past a fresh set of onlookers—thousands of them, mostly silent, many sobbing, some in full black mourning dress—until the journey ended where it had begun in Springfield, Illinois.

As peace settled across the land, many sought a chance for renewal. Henry Clapp had waited out the entire Civil War in an underground saloon. Now, like one of those locusts that remain buried for years in suspended animation, he burst forth.

Somehow he lined up new investors, scraped together the necessary funding, and managed to resuscitate the *Saturday Press*. On August 5, 1865, after half a decade's silence, the debut issue of the journal's second iteration appeared. In an editor's note, Clapp offered his sly explanation:

"What did you ever stop it for?"

"For want of money."

"Why do you revive it, then?"

"For the same reason."

Clapp picked up exactly where he'd left off. The new *SP* was everything the old one had been: clever, worldly, opinionated, and, most of all, irreverent. It featured articles such as "How to Write War Lyrics," offering helpful tips such as "You may make Slain rhyme with Again";

"Muck-a-Muck," a send-up of one of James Fenimore Cooper's noble savage tales; and a piece on new findings in astronomy, written in a faux scientific style, and asserting among other things that earthlings will soon discover an "inconceivable number of worlds . . . peopled like our own," but can take comfort in the fact that we'll be superior to them all.

By now, Clapp's original circle of writers was widely scattered. Where necessary, he simply recruited substitutes. Queen Clare was no longer in the *SP* stable; to provide a witty female perspective, he turned instead to a writer and actress named Olive Logan.

Nearly every issue carried an advertisement for Pfaff's. The saloon was now in a new location, though. Right after the Civil War ended, it moved up Broadway a few doors to No. 653. On one wall, the new Pfaff's had a mural depicting a natural scene. There was a garden out back where Charlie Pfaff kept a pet eagle, which subsisted on sauerkraut, pretzels, and other specialties of the house. "The National bird received the same nourishment as American arts and letters," according to a reminiscence, "and was fed with the same generous hand."

Clapp continued to go to the saloon every night without fail. Even though the new establishment didn't feature a separate vaulted room, it appears that Herr Pfaff furnished him with a long table once again.

Bohemianism itself remained a topic of endless discussion in the *SP*. The August 12 issue featured a poem called "Beerdrinkers Song," and a subsequent number included a brief sketch called "Life in a Bar-Room." Clapp sought, once again, to create a seductive yet intimidating tone of insiderism, always a winning journalistic formula. Clapp even published an update of a piece that had run in 1860, listing various public eminences and historical figures, divided neatly into Bohemians and those who failed to make the club. Where Washington had been deemed a Bohemian in the original article, among those who now got the nod was Lincoln: "Abraham Lincoln was a most worthy member of our order."

On nearly every page, Clapp's fierceness was also on display. Evidently, he came back with a vengeance. The new *SP*, like its predecessor, was filled with assorted nose thumbings at orthodoxy, takedowns of figures considered ponderous by Clapp, and savage critiques of books, plays, and paintings. Once again, he reserved his greatest bile for the citizens and customs of New England. His editor's note for August 19 included the following: "A teetotal correspondent in Boston . . . objects to our having printed, last week, two poems on beer. He can't bear the sight or sound of the word. He objects even to our mentioning Meyerbeer. What is to be done with such people?" ("Meyerbeer" is a reference to Giacomo Meyerbeer, a German opera composer.) The swipe is but a sample of the tireless assault Clapp continued to wage against the region of his birth.

The *SP* was off to a fast start. But what happened next is nothing short of extraordinary. Clapp managed an editorial coup for the ages. Within the space of a month, he published a pair of timeless works, by two different American masters.

First came Whitman's "O Captain! My Captain!" published in the *SP*'s November 4, 1865, issue. This ode to Lincoln is one of several that Whitman had recently completed. After putting his Civil War collection on hold, he had focused his creative energy on composing a series of fitting tributes to the assassinated president. He collected these new works in a pamphlet called *Sequel to Drum-Taps*. The pamphlet, in turn, was sewed into the binding of the existing edition of *Drum-Taps*, already printed and waiting.

Whitman sent the new collection to Clapp. Right after the war, the two men renewed their friendship, although they no longer lived in the same city. Clapp sometimes clipped interesting newspaper articles and mailed them to Whitman in Washington, a gesture that pleased the poet mightily. On at least one occasion, Whitman visited Clapp in New York.

"O Captain! My Captain!" is based on a recurring dream Lincoln supposedly had following monumental events such as Antietam and Gettysburg. He was aboard a mysterious ship quickly approaching an unknown shore. The night before the assassination, Lincoln had the dream again—or so claimed a spate of newspaper accounts. The president took this as a promising sign, perhaps related to some aspect of the newly dawned peace.

Whitman gave Lincoln's dream the tragic twist it now warranted. In his poem, the voyage is complete; the ship has arrived at that distant harbor, but at a terrible cost:

> O Captain! my Captain! our fearful trip is done,
> The ship has weather'd every rack, the prize we sought is won,
> The port is near, the bells I hear, the people all exulting,
> While follow eyes the steady keel, the vessel grim and daring;
>   But O heart! heart! heart!
>   O the bleeding drops of red,
>   Where on the deck my Captain lies,
>   Fallen cold and dead.

"O Captain! My Captain!"—rhymed and metered—is a departure from Whitman's trademark free-verse style. But a certain formality seemed necessary to properly commemorate such a somber event.

The sublime "When Lilacs Last in the Dooryard Bloom'd" was also part of the new collection. This poem in particular exhibits Whitman's rare gift for empathy. It draws on Doyle's account of the assassination. But it does so emotionally rather than literally, for it doesn't include a single specific from the event. (In the future, Whitman would rely on the details of Doyle's account, but for a purpose other than poetry.)

"Lilacs" never even mentions Lincoln by name, a brilliant stroke. Instead, it explores the *feeling* of losing "him I love," a phrase that becomes a fevered refrain. In the poem, the emotions from those magical early months of 1865 run together with those surrounding the night of April 14. What seemed such hopeful signs—the low-hanging evening star, the scent of lilacs—are understood to be ominous portents as well. Forever after, they'll have complex, ambivalent associations, joy mixed with dread:

> Ever-returning spring, trinity sure to me you bring,
> Lilac blooming perennial and drooping star in the west,
> And thought of him I love.

And then Whitman provides a further poetic complication, this one transcendent: the "him I love" comes to represent not only Lincoln but also every departed son and father and husband and brother—"all the slain soldiers of the war."

Whitman's new collection—featuring a pamphlet sewn into a previously printed volume—was referred to by an awkward title, *Drum-Taps and Sequel.* That's when it was referred to at all. It received very few reviews, although one did run in the *SP.* Written by a critic who used a single initial—F.—it was mostly negative. Clapp was up to his old any-publicity-is-good-publicity tricks. But Whitman was in no position to benefit. He wasn't able to get the collection into bookstores or, for that matter, even phrenology shops. He sold perhaps a couple hundred copies at best, directly to readers.

The work was destined to make its mark slowly, over the passage of many years. "When Lilacs Last in the Dooryard Bloom'd" was once described as "the most sweet and sonorous nocturne ever chanted in the church of the world." "O Captain! My Captain!" would emerge as the most famous poem Whitman ever wrote and, by some accountings, rates among the ten best known in the English language. The *Saturday Press* had the distinction of being the first place where it ever appeared.

Only two weeks later, Clapp published a story by Mark Twain. "Jim Smiley and His Jumping Frog" created an instant sensation. To this point, Twain's reputation was strictly regional, but after appearing first in the *Saturday Press,* his story was reprinted across the United States. "The papers are copying it far and near," reported the *Alta California.* Clapp, champion of Whitman, also gave Twain his first big national break.

Credit is also due Artemus Ward, of course. Ward had come through, keeping his promise to bring Twain's work to the attention of editors back East. The sequence of events that rescued Twain from sagebrush obscurity is like a tall tale in its own right and goes as follows: Ward had been working on another quickie book for his publisher,

Carleton. To pad it out, he contacted Twain and others he'd met on his recent tour, requesting that they send stories, brief sketches, observations about western life, anything.

Twain sent Ward the fictional tale of Jim Smiley, a mining camp dweller who enjoys betting on "rat-terriers and chicken cocks, and tom-cats, and all them kind of things." He is especially proud of Dan'l Webster, a frog that can "out-jump ary frog in Calaveras county."

The publisher couldn't see how Twain's story, or any of the bric-a-brac Ward had gathered from his western acquaintances, fitted into the book. This was supposed to be *Artemus Ward, His Travels.* Carleton decided not to use the contributions of the other authors. That meant publishing a slender volume, but no matter—Ward's previous book, while wafer-thin, had been a runaway hit. At this point, Twain's discarded story was snatched up by Clapp, who couldn't believe his good fortune.

The version that ran in the *SP* differs slightly from the now familiar tale. For one thing, it has a framing device in which the story is presented as a letter written to Ward. "Mr. A Ward," it begins, and it closes, "Yours, truly, Mark Twain." After the story became famous, the author would also change the title to "The Celebrated Jumping Frog of Calaveras County."

Twain would always feel a debt of gratitude. "The 'Jumping Frog' was the first piece of writing of mine that spread itself through the newspapers and brought me into public notice," he would recall. "Consequently, the *Saturday Press* was a cocoon and I the worm in it."

Clapp had managed an awesome literary streak for the *SP*. By January 1866, however, the journal was in a death spiral.

Clapp remained a brilliant editor. The *SP* was still a bright and clever journal. But its novelty—the second time around—quickly wore thin. The arrival of Lincoln's funeral train in Springfield had signaled the dawn of a new era. As was about to become painfully clear to Clapp, people now had a limited appetite for irony and edginess and fanciful conceits. The nation had just emerged from a war that had cost hundreds of thousands of lives. It was entering into a new period, dubbed the Brown Decades by critic Lewis Mumford, characterized by an autumnal mood of seriousness and a clear-eyed realism.

As readers began to flee the *SP,* a vicious circle was triggered. Money started to dry up, so Clapp hiked the subscription rate from three to five dollars per year, driving away still more of them. Soon advertisers joined in the exodus—though Pfaff's saloon remained stalwart—and Clapp was forced to start adjusting his page count downward. Unable to pay contributors even the usual pittance, Clapp took to reprinting old articles from prewar issues of the *SP,* including a couple of pieces by the long-departed Fitz-James O'Brien.

"I am getting too old to care much about cultivating new people," wrote Clapp in one of his editor's notes. The comment was meant in a different context, but it may as well have referred to the current state of his professional affairs.

As the *SP* floundered, the vultures began to circle. Other publications started to take shots at Clapp's journal. "Of late, however, it has sadly fallen off in interest and brilliancy," asserted the *Trenton Gazette.* Many of the attacks took aim not only at the *SP* but also, more broadly, at Bohemianism. The *Wilmington (NC) Herald* calculated that Clapp's circle, "originally composed of about a dozen literary fellows," had now declined to six. The *New York Leader* called those remaining acolytes "a peculiar mixture of the seedy, bloated, whiskey-sucking, kid-gloved, airish and pretentious."

The *SP*'s troubles provided occasion for a sort of referendum on Bohemianism. The overwhelming verdict: it had fallen very out of fashion. Such is the way of artistic movements, whether they be romantic poetry, Fauvism, or punk rock; they have their shining cultural moment, sometimes eye-blink brief, and then tail off. It took the Civil War ending, however, for real perspective to emerge. Now, a clear line existed. All at once, Bohemianism seemed a relic, a movement that had enjoyed its ascendancy in an earlier era.

When Clapp ran an article headlined "Decimal Currency, Weights, and Measures," the *SP*'s end was drawing nigh. The opening sentence reads, "By the adoption of a decimal currency, America has brought her financial computations within the four fundamental processes of arithmetic." Then, the story proceeds to walk through each of the four in excruciating technical detail. Subscribers—their ranks now greatly diminished—must have read this article with puzzlement, waiting for it to become satire or take a bizarre turn, expecting some kind of conceit to reveal itself. None was forthcoming. The story really was about decimal currency, weights, and measures. It appears that Clapp simply lifted it from another publication to use as filler. His editor's note became a source of equal mirthlessness, as he began increasingly to devote it to panicked requests for subscribers.

June 2, 1866, is the date of the *SP*'s last issue. Less than a year after restarting, it re-stopped. The final number is notably austere: thin on stories, thin on ads. Nothing really marked the sad occasion. There was no official announcement to be found anywhere in the issue, no valedictory essay by Clapp about his journal's invaluable contributions to American culture and letters. The *SP* was here. And then it was gone.

CHAPTER 17

All Fall Down

"C. Pfaff and die!"

Some anonymous wag scrawled this bit of graffiti on the wall at the new saloon, playing with the rotund proprietor's first name, Charlie, and the old saying "See Paris and die."

It may as well have been a prophecy. The years following the Civil War would be pitiless toward many of Clapp's original circle. They had lived life at full tilt, making art, seeking adventure, pushing limits, and tasting passion. Now, America's first Bohemians came tumbling down.

Sometime in the early months of 1865, during the war's grim final winter, Fitz Hugh Ludlow lost his beautiful wife. She left him, fleeing into the waiting arms of none other than the painter Albert Bierstadt.

As to when their affair began, it's impossible to pinpoint. Perhaps Bierstadt and Rosalie were already involved even before the transcontinental journey. Or maybe they got together on the first part of that trip, the part that was conducted by rail. Rosalie had gone along all the way to Atchison. It's also possible that Bierstadt was merely smitten with Ludlow's wife at the time of the journey, and feelings that he hadn't yet acted upon account for those dissonant little gestures, such as naming the camp in Yosemite "Camp Rosalie." Maybe the affair didn't start until after the painter arrived back in New York City.

Chances are no one will ever know. Bierstadt and Rosalie would always remain tight-lipped about the circumstances that brought them together; no incriminating letters between the couple—providing dates or details—are extant. The trail of this ancient adulterous affair has

245

gone very cold. But this much is clear. Rosalie walked out on Ludlow. On November 21, 1866, she married Albert Bierstadt.

The same year, Bierstadt managed a record sale of one of his monumental-scale paintings, *A Storm in the Rocky Mountains, Mt. Rosalie*. Ironically, it's based on his study of the Colorado peak he had named after Ludlow's wife during the western journey. The work fetched $20,000. This was more than Ludlow had earned from writing over the previous ten years. Bierstadt moved his new bride into a mansion built in her honor. Malkasten, as he dubbed it, sat high on a bluff overlooking the Hudson River with a commanding view that extended all the way to West Point in one direction and to Manhattan in the other. The mansion included a library, billiard room, and butler's pantry. The painter's new studio was seventy feet long with thirty-foot-high ceilings, the better to accommodate his huge canvasses. "I am the happiest man living," gloated Bierstadt, referring to his new wife, new home, bright prospects, everything.

Ludlow was simply in hell. For years, he had struggled to follow up *The Hasheesh Eater*. The cross-country journey—what a stroke of good luck it seemed at the time—had provided a worthy subject at last. He'd lined up an enthusiastic publisher, the New York–based Hurd and Houghton. Following Rosalie's departure, however, Ludlow found it difficult to finish his masterpiece. Increasingly, he lost himself in opium. While it may have helped numb his pain, it also hampered his efforts at writing. As Ludlow's life grew more troubled, he slid deeper into addiction. He fell completely out of touch with the old crowd from Pfaff's.

Relatives were horrified by what had become of the bright-eyed young man they had once known. It's perhaps a blessing that Ludlow's minister father died before the lowest ebb was reached. "I pity the strange misguided man & seek not to judge him," noted a cousin. An uncle observed that "Fitz . . . from his long-continued bad habits, is so radically dilapidated, as to demand all sorts of means & appliances to sustain him in life. It must be folly to expect that the wreck can ever be raised & repaired."

Ludlow tried valiantly. During these sad years, he did numerous stints at water-cure facilities. Such places promised treatment of myriad ailments through bathing, constant bathing, in water that was steaming or ice cold, fresh or salty, before meals or at midnight—there were scores of competing philosophies. Because he was battling a drug addiction, these water cures served as the nineteenth-century equivalent of a rehab clinic for Ludlow. But he always relapsed.

Ludlow's publisher grew impatient with the constant delays. Post–Civil War, the publishing industry was on the rebound, and travel books were a popular category. Several accounts of cross-continental journeys were published while Ludlow struggled to complete his. One, by noted journalist Samuel Bowles, not only beat Ludlow to market, but also featured the very title he had planned to use: *Across the Continent.*

When Ludlow was able to write, he drew on his original travel diary, the one brimming with learned observations, the one that he'd carefully protected with the homemade India rubber sleeve. He was also able to use the travel pieces he had earlier contributed to the *New York Post* and the *Golden Era.* Often he took entire sections directly from these accounts. But he always made a point of removing Bierstadt's name. For places in the account where Ludlow had to mention him, he employed generic terms such as "the other overlander." Ludlow made other revisions, too. For example, he changed the episode about Camp Rosalie as follows: "Here we pitched our first Yo-Semite camp,—calling it 'Camp Rattlesnake,' after a pestilent little beast of that tribe which insinuated itself into my blankets, but was disposed of by my artist comrade before it had inflicted its fatal wound upon me."

Ludlow could liken his ex-wife to a venomous snake, *disposed of* by his unnamed *artist comrade.* He could pretend this somehow had all been for the best, preventing him from receiving her *fatal wound.* But what burns through are the bitterness—and the pain.

The Heart of the Continent was finally published in the summer of 1870. Originally, it was supposed to include some of Bierstadt's studies. Instead, the book now featured a handful of amateurish sketches of stagecoaches and waterfalls and prairie dogs. They're the work of an uncredited artist. This change defeated an important part of the book's original purpose: to combine Bierstadt's sketches and Ludlow's prose in a glorious symbiosis that would benefit both their careers. There was also an issue of unfortunate timing to contend with. One of the signature events of the previous year, 1869, was the completion of the transcontinental railroad, capped by the driving of that famous golden spike joining the eastern and western portions. Traveling across the country soon became an unremarkable achievement.

Ludlow's long-delayed book received very few reviews. One did appear in the *Atlantic,* however, and it was brutal: "Since Mr. Ludlow made his explorations . . . the Heart of the Continent has been visited by such numbers of travellers that it is wellnigh as stale and battered as the heart of a coquette entering upon her fifth or six season of flirtations." The reviewer added that the book was full of "superannuated raptures about buffaloes, and sage-brush, and alkali, and antelopes, and parks, and the giant pines and domes of the Yosemite, and Brigham Young's capacity for self-government, and all the rest." And then one final twist of the knife: "It *is* rather late for Mr. Ludlow, we must confess, and we think that five hundred and six pages are a good many."

Yes, it was late. Very late. On September 12, 1870, Ludlow died in a little cottage on the shore of Lake Geneva, his sister Helen by his side. The official cause of death was tuberculosis. He'd traveled to Switzerland, hoping to find a suitable place to convalesce. By this time, though, his body was racked by years of opium abuse. Ludlow was thirty-four years old.

The final year of the Civil War found Adah Isaacs Menken in London. She had pretty well blanketed the states and territories of the Union, even dipped into Confederate-leaning Baltimore, so Great Britain was her natural next stop. Menken was becoming an international superstar at a time when the very concept—let alone that phrase—was difficult to comprehend. Then again, she had always been like a celebrity from a future era, closer in temperament to a scheming Hollywood leading lady or a jaded rock star. "I have everything I could wish for," she lamented, "but I am very miserable." The comment may as well have been her mantra.

For her London run, Menken performed *Mazeppa* at Astley's Royal Amphitheatre. An advertisement claimed that her shapely legs "would have made St. Anthony lift his eyes from his prayer book." The ante was upped once again: everything was bigger, faster, newer. For her infamous ride, she was now pursued by mechanical wolves that snapped at the horse's hooves. As she climbed a truly imposing prop mountain, more Caucasus-like than ever, she traveled past an artificial cataract that gushed real water.

Charles Dickens attended several performances of *Mazeppa*. He went backstage to meet the star; the two also crossed paths at some fancy London dinners. By now, works such as *Great Expectations, A Tale of Two Cities, David Copperfield,* and *Oliver Twist* had secured his lasting fame. Menken courted Dickens assiduously, hoping to enlist his aid in publishing a collection of her poetry. "I have the advice and patronage of the greatest literary man of England, who will revise my poems for me," she crowed in a letter to one of her handlers back in New York. She demanded that the man gather up her poems and mail them to her at once.

While in Great Britain, Menken took *Mazeppa* on the road, traveling to Birmingham, Glasgow, Leeds, and Liverpool. In Scotland, she caused such a sensation that it remained forever imprinted on the mind of a young Arthur Conan Doyle. Many years later, as the creator of Sherlock Holmes, he'd write a story called "A Scandal in Bohemia," featuring a character named Irene Adler, based on Menken. Adler is a femme fatale, described as having "the face of the most beautiful of women, and the mind of the most resolute of men." Adler is distinguished as one of the few characters capable of rattling the famous detective.

Somehow, in the midst of ceaseless touring, Menken also managed to get married yet again. During a trip back to New York, she was wed to James Paul Barkley, a rich but shadowy mining-stock speculator, whom she had met on her trip out West. (She had earlier been granted a divorce from the mousy Robert Newell.) Menken's fifth marriage lasted only three days. She fled New York, returning to Europe, carrying her ex-husband's child. The boy, born prematurely and named Louis Dudevant Victor Emmanuel Barkley, lived for only a few months.

Up and down it went for Menken. Tragedy followed hot on the heels of triumph. Over the few frantic years left to her, she would hurtle through such a rapid sequence of victories and setbacks and twists that her life lost all sense of scale and proportion.

The French, even more than the British, were wild to see Menken. So she entered into negotiations with a theatrical producer and began making arrangements to perform in Paris.

The producer felt that a new play was required. Parisian audiences weren't likely to go in for the English-language *Mazeppa*. Instead, Menken was offered the lead in *Les pirates de la Savane*. At last—a suitable dramatic vehicle. While the Tartar warrior was the source of her fame, Menken had long been hungry for a role that would allow her to be taken seriously as an artist. Ada Clare and Artemus Ward had both promised to write her such a play, but neither had come through. In fact, nearly every person with literary ability whom she encountered—and their numbers were legion—had promised to write her a play, yet none had delivered. Now it looked like her situation was about to change.

Pirates was a swashbuckling adventure tale that had made its Paris debut several years earlier. In advance of the new production, its co-writers, Ferdinand Dugué and Auguste Anicet-Bourgeois, reworked the script, adding a couple of plot contrivances. Menken's character, Leo, was turned into a mute, whose tongue had been cut out in an Indian attack. It was an elegant solution to the challenge of getting the tempestuous actress to memorize her dialogue—in French no less. Now, she could play her part without uttering a word. The playwrights also added a climactic scene, where Leo was . . . well . . . stripped down, strapped to a horse, and sent off on a wild ride.

Initially, Menken chafed at playing a role that had become nothing more than a silent French *Mazeppa*. But the chance to conquer Paris proved an even greater enticement. *Pirates* opened on December 30,

1866, at the Théâtre de la Gaîté. The play was an instant sensation. The crowd loved it, and the critics piled on the accolades. To cries of "Vive Leo!" Menken made nine curtain calls that first night. A review in *Le Moniteur Universel* praised Menken as "a very beautiful woman, svelte and admirably proportioned, who mimes with rare intelligence."

Pirates managed a run of 150 sold-out performances. In Paris, as in London, Menken devoted her time offstage to cultivating people who could help her career. Often, she was spotted out strolling in the Bois de Boulogne, arm in arm with Alexandre Dumas. The author was an old man now, easily thirty years Menken's senior, and was decades removed from his greatest successes, *The Three Musketeers* and *The Count of Monte Cristo*. He was living in a cheap flat on the boulevard Malesherbes, dependent for income on an allowance from his son.

One day, Menken and Dumas decided to visit a studio and have their picture taken together. In the photo, Menken rests her head against the author's chest, one arm wrapped around his neck. Both wear oddly amorous expressions, sleepy eyes and languid smiles, as if they have just finished making love. Or that would have been the natural conclusion—particularly in a more demure age—had anyone happened to see this very private and intimate portrait.

Predictably, *everyone* in Paris did. Somehow, the photograph was leaked to the public. One suspects that Dumas was the instigator. In his prime, he had been a lothario of epic proportions, who boasted of bedding thousands of women. Here was evidence—photographic evidence—that he'd lost none of his prowess. Menken may have been a willing party to the leaked picture, although she professed to be mortified.

Along the boulevards, newsstands did a brisk business selling copies. Doctored versions became especially popular, featuring Menken's and Dumas's heads attached to images of naked bodies in various sexual positions. Parisians delighted in crafting doggerel verse and bawdy songs about the supposed sex partners. The truth—did they or didn't they?—was immaterial. The scandal worked its magic, as so often happens, benefiting both parties. After a long, painful absence, Dumas was back in the public eye. Soon a Paris newspaper began a serialization of *The*

Knight of Sainte-Hermine, his last major novel. Menken, quite simply, was the toast of Paris.

What else was left? Menken had pretty much seen and done it all. In the summer of 1868, she withdrew from public life, suffering from a mysterious ailment. She settled into a Paris hotel room, confined to her bed. "I am lost to art and life," she told a visitor. "Yet, when all is said and done, have I not at my age tasted more of life than most women who live to be a hundred?" She spent her last days and devoted her remaining strength to battling to get her poetry collection published.

During the morning of August 10, her breathing became shallow, and a rabbi was brought to her bedside. He delivered last rites in Hebrew, and then Menken slipped away. Despite all the money she had made, the actress left nothing behind. Somehow, in her last years, she managed to squander everything on extravagances such as a custom-made coach and team of horses. In true Bohemian fashion, Menken died penniless in Paris. She was thirty-three years old, according to the best estimate.

Her passing was a major news story. "The Menken is dead," reads one obit. "The bare-faced, bare-limbed, reckless, erratic, ostracized, but gifted, kind-hearted, successful, yet ill-starred, Menken is no more. . . . She has exchanged for the stage the coffin, and for the saloon the cemetery." As the writer continued, he couldn't resist slipping in a cautionary note, a pattern with the numerous obituary notices she received: "But, alas! her soul, almost from her birth, was given over a prey to a Demon, whose earthly name is A Morbid thirst for Notoriety."

The cause of Menken's death, like the date of her birth, remains a mystery. Various accounts attributed it to tuberculosis, appendicitis, an abscess, cancer, or—most dramatically—complications from a horse-riding accident. She did have a serious onstage mishap while performing in Paris, so even this is plausible.

Only one week after her death, her poetry collection finally came out. Entitled *Infelicia* and published by the English house of John Camden Hotten, the book was rushed into stores to capitalize on the upsurge of interest following Menken's demise. Dickens had not been involved. While intrigued by Menken's stage act, he was always privately dismissive of her verse. Nevertheless, Dickens did provide a "dedication" of sorts. Menken had cobbled it together by combining passages from two of his rather formal letters to her:

> Dear Miss Menken: I shall have great pleasure in accepting your dedication. I thank you for your portrait as a highly remarkable specimen of photography. I also thank you for the verses inclosed in your note. Many such inclosures come to me, but few so pathetically written, and fewer still so modestly sent. Faithfully yours, Charles Dickens.

This appeared prominently, on the opening page of the volume. As endorsements go, it wasn't exactly ringing. *Infelicia* was soon forgotten.

Menken, too: she's buried in Paris in Montparnasse cemetery, laid to rest underneath a shade tree. In this case, though, *rest* doesn't exactly seem fitting. It's hard to picture Menken as anything but the vibrant creature she was in life. Time may have passed; the memories may have faded. But there was a moment—a few brief, fever-tinged years—when the whole world was captivated as the bold and alluring actress was strapped to a horse and sent thundering off, taking that notorious wild ride.

Adah and Artemus, Artemus and Adah: their fates had always been oddly bound together. They had often seemed to move along the same path. After the Civil War, Ward made the same decision as Menken, choosing to travel abroad in search of opportunity.

Ward arrived in London in the autumn of 1866, peddling a new act. The British public had never been exposed to *The Babes in the Wood*. But Ward felt confident that fresher, more topical material was the way to go.

His new act spoofed moving panoramas, then a very popular type of entertainment. They consisted of a long canvas (stretching for hundreds or even thousands of feet), which could be unwound from a spool, revealing a sequence of images. A forerunner of the motion picture, moving panoramas proved especially effective as the backdrop for a speaker who was describing a trip to an exotic location. A very successful one was devoted to an Arctic journey, for example, but the era's biggest hit reproduced a paddleboat voyage down the Mississippi, unspooling the sights one might see on the river while steaming along.

Ward's panorama depicted various scenes encountered on the trip to Virginia City, Nevada, and environs. Obviously, this called for a far more elaborate production than his earlier routine. In fact, it required several additional personnel such as a pianist along with what Ward called a "crankist" (someone to spool the panorama) and a "moonist" (someone to handle lighting effects). But Ward's comedic formula remained much the same. Often, he put on a befuddled air when an image didn't line up with the story he was trying to tell. He also had great fun with the amateurishness of his production. As Ward attempted to describe the beauty of the Great Salt Lake at night, for example, the moonist proved unable to hold the lantern steady, creating a chaotic play of light on the image—and driving the comedian to ever-greater distraction. Another bit involved Ward telling a dramatic western tale, accompanied by staccato runs of piano. The piano soon grew so loud, however, that the audience couldn't make out what Ward was saying. It was possible only to see his mouth moving and his hands wildly gesticulating. Just as Ward reached the climax of his tale, the piano stopped, and it was possible to hear " . . . and she fainted on Reginald's breast." Then: mock embarrassment as Ward realized the crowd had failed to follow the story. He tried again, but the pianist proved equally enthusiastic, and once again the only audible line was that final, maddeningly enigmatic " . . . and she fainted on Reginald's breast."

Crowds loved Ward's new act. His peerless instincts as a showman were once again confirmed. For the British, Ward's inimitable humor combined with scenes from the distant and intriguing American West proved a winning formula. The *Times* of London praised the comedian for jokes of "that true Transatlantic type," adding that he possessed an "air of profound unconsciousness, we may almost say melancholy, which is irresistibly droll." A publication called the *Queen* was emphatic: "The audience fairly laughed till they could laugh no more."

Old habits die hard, though. Whenever he finished a show, Ward enjoyed carousing in London until dawn, often in the company of journalists. He fell in with a set that included some writers for *Punch*. He even contributed some articles to the celebrated humor magazine. But years of following his demanding comedy act with late hours and hard drinking were starting to take their toll. "He had that unfortunate desire for the second round of applause" is how someone who knew Ward in London describes it.

Soon, Ward had grown so worn down that he had trouble performing his act. Along with a moonist and a crankist, he arranged for a pharmacist to be available backstage during shows to dispense drugs to keep him going. Although the precise varieties are unknown, he was probably taking patent medicines laced with stimulants. He even adjusted his act, contriving to do a portion of it seated to conserve his energy. Two months into his London run, however, Ward became so exhausted that he was unable to take the stage. His remaining shows had to be canceled.

A doctor was summoned, and Ward received a grim diagnosis: he was suffering from tuberculosis. His condition was startlingly advanced. Most likely, he'd been aware of his affliction for a while, but had kept it secret. It was certainly not something a popular entertainer would want known. No doubt, his condition was exacerbated by his tireless pursuit of that second round of applause.

Ward traveled first to the Isle of Jersey and then to Southampton to convalesce. It was midwinter now—not that this part of the world provides a therapeutic climate in any season. Ward was mostly confined to his room in various inns, growing progressively sicker. He'd always had a mournful streak. It must have felt sad and strange to Ward, far from New York City, away from London even, just an off-season visitor of lonely seaside resorts. "I am so fearfully weak," Artemus wrote in a letter to his agent. "I am so utterly 'gone' now the excitement is over."

On March 6, 1867, Artemus Ward died in his room at Radley's Hotel in Southampton. He was thirty-two years old.

Ward's body was placed on board the liner *Deutschland* for passage back across the Atlantic, and then on to Waterford, Maine. He was buried in the same dour little hamlet where he'd been born, the well-spring of his pioneering humor.

The deaths were piling up fast: Ludlow, Menken, and Ward were gone. It was like a Jacobean-era tragedy where all the major characters get killed off. In the autumn of 1865, George Arnold, the Poet of Beer, died at age thirty-one from undisclosed causes. Shortly thereafter, Charles Halpine, the stammerer of inspired phrases, suffered at age thirty-nine a fatal overdose of chloroform, a drug he was using recreationally. Fitz-James O'Brien, Clapp's first recruit, was by now long departed, a casualty of the Civil War. The *New York Times* was amazed by the toll: "Death has gathered the greater number of the jovial wits that wasted life under the Broadway sidewalk."

Yet not all the Pfaff's stalwarts met untimely ends. Several even managed to become respectable. William Winter settled into his job as drama critic of the *New York Tribune,* a post he would hold for forty-four years. Thomas Aldrich, Clapp's deputy on the *Saturday Press,* became the editor of the *Atlantic.* Aldrich, who as a young man wrote the line "We were all very merry at Pfaff's," would spend his later years at the very heart of the literary establishment, piloting the erstwhile *SP*'s most hated rival. After leaving New York, however, he would always describe himself as not "genuine Boston" but rather "Boston plated." To prove it, he continued to smoke a little clay pipe, a vestige of his wild youth.

Edwin Booth also managed to reach an accommodation—albeit an uneasy one—with the world. For the actor, who had traveled in Bohemian circles and was close friends with such mainstays as Ludlow and Aldrich, the time immediately after Lincoln's assassination was agonizing. Federal marshals tracked brother John to his hideout, a hay barn in the Virginia countryside. They tried to take him alive, but in the ensuing chaos a marshal opened fire. John—who wished to be loved by the Southern people, who wanted so very many things, but who held as his deepest desire "fame, I must have fame!"—was killed. The main conspirators were quickly rounded up and hung.

Edwin spent eight months holed up in his home, while death threats rained down on him and his remaining siblings. Then he took once more to the stage, working tirelessly to restore the Booth name. He managed to stay sober and proclaimed that he never touched anything stronger than milk. Through discipline to his craft, he would emerge as arguably the greatest actor of the nineteenth century, eclipsing even his father, the Mad Tragedian. But his past would prove impossible to escape. Edwin suffered terrible bouts of insomnia where he was visited by agonizing memories, what he called "the vultures."

One night in 1873, Edwin awakened at three and summoned his manservant. Together, they went down to the basement of Booth's home, where an old trunk sat waiting, gathering dust. It was filled with John's theatrical costumes. The manservant stoked the fire in the furnace. One by one, Edwin tossed in his brother's costumes, for roles such as Iago and Romeo and Hamlet. Edwin had experienced far more than his share of chaos; wherever possible, he wished to banish its traces.

Others weren't so fortunate.

In 1866, Ada Clare published a novel with a small New York house. *Only a Woman's Heart* is an overwrought tale, featuring one main character that's a thinly veiled Clare and another that's a barely disguised Louis Gottschalk (the famous pianist suspected of fathering her son, Aubrey). There's even a shipwreck that only the two lead characters survive, a flimsy conceit that allows them to wind up on a desert island where they drone on endlessly about love and art and life—and love. Reviews were savage. "Stale lager-bier cannot be a pleasing beverage even to a Bohemian, and this book is to literature what stale lager-bier is to imbibables," wrote a critic for a magazine called the *Round Table*, adding, "The authoress has no conception of a plot, no skill in dialogues, no knowledge of human nature, no acquaintance with society."

Clare was deeply wounded by her novel's reception. While there were only a handful of reviews (a slight of its own), it was enough for a consensus: *Only a Woman's Heart* was a very poor effort. This was the first time that Clare's writing had ever met with any kind of significant criticism. She had always been celebrated for her thoughtful and trenchant prose, in the *Saturday Press* and later in the *Golden Era.*

Adding to her pain: Clare must have felt robbed of glory by the vagaries of timing. Only a few years earlier, when Bohemianism was the rage, Thayer & Eldridge had planned to bring out Clare's *Asphodel* shortly after Whitman's *Leaves of Grass.* But the firm went bankrupt, and the novel was never published. It's possible that *Asphodel* was a superior work to *Only a Woman's Heart;* it's further possible that the novel was lost during the turmoil of the war (no printer's proof can be found, let alone a manuscript). Regardless, Clare decided to give up writing.

"I shall withdraw from the literary domain," she announced in a letter to a friend. Henceforth, acting would be her vocation. She adopted a stage name, Agnes Stanfield. Going forward, she would insist that theaters use it in billing her. "If the name Ada Clare appeared it would cause a constant buzz all around the country," explained Clare in another letter. While *buzz* was the word she chose, one suspects that brickbats were her real concern and that she was worried critics would be less kindly disposed toward Ada Clare than the unknown Agnes Stanfield. She wanted a new start under a new name.

Acting had never been Clare's strong suit, though. She'd already tried it during her early days at Pfaff's and had been roundly criticized for a weak and unemotive stage voice. Now in her thirties, she found it difficult to break into the profession again. About the only work Clare was able to find were bit parts in small-time productions at various regional theaters. While touring, she met a journeyman actor named J. Franklin Noyes. They were married and moved—along with Clare's teenage son, Aubrey—into a cheap Manhattan boardinghouse.

One day, early in 1874, Clare dropped by the offices of the second-rate theatrical agency that handled her bookings. The previous autumn, a financial panic had gripped the United States, and the theater business had yet to recover. Roles had become all the harder to come by. While Clare was at the offices, a little black-and-tan terrier, belonging to her agent, hopped into her lap. Clare petted the dog.

Unexpectedly, it lunged up and bit her face. Despite this unpleasant encounter, Clare succeeded in firming up a series of engagements with Lucille Western's traveling theater company.

Clare departed for a tour of cities in upstate New York such as Auburn, Buffalo, and Syracuse. At a performance in Rochester, however, she created a shocking onstage spectacle. Midway through the play *East Lynne,* she utterly abandoned her role and began raving like a lunatic. She had to be forcibly removed from the stage by police officers and was confined to a jail cell for the night. The following day, Clare was placed on a train with an escort, a fellow actor from her company, and she traveled back to New York City. She seemed calmer during the ride. Her husband was there to meet her at the station. As Clare emerged from the train, however, as the cold winter air hit her face, she began to scream in agony.

A hyperamplified sense of touch is a symptom of one of history's most dreaded afflictions, then known as hydrophobia, now as rabies. As it turns out, the little terrier had died the day after it bit Clare.

Clare was taken back to her boardinghouse. Doctors were consulted, but there was nothing to be done, save for administering opiates to numb her addled consciousness. Mercifully, she slipped into a coma and died on March 4, 1874. She was thirty-nine years old.

That such an elegant woman came to such a brutal end was hard to fathom. On learning the news, Whitman said, "Poor, poor Ada Clare—I have been inexpressibly shocked by the horrible & sudden close of her gay, easy, sunny free, loose, but *not ungood* life." Unlike so many of the departed Pfaffians, Clare didn't die without significant attachments. She left behind a spouse and a child. Aubrey would grow up to be an actor.

The Queen of Bohemia was dead. But what about the king? What became of Henry Clapp?

When the *Saturday Press* folded for the second time, it broke the old cynic's heart. For a while, Clapp managed to pick up assignments from newspapers such as the *New York Leader* and the *Daily Graphic.* As the work dried up, he turned increasingly to drink.

The final years of Clapp's life are visible only in brief flashes, like a man falling down a mine shaft. In the flickering half-light, it's possible to get intermittent glimpses as he tumbles and flails and vainly reaches out his hands. He remained in New York City, living in a series of squalid rooms. But he also did an untold number of stints in asylums, where he was thrown into a general population that included schizophrenics, victims of serious head injuries, and prostitutes suffering the last ravages of syphilis. For an alcoholic without means, that was the only treatment option available in the nineteenth century.

During one bender, police officers picked him up and took him to an asylum, where he was admitted as "Henry Clark." No one even bothered to get his name right; it didn't really matter. Clapp had outlived his fame and had outlasted many of the main figures of his circle who would have recognized him as well.

Still, as Clapp made his shambling rounds, he was sometimes spotted by one member or another from the old Pfaff's set. These little glimpses are terribly sad. He was seen on the Bowery selling some of his clothes for liquor money. Another person saw him walking along Broadway, looking "shriveled and shabby and wretchedly forlorn" and "unknown and unnoticed in the hurrying crowd." Still another described encountering Clapp and being stunned to realize that the old man was in "actual want." *Actual want:* those two little words speak volumes. This wasn't the salad days' pennilessness that some of his young acolytes tried on for style. Unable to find work, bedeviled by alcoholism, Clapp had slipped into genuine, crushing poverty.

The asylum stays became more frequent and longer. Over time, Clapp got in the habit of writing to old friends, seeking money for incidentals that could be bought at the institutions' commissaries. A letter to Edmund Stedman, a journalist and onetime Pfaffian, concludes, "And now, my dear fellow, if you can send me a few dollars to buy tobacco, pipes, newspapers . . . etc, you will make me a happier man than I have been for years, though I am in a Lunatic Asylum." Stedman sent him five dollars. Desperate for money, Clapp even wrote to Frederick Douglass, someone he'd last known decades earlier when they had both lived in Lynn, Massachusetts. Douglass also sent Clapp a few dollars and would later recall: "He was a witty and pungent writer and speaker and for a time did good service to the antislavery cause."

Clapp doesn't appear to have written to Whitman. Perhaps the two had drifted apart again, or maybe this represented a last morsel of pride, Clapp not wanting the poet who had brought him glory to see him in such an abject state of need. Whitman, for his part, would always remember Clapp fondly: "Henry Clapp stepped out from the crowd of hooters—was my friend: a much needed ally." On another occasion, the poet would say, "He did honorable with me every time."

Clapp did keep up with Charlie Pfaff, though. For years, the cheerful old proprietor fed him meals gratis. It was the least Pfaff could do; Clapp had done so much to promote his reputation as a saloon keep. Pfaff refused to serve Clapp alcohol at his establishment—or tried to anyway. But it was hopeless; whenever he had any funds, Clapp went on a fresh bender and always wound up institutionalized once more.

A last flickering glimpse finds Clapp at the asylum on Ward's Island in Manhattan's East River. It was a regular drying-out spot for him. The asylum had a small library, an amenity of which Clapp took thorough advantage. One of the books he checked out was Thackeray's last novel, *The Adventures of Philip on His Way Through the World: Shewing Who Robbed Him, Who Helped Him, and Who Passed Him By*. Clapp was also thrilled to discover a cache of yellowed back issues of magazines in the library. "I have been feasting, this last few days, on old and odd no's of the *Galaxy* and *Harper*," he wrote to Stedman. Even in this grimmest of places, Clapp held fast to his passion for the arts, remained curious about the world, and he must have had plans, and on his best days hopes, and—

Clapp died on April 10, 1875. He was sixty years old.

There was a brief flutter of obituaries, a last taste of the attention that had so eluded him in the last years of his life. "With the death of Henry Clapp," reads one in the *Boston Globe*, "fades the memory of one of the most peculiar cliques of roystering literary characters ever known," adding, "The rest of the Colony that once met at Pfaff's beer saloon on Broadway, to enliven the midnight hour with songs and jokes and reckless repartee, are either dead or dispersed or turned respectable."

For a while, Clapp's body lay in a pauper's grave before it was removed to Nantucket and placed in a little cemetery overlooking the sea.

Born a Puritan, Clapp died a Bohemian.

CHAPTER 18

"Those Times, That Place"

WHITMAN CONTINUED ON, through the presidencies of Johnson, Grant, Hayes, Garfield, Arthur, Cleveland, and Harrison. He was still around for the last bare-knuckle prizefight and the first five-and-dime, for the advent of electric bulbs and Coca-Cola, standardized time zones and the Brooklyn Bridge. He even managed to make one final visit to Pfaff's. Fellow Bohemians such as Ludlow, Menken, and Ward never even saw forty. It's quite likely that they didn't manage a single gray hair. Whitman watched his hair turn gray to white, and his blue eyes became highly changeable, now filled with sadness and, in the next moment, flooded with joy. There had been so much—time and people and change—just so much.

For many years, Whitman remained in Washington, DC. During the late 1860s and early 1870s, following Lincoln's assassination and the Civil War, he had built a life there for himself. He had moved into a new attic room, at 472 M Street, though it wasn't much different from his previous garrets. He settled into a new government clerkship, working in another undemanding job for the US attorney general's office, not such a departure from his earlier posts. Whitman enjoyed frequent month-long leaves. He was even allowed to draw on the departmental stationery supply for use in his own writing.

What distinguished this job, however, was the length of his tenure. Whitman spent seven years in the attorney general's office. It's hard to imagine him as a civil servant, yet this job was among his life's constants for a very long time. One of his primary duties was making copies of official correspondence. (In the days before mimeographs and photocopiers, this was a necessary though thankless task.) Whitman dutifully copied thousands of letters related to the department's busy docket of legal cases, filled with terminology such as "binding stipulation," "writ of error," and *nolle prosequi.*" A typical letter ends with a little flourish: "I am Sir, with great respect, your obedient serv't, Henry Stanbery, Attorney General." But even the attorney general's signature was in Whitman's distinctive hand. (It's merely a copy, after all, for the department's records.) The poet of the body and the soul was also a government clerk, third class, making $1,600 per year.

Whitman also kept up with his hospital visits. That was one of the reasons he held fast to a job that left him ample free time. After the war ended, though, the sense of frantic mission lifted. A handful of badly wounded soldiers remained in the hospitals, but eventually they either died or recovered, returning to civilian life as farmers and bakers and factory workers. Only a few chronic cases lingered on. Gradually, Whitman reduced the frequency of his visits until he was going only on Sunday afternoons, just a remnant from a sad time fast receding. So much from those days was receding.

But Whitman and Peter Doyle remained steadfast. Each day, after finishing work, Whitman would stand in front of his building on Pennsylvania Avenue, waiting for Doyle's omnibus. He'd climb aboard and ride back and forth until the shift was over. Often Whitman would help out, ringing the bell or assisting passengers as they got on and off. He'd salute the drivers of the other omnibuses as they rolled past.

Whitman and Doyle continued their habit of long walks, only now it was as if the world had opened up. The war was over, and they could go anywhere, walk as far as they wished. Sometimes, they crossed the Anacostia River via the Navy Yard Bridge, then ambled along its banks to a ferry point where they would set off for Virginia, then more ambling, this time along the Potomac banks, before crossing back into the district by way of the Long Bridge. That's a roughly eight-mile circuit. "Often we would go on for some time without a word, then talk—Pete a rod ahead or I a rod ahead," Whitman would recall. "Oh! the long, long walks, way into the nights!—in the after hours—sometimes lasting till two or three in the morning! The air, the stars, the moon, the water—what a fulness of inspiration they imparted!—what exhilaration! And there were the detours, too—wanderings off into the country out of the beaten path."

In Doyle's recollection: "We took great walks together—off towards or to Alexandria, often. . . . We would talk of ordinary matters. . . . He never seemed to tire." Whitman would point out the stars to Doyle. He knew all the constellations, Canis Major, Cassiopeia, and the hunter, Orion. "My love for you is indestructible," he promised Doyle.

For Whitman, these years in Washington right after the Civil War were a sweet time, full of calm. This wasn't one of his most productive periods, at least when measured against the whirlwind pace he'd sometimes achieved. No matter. For Whitman, perhaps, the lack of fever—in his personal life, in the life of the nation—simply didn't lend itself to the act of creation.

Ironically, it's during this time that Whitman's reputation as a poet began to grow. In 1867, he brought out a new volume of *Leaves of Grass.* This was the first one since 1860, when Thayer & Eldridge had published the third edition. During the intervening years, pirated versions, such as Horace Wentworth's, had helped keep interest alive. Whitman took his old familiar route, self-publishing the latest *Leaves.* It was the first to contain his Civil War poetry, such as "O Captain! My Captain!" and "When Lilacs Last in the Dooryard Bloom'd." Otherwise, there were only six new poems. *Leaves,* fourth edition, was a commercial flop that garnered very few reviews—an all too common outcome for Whitman's work.

Yet somehow, he was finding his way to readers. The sense of opposition that his poetry always managed to spark created a potent interplay between those who thought he merited obscurity and those who felt he'd been dealt a grave artistic injustice. The very fact that *Leaves of Grass* was dismissed in some quarters served as the proof for others that it was a masterpiece.

In 1874, Emerson published an exhaustive 534-page collection meant to settle for all time the question, *What are the greatest poems ever written?* It was titled *Parnassus* after the mountain that symbolized poetry in ancient Greece. Virgil, Dante, and Chaucer were well represented in the collection, as were such homegrown talents as Whittier and Longfellow. There was even a selection from Forceythe Willson, a contemporary American poet deemed "remarkable" by Emerson. But no Whitman: Emerson, it seems, had never forgiven him for becoming a Bohemian, and the collection didn't include a single poem from the man he'd once greeted at the beginning of a great career.

But around the same time that Whitman was denied the rare air of *Parnassus,* he received a flattering accolade. He was asked to read a poem at Dartmouth's 1872 commencement ceremony. He composed one just for the occasion, entitled "As a Strong Bird on Pinions Free." It was the first invitation Whitman had ever received to read at a university. It came courtesy of a student committee that was hoping to rile some of the more conservative members of the faculty. That didn't happen. Whitman read his poem without Dartmouth descending into contention or chaos. But it was the student committee's gesture that mattered.

Increasingly, Whitman was becoming a divisive cultural symbol, one that separated the broad-minded from the stodgy—and very often the young from the old. The fustiest critics, the most doddering professors, could be reliably counted on to pronounce his poetry obscene. That left the younger generation all the more enticed. The fact that *Leaves of Grass* was difficult to find added to the mystique; only a handful of copies—in a quirky array of printings—were in circulation. Dog-eared editions moved across university campuses, passed from one student to another.

Whitman's poetry also created an international split, the United States versus Europe. Or, more precisely: Europe versus the United States. Across the Atlantic, there was a growing movement to give Whitman the recognition denied in his native land. *Those Americans,* went a common conceit, *they aren't even aware that a great poet is in their midst.* While Whitman labored as a government clerk, poems from *Leaves of Grass* were translated into Russian and German. English poet Algernon Swinburne wrote an encomium, "To Walt Whitman in America."

Back and forth it went. Overlook Whitman, seek out Whitman; disregard him, give him his due; there was no single event, no sudden breakthrough, but it was this process, this tension, that by slow degrees began to push forward his fame.

One of the most impassioned Whitman defenders was William O'Connor, host of the Sunday-night get-togethers Whitman frequented during the Civil War. Though O'Connor had held a milquetoast salon, as a polemicist he proved nothing short of ferocious. He wrote a forty-six-page pamphlet in which he took on the doubters, what he referred to as "the bigots, the dilettanti, the prudes and the fools." By contrast, he cast Whitman in near-saintly terms:

> He has been a visitor of prisons; a protector of fugitive slaves; a constant voluntary nurse, night and day, at the hospitals, from the beginning of the war to the present time; a brother and friend through life to the neglected and the forgotten, the poor, the degraded, the criminal, the outcast; turning away from no man for his guilt, nor woman for her vileness. His is the strongest and truest compassion I have ever known.

Time was, Henry Clapp had been Whitman's champion, publishing and promoting his work. O'Connor was something altogether different. Unquestionably, Whitman's service in the hospitals was noble, and his compassion for the wounded soldiers was truly remarkable. But *visitor of prisons? Protector of fugitive slaves?* O'Connor was Whitman's mythologizer, the most capable of several who would assume that role, and the title he gave his pamphlet, *The Good Gray Poet,* would become an enduring image.

On January 23, 1873, sometime around three in the morning, Whitman awoke in his attic room to find that he couldn't move his left arm and leg. There wasn't any pain, though, so he didn't give it further thought and soon drifted back to sleep. Come morning, he was horrified to discover that the entire left side of his body was paralyzed. He was stranded in his bed and grew increasingly panicked. "After several hours, some friends came in," he recalled, "and they immediately sent for a doctor."

Whitman had suffered a stroke. He was only fifty-three years old, though his health had been in decline for many years, had never really been the same since the war. To his mind, the cause of his stroke would always be the "hospital poison" that he'd absorbed at the time. In a way, this may even have been true. The stress of that experience certainly could have exacerbated what appears to be serious and undiagnosed hypertension.

Doyle and various friends took turns nursing Whitman. The paralysis began to lift, and in a matter of days he was able to get around, though slowly and with help. After only a few months, he even returned to his job. The stroke—or "whack," as Whitman called it— didn't affect his speech and doesn't appear to have diminished his mental acuity. But it had lasting physical effects. His left leg would remain pretty much useless. For the rest of his life, he would walk with a cane, dragging his left foot.

Then more bad news: Whitman learned that his mother was dying. She had moved in with his brother George in Camden, New Jersey, where he now worked as a pipe inspector. On May 20—just four months after his stroke—he rushed to her bedside. Three days later, she died. She left behind a note composed for her children: "Farewell my beloved sons farewell I have lived beyond all comfort in this world dont mourn for me my beloved sons and daughters farewell my dear beloved Walt."

Whitman decided to stay on for a while with George and his wife. There had been so much tumult; a rest was sure to do him good. He arranged for a two-month leave from his job. When the time was up, he managed to extend the leave, staying on with George. This may seem a curious decision, especially since it kept Whitman apart from Doyle.

But other circumstances may have weakened their bond. Lately, they had contended with plenty. Whitman's stroke had made their twenty-four-year age difference stark. Doyle was still a young man;

Whitman, all at once, was an old man, even one who required nursing care. Doyle gave Whitman a cane, a thoughtful but awkward gesture. For Whitman, this practical gift must have been a painful reminder, and for his regular, everyday cane, he relied on a different one. There are hints, too, of other troubles between the couple. Whitman may have wanted a deeper commitment; perhaps he even hoped they could move in together. Doyle felt pulled by obligations. He had family in Washington and was also charged with helping care for his mother, who was in declining health.

Whitman kept extending his leave until eventually he'd been away for a year, too long, even by the lax standards of his employer. His position at the attorney general's office was officially terminated. It's then that Whitman made a fateful decision. He chose to remain in Camden.

For Whitman, there was something comfortingly familiar about this industrial city on the banks of the Delaware River. Camden played Brooklyn to Philadelphia's Manhattan. And its big sister city was accessible via a quick ferry ride, a trip that Whitman made frequently. He'd traversed Broadway as a young man, moved through Boston as he typeset the 1860 *Leaves of Grass,* seemingly gotten to know every lane and byway of Washington in wartime and after. Now a great pleasure was to hail a stage and make his way up and down Philadelphia's Market Street.

Whitman took over a small bedroom in his brother's house. He continued writing poetry. But his abilities as an artist had greatly diminished. Some new poems such as "Passage to India" are deeply affecting. As Whitman pressed forward as an artist, however, almost everything he wrote suffered in comparison to the impossible standard of his earlier work. Many years before, he had told his editor Charles Eldridge, "I shall range along the high plateau of my life & capacity for a few years now, & then swiftly descend." Even then, Whitman had known. At the very top of his power, he was aware of what a lofty place he'd reached, and he recognized that such creativity simply could not be sustained.

Still, he continued to bring out versions of *Leaves of Grass.* In the course of his lifetime, he would publish seven separate editions of what

he called "that *unkillable* work." During the postwar years, each succes-
sive version contained only a small number of new poems. Otherwise,
Whitman made continual—and usually tiny—revisions to the existing
poems, such as "Song of Myself" and "Out of the Cradle Endlessly
Rocking." A growing fondness for apostrophes, for example, prompted
Whitman to change words such as *buzzed* to *buzz'd* in later editions.
He tinkered endlessly with poem titles and reshuffled their sequence,
seeking fresh thematic groupings. The grand cathedral had been built
years before. Now, it was a matter of making small adjustments.

But he kept working. Eventually, he'd be listed by his profession
("Walt Whitman, poet") in the Camden city directory. He even be-
gan to derive a modest income from *Leaves of Grass*. For a while, he
sold the self-published volume by mail, handling the order fulfillment
himself. Then, for the later editions, he was able to line up commercial
publishers such as David McKay, a small Philadelphia press. They paid
him royalties on every copy sold. In a good year, he could earn $1,000,
though there were plenty of lean years. Whitman never required much
money. Emerson was right: he was a Bohemian.

From Camden, Whitman also realized his long-held ambition to
become a "wander-speaker." Each year, he delivered a lecture about
Abraham Lincoln's death. It was always on or around April 15 (the
anniversary of his passing), and it was usually in Philadelphia or New
York, though once in Boston. The strain of standing was too much
for Whitman, so he gave his speech seated. He'd put on his spectacles,
which, out of vanity, he never wore for any of the countless photo-
graphs taken during his latter years. He'd consult his notes, which he'd
pasted to the pages of a book of poetry entitled *The Bride of Gettysburg*.
That way they would be harder to scatter or misplace. And there was an
added advantage: If he happened to glance at his notes during a speech,
he would appear to the audience to be paging through a book.

Whitman spoke slowly, in an unusually low, quavering voice—not
exactly a natural orator. But he had his wiles. The auditorium would
grow hushed as he described "the muffled sound of a pistol shot" and
the fleeing Booth "catching his boot heel in the drapery of the Amer-
ican flag" before landing on the stage, looking around with "those

basilisk eyes flashing," and shouting "these words: 'Sic Semper Tyrannis.'" What always struck audiences was the immediacy of the scene Whitman painted. "He related the death of Abraham Lincoln quite simply," noted one attendee, "as though the event had taken place the evening before. Not a gesticulation, no raising of the voice." The attendee added that Whitman's account possessed an authority, gave the impression that "I was there; everything happened to me."

Only Whitman hadn't been there. He was, of course, relying on Doyle's long-ago account of the event. With each passing year, the two men had drifted further apart. There would be other romances for Whitman in Camden, but none would ever manage a rival claim to the poet's heart. Doyle took a job as a brakeman on the Baltimore & Potomac Railroad, making late-night runs up and down the mid-Atlantic corridor, sometimes passing only miles from where Whitman lay in his bed. Indeed, there would come a point when Whitman entirely lost track of Doyle, had no idea as to the whereabouts of the man to whom he'd once professed eternal love. "He is a bird of passage," mused Whitman, adding, "I would not know how to reach him now."

Whitman lived with George for nearly eleven years. Then he bought a home of his own in Camden. It was a modest wood-frame house, painted brown, and located at 328 Mickle Street. Whitman appreciated the shade tree out front and the lilac bushes in the backyard. The house cost $2,000, an amount that Whitman cobbled together from his modest royalties, meager savings, and a loan from a businessman acquaintance.

Whitman had accumulated very little furniture. On first moving in, he used an overturned box as a kitchen table. But then he cut a deal with Mary Davis, a widow who lived nearby. In exchange for her furniture and her agreement to perform cooking and housekeeping duties, Whitman invited the widow Davis to live with him rent free. She also brought along assorted pets, including a dog, a cat, and a canary, which she placed in a cage that hung from the kitchen ceiling. Whitman would repair to the little front room—what he jokingly called the "parlor"—and sit in a rocking chair, soaking up the comfort of his household's clutter and activity.

During the years in Camden, Whitman played host to a steady stream of distinguished visitors. Oscar Wilde, Bram Stoker, and an ancient Longfellow crossed the Delaware to see him. At home and overseas, his fame kept growing. Vincent Van Gogh painted his *Starry Night* after reading *Leaves of Grass* in translation, even took the title from one of Whitman's poems. The mythologizers only multiplied. One in particular, Richard Maurice Bucke, the superintendent of an insane asylum in London, Ontario, made repeated visits to Camden while formulating his theory of cosmic consciousness. It held that select individuals throughout history—Buddha, Shakespeare, Muhammad, Saint Paul, and Walt Whitman—had evolved to a plane higher than the rest of humankind. Bucke was thrilled to discover that the poet existed "in an upper spiritual stratum above all mean thoughts, sordid feelings, earthly harassments. He resembled hardly at all ordinary men, but lived in a different world and was governed by entirely different thoughts and feelings and considerations."

That was of little solace when Whitman had a cold, felt lonely, was exhausted. He pressed on, past loss and recompense and loss again, through the indignities of aging and the pleasures of adulation.

Along the way, he paid one final visit to Pfaff's. On August 16, 1881, during a trip to Manhattan, he stopped by the saloon. The place had moved yet again, this time to 9 West 24th Street, and with the passage of the years it had grown respectable. Pfaff was still the proprietor, rounder now, grayer now, but jolly as ever. Herr Pfaff went and retrieved a bottle of the establishment's finest wine. He poured a glass for Whitman and took a seat across from him. Then they talked about the old times, about that little vaulted room in the Broadway basement, and about the Bohemians, Clapp, Clare, O'Brien, and the rest, most dead, all gone. "Ah, the friends and names and frequenters," marveled Whitman, "those times, that place."

Whitman sat for a pleasant hour, sipping wine and reminiscing. Then the old poet bid farewell to Herr Pfaff. He made his way slowly through the saloon and out into Manhattan, where he was once more amid the throng, the millions, toiling, striving, alive.

ACKNOWLEDGMENTS

"Have you ever heard of Pfaff's saloon?"

I was asked this question by Terry Alford, a history professor at Northern Virginia Community College. My answer: no. So I did some research and was intrigued. After some further digging, I became fascinated. Before I knew it, I was writing a book about Pfaff's and its circle of Bohemian artists. Thanks to an offhand question, I dove into a project that has filled my past two years with focus, passion, challenge, and discovery. Had Dr. Alford not asked me about Pfaff's, I would never have set off on this particular writing journey. From the seed of an idea to bound book, this has been a collaborative process. A whole lot of people helped me along.

It was a pleasure to work yet again with the talented team at Da Capo Press. Publishing is a notoriously transient industry, so it's a rare luxury to be able to rely on the same set of people, book in, book out. Merloyd Lawrence, my editor, has been a tireless champion of this project, which she dubbed "Walt and the rowdies." She helped shape this book, bringing big-picture vision while also lending small, deft touches. Lissa Warren, publicist extraordinaire, works hard—and works magic—getting books much-needed attention in this era of gifs, tweets, and selfies. Thanks to Jonathan Sainsbury for another stunning cover; to Annette Wenda, for another fine-tooth copyediting job; and to Sean Maher for continued marketing expertise. Brent Wilcox and Cindy Young deserve high praise for designing the book's stylish interior. My appreciation to marathon-runner Carolyn Sobczak for moving the book smoothly through production without even breaking a sweat. For his good efforts and support, I also wish to thank my agent, Don Fehr at Trident Media Group.

Another team that I'm thrilled to be part of is the Gotham Biographers Group. This is a small, intimate group; besides me, it consists of eight other writers, and very accomplished ones I might add: Kate Buford, Ina Caro, Betty Boyd Caroli, Gayle Feldman, Anne Heller, Carl Rollyson, Stacy Schiff, and Will Swift. Writing a biography (a group bio, in my case) has its own unique set of challenges. It's a great help—great comfort too—to be able to turn to a circle of writers for advice. Thanks GBG: I've gained so much from our free-flowing, generous-spirited discussions. Guess one might say this is our version of Pfaff's, though decidedly less decadent (we haven't had any drunken fist-fights . . . yet).

While researching this book, I spent a vast amount of time at libraries and archives. I made some great discoveries—and appreciate the help of the many knowledgeable staff members I consulted—at the following places: Brown University's Hay Library, Columbia University's Butler Library, Harvard's Houghton Library, the Library of Congress, New York Public Library, St. John's University library, and Union College's Schaffer Library. I also made use of a couple of excellent online archives that merit mention. The Vault at Pfaff's, maintained by Lehigh University, is an excellent resource, featuring brief biographies of America's first Bohemians and also a complete set of the *Saturday Press*, a hugely influential nineteenth-century journal that is, regrettably, very difficult to find. The Walt Whitman Archive is also superb, as a Web-based repository where it's possible to do everything from scroll page by page through a rare 1855 edition of *Leaves of Grass* to read documents Whitman copied as a clerk in the US Attorney General's office.

As always, I want to thank my parents, Rex and Donna Martin. Officially they are, respectively, a semiretired philosophy professor and a semiretired editor (they also remain about the busiest people I know). While working on this book, I turned to them frequently for their considerable knowledge and expertise. Even more often, I fell back on their unwavering love and understanding. Thanks Mom and Dad! I also want to thank my in-laws, Sylvia Charlesworth and Jerry Kressman, aka Mr. K. Their enthusiasm and support is so appreciated—always gives me a lift.

I'll close with a great big thanks to my wife, Liza Charlesworth, and my twelve-year-old twin sons, Dash and Theo. My household is very active and *very loud*: baseballs fly, electric guitars blare. But my family is also my finest collaboration, and for that I am very grateful.

NOTES

ABBREVIATIONS KEY

CW   *The Collected Writings of Walt Whitman,* a multivolume set published by New York University Press

HTC   Harvard Theatre Collection, Houghton Library, Cambridge, MA

LOC   Library of Congress, Washington, DC

SP   *Saturday Press,* the Vault at Pfaff's digital archive, Lehigh University, Bethlehem, PA

WW   Walt Whitman

WWC   Horace Traubel, *With Walt Whitman in Camden,* vols. 1–9, accessed online at the Walt Whitman Archive

NOTE ON WHITMAN POETRY

Whitman published seven editions of *Leaves of Grass,* a work that evolved over time with changes to poems' titles, changes to syntax, sometimes even changes of wording. With this in mind, I've chosen to reproduce passages that are true to how the poems originally appeared. For example, if I'm quoting from a poem that first appeared in the 1855 edition, I consulted that edition as the source. I relied on the following:

Leaves of Grass (1855): page-by-page photographs of an original printing of the book, accessed online at the Walt Whitman Archive (Brooklyn: Rome Brothers, 1855).

Leaves of Grass (1860): *The 150th Anniversary Facsimile Edition*, edited by Jason Stacy (Iowa City: University of Iowa Press, 2009).

Leaves of Grass (final edition): edited by Sculley Bradley and Harold Blodgett (New York: W. W. Norton, 1973). This is a complete Whitman collection that features all the poems from the "deathbed edition" of 1891–1892, plus some additional annexes of poetry and unpublished works.

INTRODUCTION:
A VISIT TO PFAFF'S

3   **"Pfaff's 'Bohemia' was never":** Thomas Donaldson, *Walt Whitman the Man* (New York: Francis P. Harper, 1896), 208.

CHAPTER 1:
BOHEMIA CROSSES THE ATLANTIC

5   **November 11, 1814:** Clapp genealogical details from Ebenezer Clapp, comp., *The Clapp Memorial: Record of the Clapp Family in America* (Boston: David Clapp & Son, 1876).

5   **The Nantucket of Clapp's youth:** Description of Nantucket in this era from multiple sources, including Nathaniel Philbrick, *In the Heart of the Sea: The Tragedy of the Whaleship* Essex (New York: Penguin Books, 2000).

5   **New England ancestry to 1630:** Clapp, *Clapp Memorial,* 3.

6   **"Spare-the-Rod-spoil-the-Child Academy":** *SP,* November 13, 1858.

6   **Admiral Sir Isaac Coffin:** Details about this school from multiple sources, including Margaret Moore Booker, *The Admiral's Academy: Nantucket Island's Historic Coffin School* (Nantucket, MA: Mill Hill Press, 1998).

6   **Clapp took two voyages:** *Brooklyn Eagle,* May 25, 1884.

6   **"I venture the assertion":** Henry Clapp Jr., *The Pioneer; or, Leaves from an Editor's Portfolio* (Lynn, MA: J. B. Tolman, 1846), 73.

6   **"pacific business, viz:":** Ibid., 46.

7   **"liked to say startling things":** Charles Congdon, *Reminiscences of a Journalist* (Boston: James R. Osgood, 1880), 173.

7   **Clapp was convicted:** *Massachusetts Spy,* April 1, 1846.

7   **"like snapping glass":** William Shepard, ed., *Pen Pictures of Modern Authors* (New York: G. P. Putnam's Sons, 1882), 162.

7   **"a wily creature":** William Lloyd Garrison to Henry Clarke Wright, March 1, 1847, Boston Public Library Anti-Slavery Collection, accessed online.

8   **"faith in man":** Clapp, *The Pioneer,* 5.

8   **In August 1849:** Clapp is listed as an attendee in the *Report of the Proceedings of the Second General Peace Congress* (London: Charles Gilpin, 1849), 99.

8   **"I could say *oui*":** *SP,* November 27, 1858.

8   **The term *Bohemian*:** Discussion of Bohemianism from multiple sources, including Jerrold Siegel, *Bohemian Paris: Culture, Politics, and*

the Boundaries of Bourgeois Life, 1830–1930 (Baltimore: Johns Hopkins University Press, 1986).

9   **"Everything that had an arm":** *SP,* December 4, 1858.

10   **an estimated forty-five hundred cafés:** W. Scott Haine, *The World of the Paris Café: Sociability Among the French Working Class, 1789–1914* (Baltimore: Johns Hopkins University Press, 1996), 3.

10   **"a consistency between a liquid":** *SP,* January 8, 1859.

10   **"Thank you, gentlemen":** *SP,* November 20, 1858.

11   **"secured a nice little nook":** *SP,* December 25, 1858.

12   **The unlikely catalyst was Henry Murger:** Portrait of Murger from multiple sources, including Malcolm Easton, *Artists and Writers in Paris: The Bohemian Idea, 1803–1867* (London: Edward Arnold, 1964).

13   **"The public is being moved":** Robert Baldick, *The First Bohemian: The Life of Henry Murger* (London: Hamish Hamilton, 1961), 124.

13   **"Everything is, so to speak":** Ibid., 125.

14   **"La Bohème, c'est nous":** Théodore Barrière and Henry Murger, *La vie de Bohème* (Paris: Calmann Lévy, 1878), 11.

14   **"Oh, my youth":** Ibid., 104.

15   **"Temperance secured for us":** *SP,* December 11, 1858.

15   **"more good sense":** *SP,* January 1, 1859.

15   **"There was a charm":** *SP,* January 8, 1859.

16   **returned to America late in 1853:** Several sources agree on this date, including Mark Lause, *The Antebellum Crisis and America's First Bohemians* (Kent, OH: Kent State University Press, 2009), 17.

CHAPTER 2:
A LONG TABLE IN A VAULTED ROOM

17   **In 1856 he happened upon:** Multiple sources agree on this date, including Rufus Rockwell Wilson, *New York in Literature: The Story Told in the Landmarks of Town and Country* (Elmira, NY: Primavera Press, 1947), 63.

17   **located elsewhere on Broadway:** For the year 1856, *Wilson's Business Directory of New York City* lists Pfaff's at 683 Broadway.

17   **No. 647, a few doors north:** For address, see advertisements in *Saturday Press* such as September 24, 1859.

18   **possible to get a full meal:** Discussion of Pfaff's fare and drinks from multiple sources, including *New York Times,* April 26, 1890.

19   **"one of the first men":** *Philadelphia Inquirer,* November 27, 1892.

19   **very first recruit was Fitz-James O'Brien:** Wilson, *New York in Literature,* 63.

19   **There was no better choice:** Description of O'Brien from multiple sources, including Francis Wolle, *Fitz-James O'Brien: A Literary Bohemian of the Eighteen-Fifties* (Boulder: University of Colorado Studies, 1944).

21   **"Haste is evident":** *Critic,* February 26, 1881.

21   **"No American writer":** *New York Tribune,* March 6, 1881.

22   **"a certain kind of magnetism":** Junius Henri Browne, *The Great Metropolis: A Mirror of New York* (Hartford, CT: American, 1869), 152.

22   **among the early notables:** Descriptions of Charles Halpine, George Arnold, and Thomas Nast from multiple sources, including *The Vault at Pfaff's: An Archive of Art and Literature by New York City's Nineteenth-Century Bohemians,* maintained online by Lehigh University.

22   **Halpine regularly amazed:** Description of his inspired stuttering from Louis Starr, *Bohemian Brigade: Civil War Newsmen in Action* (New York: Alfred A. Knopf, 1954), 9.

22   **"Here, / With my beer":** *SP,* January 1, 1859.

23   **"altogether the most showy":** *Putnam's* magazine quoted in the New York Public Libraries Online Exhibition Archive.

23   **"Saints and sinners":** Browne, *Great Metropolis,* 341.

24   **The heart of Broadway:** Description of Broadway from multiple sources, including David Dunlap, *On Broadway: A Journey Uptown over Time* (New York: Rizzoli, 1990).

24   **Mary Todd Lincoln:** Edwin Burrows and Mike Wallace, *Gotham: A History of New York City to 1898* (New York: Oxford University Press, 1999), 878.

24   **"'I lodge in Bleecker street'":** Browne, *Great Metropolis,* 379.

25   **found himself *on the rock*:** Details about O'Brien's desperation from multiple sources, including William Winter, *Old Friends: Being Literary Recollections of Other Days* (New York: Moffat, Yard, 1909).

26   **"One of Harper's Authors":** Eugene Lalor, "The Literary Bohemians of New York City in the Mid-Nineteenth Century" (PhD diss., St. John's University, 1976), 29.

26   **"Just at that period death":** William Winter, ed., *The Poems and Stories of Fitz-James O'Brien* (Boston: James R. Osgood, 1881), lv.

27   **"born, like Baudelaire":** Joseph Wood Krutch, *Edgar Allan Poe: A Study in Genius* (New York: Alfred A. Knopf, 1926), 192.

27   **dedicated area in his lager house:** Description of Pfaff's vaulted room from multiple sources, including *Philadelphia Inquirer,* November 27, 1892.

28   **"King of Bohemia":** Albert Parry, *Garrets and Pretenders: A History of Bohemianism in America* (New York: Covici, Friede, 1933), 44.

28   **"Cater-wall Street":** Ibid., 45.

28   **"aimed at nothing":** Mark Antony de Wolfe Howe, *Memories of a Hostess* (Boston: Atlantic Monthly Press, 1922), 185.

28   **"spied the intruder":** *American Magazine,* January 1896.

29   **"never spared each other":** Winter, *Old Friends,* 96.

29   **"Those were merry and famous nights":** Browne, *Great Metropolis,* 156.

29   **"of quip, and quirk":** *SP,* December 3, 1859.

CHAPTER 3:
WHITMAN AT A CROSSROADS

31   **likely sometime in 1858:** While some accounts date Whitman's first appearance at Pfaff's to 1859, others say he first showed up there in 1858. There is convincing evidence for 1858, such as a *Brooklyn Daily Times* article he wrote that year that shows familiarity with Bohemianism. See Emory Holloway, *Free and Lonesome Heart: The Secret of Walt Whitman* (New York: Vantage Press, 1960), 88.

31   **"greatest poet":** *Leaves of Grass* (1855), v, reproduction of an original printing, accessed online at the Walt Whitman Archive.

32   **"as good talk around the table":** *Brooklyn Daily Eagle,* July 11, 1886.

32   **"rubbing and drubbing":** *WWC,* 3:116.

32   **"My own greatest pleasure":** Ibid., 1:417.

32   **"That's the feller!":** William Winter, *Old Friends: Being Literary Recollections of Other Days* (New York: Moffat, Yard, 1909), 91.

32   **"The ravishing charm":** Ibid.

33   **"I have often said":** *WWC,* 2:375.

33   **Born in 1819:** Account of Whitman's early years from multiple sources, including Gay Wilson Allen, *The Solitary Singer: A Critical Biography of Walt Whitman* (Chicago: University of Chicago Press, 1955).

34   **"To cure a tooth ache":** WW quoted in the *Atlantic,* November 1903.

34   **"honorable nonsense":** Ibid.

36   ***bender, bummer, spree,* and *shin-dig*:** Terms from Whitman's *Primer of Words* mentioned in Justin Kaplan, *Walt Whitman: A Life* (New York: Perennial, 1979), 229.

36   **Phrenology is a pseudoscientific theory:** Description of phrenology from multiple sources, including David Reynolds, *Walt Whitman's America: A Cultural Biography* (New York: Vintage Books, 1995).

37   **"Know thyself":** "The Fowler Brothers" at Harvard.edu, accessed online.

37   **gallery of plaster casts:** Advertisement for Fowler & Wells in *Wilson's Business Directory of New York City* (1850), v.

37   **Whitman rated an exemplary 6.5:** Details of WW's phrenological reading from *Leaves of Grass,* 1856 edition (Brooklyn, 1856), 362, reproduction of an original printing, accessed online at the Walt Whitman Archive.

38   **"great pressure, pressure from within":** Allen, *Solitary Singer,* 147.

38   **"adjudged already to deserve":** *CW, Notebooks and Unpublished Prose Manuscripts,* 5:1744.

38   **"the gush, the throb":** *WWC,* 2:25.

38   **"wrote, rewrote, and re-rewrote":** John Trowbridge, *My Own Story* (Boston: Houghton Mifflin, 1903), 367.

38   **"the book arose out of my life":** Curtis Hidden Page, ed., *The Chief American Poets* (Boston: Houghton Mifflin, 1905), 686.

38   **a treble entendre:** Notion that "leaves of grass" is a treble entendre from multiple sources, including Jerome Loving, *Walt Whitman: The Song of Himself* (Berkeley: University of California Press, 1999), 179.

39   **"The proof of a poet":** *Leaves* (1855), xii.

39   **"Do I contradict myself?":** Ibid., 55.

40   **selling 30,000 copies:** Matthew Bevis, ed., *The Oxford Handbook of Victorian Poetry* (Oxford: Oxford University Press, 2013), 783.

40   **to sell 300,000 copies:** Reynolds, *Walt Whitman's America,* 315.

40   **"a curious and lawless":** *Putnam's,* September 1855.

40   **"There is neither wit":** *Boston Intelligencer,* May 3, 1856.

40   **"Walt Whitman is as unacquainted":** *Critic,* quoted in *Leaves* (1856), 375.

41   **"I am not blind":** Ralph Waldo Emerson to Whitman, July 21, 1855, quoted in ibid., 345.

41   **"an emperor":** George Rice Carpenter, *Walt Whitman* (New York: Macmillan, 1909), 76.

41   **"The writer shall not dig":** James Elliot Cabot, *A Memoir of Ralph Waldo Emerson* (Boston: Houghton Mifflin, 1890), 2:450.

41   **a "cold, fastidious" person:** Emerson to Thomas Carlyle, July 31, 1841, in *The Correspondence of Thomas Carlyle and Ralph Waldo Emerson, 1834–1872* (Boston: Houghton Mifflin, 1899), 1:366.

42   **"the courtly muses of Europe":** *The American Scholar: An Address Delivered by Ralph Waldo Emerson Before the Phi Beta Kappa Society at Cambridge, August 1837* (New York: Laurentian Press, 1901), 56.

42   **"He shouted for a 'tin mug'":** Edward Carpenter, *Days with Walt Whitman* (New York: Macmillan 1908), 167.

43   **"Here are thirty-two Poems":** *Leaves* (1856), 346.

43   **overcome with hot passion:** Ted Genoways, *Walt Whitman and the Civil War* (Berkeley: University of California Press, 2009), 29.

43   **"Every thing I have done":** *CW, Notebooks and Unpublished Prose Manuscripts,* 1:167.

44   **"not become famous yet":** Elihu Vedder, *The Digressions of V.* (Boston: Houghton Mifflin, 1911), 226.

44   **"I don't know if ":** *WWC,* 3:118.

45   **"I like your tinkles":** Winter, *Old Friends,* 140.

45   **"bovine air of omniscience":** Ibid., 141.

45   **"Willy is a young Longfellow":** Albert Parry, *Garrets and Pretenders: A History of Bohemianism in America* (New York: Covici, Friede, 1933), 41.

45   **"It is now time to *stir*":** Allen, *Solitary Singer,* 216.

45   **"eats dirt and excrement":** Justin Kaplan, ed., *Walt Whitman: Poetry and Prose* (New York: Library of America, 1982), 1310.

46   **"I would be much pleased":** Ibid., 1308.

46   **"wander-speaker":** *CW, Notebooks and Unpublished Prose Manuscripts,* 4:1554.

46   **"I desire to go by degrees":** Allen, *Solitary Singer,* 219.

46   **"henceforth my employment":** Ibid.

46   **"What wit, humor, repartee":** Thomas Donaldson, *Walt Whitman the Man* (New York: Francis P. Harper, 1896), 208.

CHAPTER 4:
HASHISH AND SHAKESPEARE

47   **"We were all very merry":** *SP,* December 24, 1859.

48   **James Buchanan was president:** Description of Buchanan from multiple sources, including James Taranto, ed., *Presidential Leadership: Rating the Best and Worst in the White House* (New York: Wall Street Journal Books, 2004).

48   **A particularly deranged episode:** Description of February 5, 1858, melee in Congress from multiple sources, including James McPherson, *Battle Cry of Freedom* (New York: Oxford University Press, 1988), 168.

49   **Buchanan, arguably the worst:** Assertion from multiple sources, including *US News & World Report,* July 13, 2010, which ranks Buchanan as the worst.

49   **Dred Scott, often considered the nadir:** Assertion from multiple sources, including Ethan Greenberg, *Dred Scott and the Dangers of a Political Court* (Lanham, MD: Lexington Books, 2009).

49   **"hot passions" and "inertia":** *CW, Prose Works, 1892,* 2:498.

49   **"What historic denouements":** Justin Kaplan, ed., *Walt Whitman: Poetry and Prose* (New York: Library of America, 1982), 1325.

49   **"some great emergency":** *CW, Notebooks and Unpublished Prose Manuscripts,* 4:1554.

50   **"overcharged Leyden jar":** Fred Pattee, *The Feminine Fifties* (New York: D. Appleton–Century, 1940), 4.

50   **a formidable conversationalist:** Description of Ludlow's conversational powers from multiple sources, including *New York Evening Mail,* December 24, 1870.

51   **"the smartest and most learned boy":** Donald Dulchinos, *Pioneer of Inner Space: The Life of Fitz Hugh Ludlow* (New York: Autonomedia, 1998), 25.

51   **"childhood's sweetest flavor":** *Golden Era,* November 22, 1863.

51   **"Fitz Hugh, I mean you":** Andrew Shores, "Fitz Hugh Ludlow, a Biography" (Union College, June 1980), 6.

51   **"whole gamut of queer agents":** Fitz Hugh Ludlow, *The Hasheesh Eater: Being Passages from the Life of a Pythagorean* (New York: Harper & Brothers, 1857), 17.

51   **"When the circuit":** Ibid., 17.

52   **"A most pleasurable and harmless":** *Harper's,* October 16, 1858.

52   **what he called a "bolus":** Ludlow, *Hasheesh Eater,* 19.

52   **"I am in eternity":** Ibid., 33.

52   **eat cayenne pepper:** Helen Ludlow, sketch about her brother Fitz Hugh, Special Collections, Union College Schaffer Library.

53   **"The Nile! The Nile!":** Ludlow, *Hasheesh Eater,* 93.

53   **"Life became with me":** Ibid., 196.

53   **he was fined $1.12:** Dulchinos, *Pioneer of Inner Space,* 44.

53   **"hot and hissing whisper":** Ludlow, *The Hasheesh Eater,* 125.

53   **"unseen tongues syllabled":** Ibid., 125.

53   **"Slowly thus does midnight":** Ibid., 202.

53   **"like a heavy tragedy":** Ibid., 86.

54   **"research," not "indulgence":** Ibid., 17.

54   **"For me, henceforth, Time":** Dulchinos, *Pioneer of Inner Space,* 90.

54   **"and Johnny must needs experiment":** William Roscoe Thayer, *The Life and Letters of John Hay* (Boston: Houghton Mifflin, 1915), 1:47.

55   **"where I used to eat Hasheesh":** John Hay, *A Poet in Exile: Early Letters of John Hay* (Boston: Houghton Mifflin, 1910), 23.

55   **went through three printings:** Publishing details of *The Hasheesh Eater* from Dulchinos, *Pioneer of Inner Space,* 90.

55   **"Her form, the freshly blossomed":** Fitz Hugh Ludlow, "Our Queer Papa," *Harper's New Monthly Magazine,* November 1858.

55   **"slight, bright-eyed, alert":** *Harper's New Monthly Magazine,* December 1870.

56   **Ludlow began to secretly dabble:** Helen Ludlow to Rev. Leander Hall, June 1, 1876, Special Collections, Union College Schaffer Library.

56   **During the autumn of 1858:** Gene Smith, *American Gothic: The Story of America's Legendary Theatrical Family—Junius, Edwin, and John Wilkes Booth* (New York: Simon & Schuster, 1992), 70.

56   **The elder Booth:** Description of Junius Brutus Booth from multiple sources, including Eleanor Ruggles, *Prince of Players: Edwin Booth* (New York: W. W. Norton, 1953).

57   **"His genius was to me":** *CW, Prose Works, 1892,* 2:597.

58   **"You see before you":** James Cross Giblin, *Good Brother, Bad Brother: The Story of Edwin Booth & John Wilkes Booth* (New York: Clarion Books, 2005), 23.

58   **"Come see Edwin Booth":** Ibid., 47.

59   **"I think I am a little quieter":** Otis Skinner, *The Last Tragedian: Booth Tells His Own Story* (New York: Dodd, Mead, 1939), 8.

59   **"I was neglected":** Ibid., 84.

59   **"Mr. Booth, who was cast":** Stanley Kimmel, *The Mad Booths of Maryland* (New York: Dover, 1969), 122.

59   **called his friend a "splendid savage":** Ruggles, *Prince of Players,* 127.

59   **"I wish I could write":** Skinner, *Last Tragedian,* 92.

60   **John was five years younger:** Description of John Wilkes Booth as a boy from multiple sources, including Asia Booth Clarke, *John Wilkes Booth: A Sister's Memoir* (Jackson: University Press of Mississippi, 1996).

60   **"loved of the Southern people":** Ibid., 77.

60   **"I must have fame, fame!":** Gordon Samples, *Lust for Fame: The Stage Career of John Wilkes Booth* (Jefferson, NC: McFarland, 1982), 20.

61   **"There was that touch":** Ibid., 7.

61   **He took up with a militia:** John Wilkes Booth at John Brown's hanging from multiple sources, including Michael Kauffman, *American Brutus: John Wilkes Booth and the Lincoln Conspiracies* (New York: Random House, 2004).

61   **"I John Brown":** Tony Horwitz, *Midnight Rising: John Brown and the Raid That Sparked the Civil War* (New York: Henry Holt, 2011), 256.

62   **"Poor Walt!":** *WWC,* 1:237.

CHAPTER 5:
BOLD WOMEN AND WHITMAN'S BEAUTIFUL BOYS

63   **spots exclusively for women:** Discussion of these from multiple sources, including Edwin Burrows and Mike Wallace, *Gotham: A History of New York City to 1898* (New York: Oxford University Press, 1999).

64   **purchase a "growler":** Christine Sismondo, *America Walks into a Bar: A Spirited History of Taverns and Saloons, Speakeasies, and Grog Shops* (New York: Oxford University Press, 2011), 222.

64   **A lady's entrance:** *History Today,* February 1995.

64   **calling it "Stag-Nation":** *SP,* September 2, 1865.

65   **Clare was born:** Account of her youth from multiple sources, including Gloria Goldblatt, "Ada Clare: Queen of Bohemia" (unpublished manuscript, 1990, Billy Rose Theatre Collection, New York Public Library for the Performing Arts).

65   **Ada Agnes McElhenney:** While most accounts claim that her birth name was Jane McElhenney, it was Ada Agnes McElhenney, according to an authoritative account, ibid.

65   **"a series of little acts":** Ibid., 22.

66   **"one of the most beautiful":** Albert Parry, *Garrets and Pretenders: A History of Bohemianism in America* (New York: Covici, Friede, 1933), 17.

66   **"evil influences":** *American Magazine,* January 1896.

66   **"a tyrant and slayer":** *SP,* November 17, 1860.

66   **"a frankness of speech":** Goldblatt, "Ada Clare," iv.

66   **"right nose for a trim":** Charles Warren Stoddard, "Ada Clare, Queen of Bohemia," *National Magazine,* September 1905.

67   **"an amiable audience":** Louis Moreau Gottschalk, *Notes of a Pianist* (Philadelphia: J. B. Lippincott, 1881), 240.

67   **"the most charming types":** Ibid., 287.

67   **"Miss Ada Clare and son":** *National Magazine,* September 1905.

68   **"I thought I was an oracle":** *SP,* July 16, 1859.

68   **"Remember me while I":** Francis Wolle, *Fitz-James O'Brien: A Literary Bohemian of the Eighteen-Fifties* (Boulder: University of Colorado Studies, 1944), 130.

68   **"It was an immaculate":** Goldblatt, "Ada Clare," iv.

68   **summer of 1859:** Multiple sources cite this as the date of Menken's first visit to Pfaff's, including Mark Lause, *The Antebellum Crisis and America's First Bohemians* (Kent, OH: Kent State University Press, 2009), 57.

68   **Clare gets credit:** Goldblatt, "Ada Clare," 111.

69   ***Dolores Adios Los Fuertes:*** Bernard Falk, *The Naked Lady: Life Story of Adah Menken* (London: Hutchinson, 1934), 24.

69   ***granddaughter of a Revolutionary War hero:*** *New York Times,* September 6, 1868.

69   ***orphan in a convent:*** Wolf Mankowitz, *Mazeppa: The Lives, Loves, and Legends of Adah Isaacs Menken* (London: Blond & Briggs, 1982), 13.

69   ***She translated the "Iliad":*** Richard Northcott, *Adah Isaacs Menken: An Illustrated Biography* (London: Press Printers, 1921), 5.

69   **"She speaks French, Spanish":** *Wisconsin Daily Patriot,* May 2, 1860.

69   **Marie Rachel Adelaide:** *New York Times,* September 6, 1868.

69   **June 15, 1835:** Multiple accounts agree, including the most authoritative Menken biography, Michael Foster and Barbara Foster, *A Dangerous Woman: The Life, Loves, and Scandals of Adah Isaacs Menken* (Guilford, CT: Lyons Press, 2011).

70   **a bareback rider:** Ibid., 21.

71   ***"Will* He *never come?":*** Gregory Eiselein, ed., *Infelicia, and Other Writings: Adah Isaacs Menken* (Peterborough, Ontario: Broadview Press, 2002), 130.

71   **"She is a sensitive poet":** Jewish Virtual Library, accessed online.

72   **"Adah was a symbol":** Article by R. H. Newell, publication and date unknown, Brown University, John Hay Library, Special Collections.

72   **"A woman of personal attractions":** James Murdock, *The Stage* (Philadelphia: J. M. Stoddart, 1880), 286.

72   **"full of southern passion":** Alan Lloyd, *The Great Prize Fight* (London: Souvenir Press, 1977), 2.

73   **"The girls have been":** *WWC,* 3:117.

74   **"no inconsiderable share":** Walt Whitman, *New York Dissected* (New York: Rufus Rockwell Wilson, 1936), 131.

74   **in separate compartments:** For a thoughtful discussion of how the two separate rooms at Pfaff's mirror the divisions Whitman maintained in his personal life, see Karen Karbiener's essay "Whitman at Pfaff's," published in *Literature of New York,* edited by Sabrina Fuchs Abrams (Newcastle upon Tyne, UK: Cambridge Scholars, 2009).

74   **"the shrine to which":** Parry, *Garrets and Pretenders,* 17.

74   **"There was no formality":** Thomas Donaldson, *Walt Whitman the Man* (New York: Francis P. Harper, 1896), 208.

74   **Café Lafitte in Exile:** Discussion of history of gay bars from multiple sources, including Sismondo, *America Walks into a Bar.*

75   **two men even lived together:** Fred Vaughan to WW, November 16, 1874, WW Papers, Charles E. Feinberg Collection, LOC.

75   **one of the people he showed it to:** Ibid.

76   **"I never stole, robbed, cheated":** Fred Vaughan to WW, undated letter believed to be from the early 1870s, WW Papers, Feinberg Collection, LOC.

76   **"My love my Walt":** Fred Vaughan to WW, November 16, 1874, WW Papers, Feinberg Collection, LOC.

76   **group of young men that included Fred Gray:** Some accounts of Whitman's life represent this group as more formal than it was, referring to it as the "Fred Gray Association." This is based on a misinterpretation of a letter Whitman wrote in which he referred to "my friends of Fred Gray association" (lower case *association*). See WW to William O'Connor, September 11, 1864, in *CW, The Correspondence,* 1:241.

76   **described them as "beautiful":** *CW, Notebooks and Unpublished Prose Manuscripts,* 1:454.

76   **"quiet lambent electricity":** WW to Hugo Fritsch, October 8, 1863, *CW, The Correspondence,* 1:158.

76   **"my darlings and gossips":** WW to Nathaniel Bloom and Fred Gray, March 19, 1863, ibid., 82.

76   **"my darling, dearest boys":** Ibid., 84.

76   **"the unconscious, uncultured, natural types":** Edward Carpenter, *Days with Walt Whitman* (New York: Macmillan, 1908), 67.

77   **"Tom Egbert, conductor":** *CW, Notebooks and Unpublished Prose Manuscripts,* 2:481.

77   **"Mark Graynor, young":** Ibid., 489.

77   **"Saturday night Mike Ellis":** Ibid., 1:454.

77   **"Dan'l Spencer . . . ":** Ibid., 2:487.

CHAPTER 6:
THE *SATURDAY PRESS*

80   **"next door to the *Saturday Press*":** *SP,* August 27, 1859.

80   **Boston remained the nation's cultural capital:** Discussion from multiple sources, including Stephen Puleo, *A City So Grand: The Rise of an American Metropolis, Boston, 1850–1900* (Boston: Beacon Press, 2004).

80 **"It was impossible to fire":** Elizabeth Webber and Mike Feinsilber, *Merriam-Webster's Dictionary of Allusions* (Springfield, MA: Merriam-Webster, 1999), 31.

81 **The *Atlantic* was "born mature":** Van Wyck Brooks, *The Flowering of New England, 1815–1865* (New York: E. P. Dutton, 1936), 484.

81 **according to one count:** Frank Luther Mott, *A History of American Magazines, 1850–1865* (Cambridge, MA: Harvard University Press, 1957), 495.

81 **"conversation set in":** M. A. DeWolfe Howe, *The "Atlantic Monthly" and Its Makers* (Boston: Atlantic Monthly Press, 1919), 23.

81 **"firm but courteous":** Mark Lause, *The Antebellum Crisis and America's First Bohemians* (Kent, OH: Kent State University Press, 2009), 78.

81 **"will not rank itself":** *Atlantic Monthly,* November 1857.

81 **"He was brilliant and buoyant":** William Winter, *Old Friends: Being Literary Recollections of Other Days* (New York: Moffat, Yard, 1909), 58.

82 **"often sparkled with wit":** Junius Henri Browne, *The Great Metropolis: A Mirror of New York* (Hartford, CT: American, 1869), 58.

82 **"the organ of Bohemia":** *Philadelphia Express* quoted in *SP,* December 31, 1859.

82 **"I had not seen":** *SP,* November 13, 1858.

82 **"prince would most undoubtedly":** *SP,* January 1, 1859.

83 **"Ode to a Tobacco Pipe":** Ibid.

83 **"Beer":** *SP,* January 1, 1859.

83 **"All of Washington's greatness":** *SP,* June 16, 1860.

83 **"The Bohemian was by nature":** *SP,* February 11, 1860.

84 **"The number of things":** *SP,* January 14, 1860.

84 **"the great body of men":** *SP,* March 17, 1860.

84 **"There is a horribly pernicious":** *SP,* May 19, 1860.

85 **"a specimen of what":** *SP,* May 28, 1859.

85 **"wasted two hours":** Lause, *The Antebellum Crisis,* 78.

85 **"New York is such":** *SP,* July 21, 1860.

85 **"A most frightful mass":** *SP,* July 7, 1860.

86 **"The December [1858] number":** *SP,* December 25, 1858.

86 **he called "fresh blood":** Laura Stedman and George Gould, *Life and Letters of Edmund Clarence Stedman* (New York: Moffat, Yard, 1910), 2:208.

87 **"Go to Pfaff's!"** *SP,* September 24, 1859.

87 **"'Twas the voice":** Winter, *Old Friends,* 294.

88 **"You may not know it":** *SP,* October 29, 1859.

88 **"Men of an indomitable":** *Harper's New Monthly Magazine,* October 1859.

88 **"The true Bohemian":** *New York Times,* January 6, 1858.

89 **"This is the capital":** *Boston Saturday Express* article reprinted in *SP,* December 3, 1859.

90 **"It is not too much":** William Dean Howells, *Literary Friends and Acquaintences: A Personal Retrospect of American Authorship* (New York: Harper & Brothers, 1917), 70.

90 **"The thought of Boston":** Ibid., 71.

90 **"Oh, a couple of shysters":** Ibid.

90 **"I felt that as":** Ibid., 72.

91 **"We were joined by":** Ibid., 72–73.

91 **"I did not know":** Ibid., 74.

91 **published in an 1895 *Harper's*:** The material cited above that Howells used in his book *Literary Friends and Acquaintances* first appeared in his article for *Harper's New Monthly Magazine,* June 1895.

92 **"Answering, the sea":** Note that the passage reprinted in this book is meant to be identical to how the poem appeared in the *Saturday Press* of December 24, 1859. Subsequent versions, from other Whitman editions, may differ slightly in terms of line breaks, punctuation, and spacing.

CHAPTER 7:
LEAVES, THIRD EDITION

95 **"Dear Sir. We want":** Thayer & Eldridge to WW, February 10, 1860, WW Papers, Charles E. Feinberg Collection, LOC.

95 **The firm Thayer & Eldridge**: Description from multiple sources, including Albert von Frank's essay "The Secret World of Radical Publishers: The Case of Thayer and Eldridge of Boston," in *Boston's Histories: Essays in Honor of Thomas H. O'Connor* (Boston: Northeastern University Press, 2004).

96 **They signed her right up:** Gloria Goldblatt, "Ada Clare: Queen of Bohemia" (unpublished manuscript, 1990, Billy Rose Theatre Collection, New York Public Library for the Performing Arts), 137.

96 **more like York Minster cathedral:** Justin Kaplan, *Walt Whitman: A Life* (New York: Perennial, 1979), 230.

96 **"inchoates," as he put it, or "little pittance editions":** *SP,* January 7, 1860.

97 **"Founding a new American Religion":** *CW, Notebooks and Unpublished Prose Manuscripts,* 6:2046.

97 **"Shall I make":** Kaplan, *Walt Whitman,* 228.

98   **Within a month:** Details of Whitman's Boston stay from multiple sources, including Ted Genoways, *Walt Whitman and the Civil War: America's Poet During the Lost Years of 1860–1862* (Berkeley: University of California Press, 2009).

98   **The typefaces for the volume:** Ed Folsom, "Whitman Making Books/ Books Making Whitman: A Catalog and Commentary," accessed online at the Walt Whitman Archive.

98   **Whitman's clusters mirror:** For astute analysis on WW's compartmentalized life and how that affected his poetry, see Karen Karbiener's essay "Whitman at Pfaff's," published in *Literature of New York,* edited by Sabrina Fuchs Abrams (Newcastle upon Tyne, UK: Cambridge Scholars, 2009).

99   **"The printers and foremen":** WW to Jeff Whitman, May 10, 1860, *CW, The Correspondence,* 1:52.

99   **"seems to me":** WW to Jeff Whitman, April 1, 1860, ibid., 51.

99   **"I quite long for it":** Jeff Whitman to WW, April 3, 1860, ibid., 51.

100   **"Moral Sentiment":** Genoways, *Walt Whitman and the Civil War,* 28.

100   **As the two men strolled:** Details of WW's walk with Emerson from multiple sources, including the *Conservator,* May 1896.

100   **"It was an argument-statement":** *Critic,* December 3, 1881.

100   **"I need not say":** Henry Clapp Jr. to WW, March 27, 1860, WW Papers, Feinberg Collection, LOC.

101   **"What I can do for it":** Clapp to WW, May 12, 1860, printed in *WWC,* 4:196.

101   **"Emerson's face always seemed":** *WWC,* 2:105–106.

101   **"great hopes of Whitman":** Clara Barrus, *Whitman and Burroughs: Comrades* (Boston: Houghton Mifflin, 1931), 38.

101   **"7 cents for a cup":** WW to Jeff Whitman, May 10, 1860, *CW, The Correspondence,* 1:53.

101   **"For when Father Taylor":** *CW, Prose Works, 1892,* 2:551.

102   **"physiognomies, forms, dress, gait":** Ibid.

102   **One other notable event:** Details of Sanborn extradition hearing and WW's attendance at the event from multiple sources, including *Boston's Histories: Essays in Honor of Thomas H. O'Connor* (Boston: Northeastern University Press, 2004).

102   **"wearing his loose jacket":** Ibid., 60.

102   **The official publication date:** Genoways, *Walt Whitman and the Civil War,* 41.

103   **"love-flesh swelling":** *Leaves of Grass* (1860), 295.

103   **"slow rude muscle":** Ibid., 303.

103 **"delirious juice" and "limitless limpid jets":** Ibid., 295.

103 **"bellies pressed and glued":** Ibid., 305.

104 **"One flitting glimpse":** Ibid., 371.

105 **"essentially the greatest poem":** *Leaves of Grass* (1855), iii, repro-duction of an original printing, accessed online at the Walt Whitman Archive.

105 **"And a shrill song":** *Leaves of Grass* (1860), 10.

105 **"States! Were you looking":** Ibid., 349.

105 **"Inextricable lands! the clutched together!":** Ibid., 18.

105 **"Smut in Them":** *Springfield (MA) Daily Republican,* June 16, 1860, accessed online at the Whitman Archive.

105 **"Walt. Whitman's Dirty Book":** *Cincinnati Commercial,* November 29, 1860.

105 **"Mr. Whitman sees nothing vulgar":** *New York Times,* May 19, 1860.

106 **"Why, these 'poems'":** *Boston Wide World,* December 8, 1860, accessed online at the Whitman Archive.

106 **drunk in a "cellar":** *Westminster Review,* October 1, 1860, accessed on-line at the Whitman Archive.

106 **"Clapp seemed almost":** Frances Winwar, *American Giant* (New York: Harper and Bros., 1941), 228.

106 **"little Willie, weakest":** Van Wyck Brooks, *The Times of Melville and Whitman* (New York: E. P. Dutton, 1947), 213.

106 **"that odoriferous classic":** William Winter, *Old Friends: Being Literary Recollections of Other Days* (New York: Moffat, Yard, 1909), 89.

107 **"I celebrate the Fourth":** *SP,* July 7, 1860.

107 **"I Happify Myself":** *SP,* June 2, 1860.

108 **"Henry was right":** *WWC,* 1:237.

CHAPTER 8:
YEAR OF METEORS

109 **For Adah Menken:** Update of Menken's 1860 activities from multi-ple sources, including Michael Foster and Barbara Foster, *A Dangerous Woman: The Life, Loves, and Scandals of Adah Isaacs Menken* (Guilford, CT: Lyons Press, 2011).

110 **The sport was especially:** Details about bare-fisted boxing from multi-ple sources, including Alan Lloyd, *The Great Prize Fight* (London: Sou-venir Press, 1977).

111 **On January 4, high noon:** *New York Times,* January 4, 1860.

111 **"Spirits, porter, gross feeding":** *Fistiana; or, The Oracle of the Ring* (London: Wm. Clement, 1841), 93.

111   **called slaveholders "tyrannical":** Hinton Helper, *The Impending Crisis of the South: How to Meet It* (New York: A. B. Burdick, 1860), 25.

111   **"lords of the lash":** Ibid., 43.

111   **"The first and most sacred":** Ibid., 27.

112   **"We want negroes cheap":** Eric Walther, *William Lowndes Yancey: The Coming of the Civil War* (Chapel Hill: University of North Carolina Press, 2006), 217.

113   **"I pronounce the gentleman":** *The Congressional Globe: The Debates and Proceedings,* 36th Cong., 1st sess. (Washington, DC: Office of John C. Rives, 1860), 1032.

113   **"Every man in both houses":** James Hammond to Francis Lieber, April 19, 1860, letter printed in *The Life and Letters of Francis Lieber,* edited by Thomas Sergeant Perry (Boston: James R. Osgood, 1882), 310.

114   **"The sporting fraternity talk":** *Plattsburgh (NY) Republican,* February 4, 1860.

114   **"Commonplace people and commonplace events":** *New-York Illus-trated News,* March 17, 1860.

114   **referred to Menken as "Mrs. Heenan":** WW to Henry Clapp Jr., June 12, 1860, *CW, The Correspondence,* 1:55.

115   **"an elephant for fifty quid":** Lloyd, *Great Prize Fight,* 25.

115   **During the early rounds:** Round-by-round account from multiple sources, including 1860 story from *Bell's Life,* a British sporting jour-nal, reprinted in Bob Mee, *Bare Fists* (Woodstock, NY: Overlook Press, 2001), 149–160.

116   **"Tom got a hot 'un":** From *Bell's Life* story reprinted in Mee, *Bare Fists,* 153.

118   **"a little faster than":** *New York Herald,* July 20, 1860.

118   **"like two chariots of fire":** *New York Post,* July 21, 1860.

118   **earth-grazing meteor procession:** Scientific details and details about the rarity of these events from Don Olson, physics professor, Texas State University–San Marcos, e-mail exchange with author, January 29, 2014.

118   **"most sublime spectacle":** *New York Herald,* July 22, 1860.

118   **"A Forerunner of Ruin?":** *Philadelphia Inquirer,* July 23, 1860.

118   **"Year of Meteors":** *Leaves of Grass* (final edition), 238–239.

119   **Abraham Lincoln was elected:** Account of 1860 election from multi-ple sources, including David Potter, *The Impending Crisis: America Be-fore the Civil War, 1848–1861* (New York: Harper Colophon, 1976).

120   **"*We* can make it *pay*":** Thayer & Eldridge to WW, August 17, 1860, WW Papers, Charles E. Feinberg Collection, LOC.

120 **"All that is wanted":** *SP,* November 10, 1860.

120 **"a scrape the horror":** Henry Clapp Jr. to WW, March 27, 1860, printed in *WWC,* 1:237.

120 **"We go by the board":** William Thayer to WW, December 5, 1860, WW Papers, Feinberg Collection, LOC.

120 **costly to Ada Clare:** Gloria Goldblatt, "Ada Clare: Queen of Bohemia" (unpublished manuscript, 1990, Billy Rose Theatre Collection, New York Public Library for the Performing Arts), 137–138.

121 **"in a rocket way":** WW to Jeff Whitman, May 10, 1860, *CW, The Correspondence,* 1:52.

121 **Lincoln made a stopover:** Lincoln's visit to New York was in February 1861. But the event seems to fit properly in this chapter since it occurred during those nervous months before the Civil War began.

122 **"a capital view of it all":** *CW, Prose Works, 1892,* 2:500–501.

122 **"Two characters as / of a Dialogue":** *CW, Notebooks and Unpublished Prose Manuscripts,* 1:436.

123 **estimated at fifty thousand:** *New York Daily Tribune,* August 14, 1860.

123 **"Adah, as she walks":** *Macon Daily Telegraph,* October 5, 1860.

124 **"Drifts That Bar My Door":** Adah Isaacs Menken, *Infelicia* (Philadelphia: J. B. Lippincott, 1868), 67–68.

124 **"Gives the most varied":** *New York Herald,* December 13, 1860.

124 **"I can not sew":** Allen Lesser, *Enchanting Rebel: The Secret of Adah Isaacs Menken* (Philadelphia: Ruttle, Shaw & Wetherill, 1947), 53.

125 **"absorbed all of good":** Adah Isaacs Menken, note addressed "To the Public," dateline Jersey City, New Jersey, December 29, 1860, HTC.

125 **Stephen Masset:** The identity of the person that saved Menken's life has always been a source of mystery and confusion. A convincing case that it was Masset is made by Foster and Foster in *Dangerous Woman,* 107–108.

CHAPTER 9:
BECOMING ARTEMUS WARD

127 **Charlie Brown:** Born Charles Brown, on becoming a famous newspaper columnist, he started using a middle name and added an *e* to his last name, becoming Charles Farrar Browne. His nickname was spelled both *Charlie* and *Charley.* I've chosen to use *Charlie Brown,* which appears to be the most frequent spelling, especially among those who knew him in his youth. See, for example, *Annals of the Early Settlers of Cuyahoga County* (Cleveland: Early Settlers Association, 1928), 26.

127 **On January 1, 1861:** John Pullen, *Comic Relief: The Life and Laughter of Artemus Ward* (Hamden, CT: Archon Books, 1983), 34.

128 **napkin into a puppet:** *American Magazine,* January 1896.

128 **names like Abraham:** Relatives names taken from *The History of Waterford County, Maine* (Portland, ME: Hoyt, Fogg & Donham, 1879).

128 **Brown hid a deck:** James Austin, *Artemus Ward* (New York: Twayne, 1964), 21.

128 **sending fake letters:** *Scribner's Monthly,* May 1881.

128 **"Is Cats to Be Trusted?":** Frederick Hudson, *Journalism in the United States, from 1690 to 1872* (New York: Harper & Brothers, 1873), 692.

129 **"To promote cheerfulness":** Pullen, *Comic Relief,* 21.

129 **"The Dandy Frightening the Squatter":** See J. R. LeMaster and James Wilson, eds., *The Mark Twain Encyclopedia* (New York: Routledge, 1993), 203.

130 **Brown also managed:** Discussions of Brown's first published effort from multiple sources, including Edward Hingston, *The Genial Showman: Being Reminiscences of the Life of Artemus Ward* (London: John Camden Hotten, 1871).

130 *Plain Dealer's* **local editor:** Account of Ward's early days at the paper from multiple sources, including *Scribner's Monthly,* May 1881.

130 **"noncents":** *Artemus Ward, His Book* (New York: Carleton, 1862), 90. Note: Fractured spellings taken from *Plain Dealer* columns reprinted in this work.

130 **"puncktooaly":** Ibid., 82.

130 **"Decleration of Inderpendunse":** Ibid., 39.

131 **"glowrius":** Ibid., 67.

131 **"confisticate":** Ibid., 194.

131 **Presently, *Vanity Fair*:** Description of publication from multiple sources, including Frank Luther Mott, *A History of American Magazines, 1850–1865* (Cambridge, MA: Harvard University Press, 1957), 520–529.

131 **asked for $1,200:** Pullen, *Comic Relief,* 33.

132 **"Quiet as he seemed":** Charles Godfrey Leland, *Memoirs* (New York: D. Appleton, 1893), 235.

132 **"It is late, sir":** William Winter, *Old Friends: Being Literary Recollections of Other Days* (New York: Moffat, Yard, 1909), 287.

133 **"He possessed":** Ibid., 285.

133 **"vishus beest":** *Artemus Ward, His Book,* 67.

133 **"He came with about":** *North American Review,* April 1889.

133   **alter his appearance:** Description of this from multiple sources, in-
       cluding Pullen, *Comic Relief,* 41–42.

CHAPTER 10:
"THE HEATHER IS ON FIRE"

135   **Southern soldiers had fired:** Account of attack on Fort Sumter from
       multiple sources, including James McPherson, *Battle Cry of Freedom*
       (New York: Oxford University Press, 1988).

136   **"I can almost see":** *CW, Prose Works, 1892,* 1:24.

137   **"The heather is on fire":** McPherson, *Battle Cry of Freedom,* 274.

137   **"My soul swells":** William Thayer to WW, April 19, 1861, WW Pa-
       pers, Charles E. Feinberg Collection, LOC.

137   **"The excitement caused":** *Brooklyn Eagle,* April 20, 1861.

138   **"tempest of cheers":** *Atlantic,* June 1861.

138   **"I have this hour":** Emory Holloway, *Free and Lonesome Heart: The
       Secret of Walt Whitman* (New York: Vantage Press, 1960), 121.

138   **"Could there be anything":** Clara Barrus, *Whitman and Burroughs:
       Comrades* (Boston: Houghton Mifflin, 1931), 339.

139   **"Regiment of Beaux":** Francis Wolle, *Fitz-James O'Brien: A Literary Bo-
       hemian of the Eighteen-Fifties* (Boulder: University of Colorado Studies,
       1944), 215.

139   **"Why, when I am":** Ibid., 220.

139   ***Bohemian* became synonymous with *journalist:*** For a discussion of
       this, see Junius Henri Browne, *The Great Metropolis: A Mirror of New
       York* (Hartford, CT: American, 1869), 151.

140   **Pfaff's habitué to war correspondent:** For names of some of the writ-
       ers who made this transition, see Louis Starr, *Bohemian Brigade: Civil
       War Newsmen in Action* (New York: Alfred Knopf, 1954), 9.

140   **"The sights now there":** *Leaves of Grass* (final edition), 678.

141   **"the harvest time for theaters":** Asia Booth Clarke, *John Wilkes Booth:
       A Sister's Memoir* (Jackson: University Press of Mississippi, 1996), 81.

141   **"I remember well":** *New York Times,* January 20, 1875.

142   **"He was a queer fellow":** *WWC,* 4:485.

142   **story of Ivan Mazeppa:** Details about Mazeppa, the historical figure,
       from multiple sources, including Hubert Babinski, *The Mazeppa Leg-
       end in European Romanticism* (New York: Columbia University Press,
       1974).

143   **English playwright Henry Milner:** Details about Milner from multi-
       ple sources, including Michael Foster and Barbara Foster, *A Dangerous*

Woman: The Life, Loves, and Scandals of Adah Isaacs Menken (Guilford, CT: Lyons Press, 2011).

144   ***Mazeppa* opened on June 7, 1861:** Details about the Albany production from H. P. Phelps, *Players of a Century: A Record of the Albany Stage* (New York: Edgar S. Werner, 1890).

144   **"crowded from pit to dome":** Ibid., 317.

145   **"It had to be seen":** Wolf Mankowitz, *Mazeppa: The Lives, Loves, and Legends of Adah Isaacs Menken* (London: Blond & Briggs, 1982), 20.

145   **"I was not impressed":** Undated reminiscence by a person named Baize from HTC.

145   **"resting on the bare back":** Adah Isaacs Menken, "Some Notes on Her Life in Her Own Hand," Special Collections, John Hay Library, Brown University.

146   **"My business here is wonderful":** Menken to John Augustin Daly, July 18, 1862, HTC.

146   **"'went it' pretty rapid":** Ibid.

146   **"It won't do to be married":** Ibid.

147   **"Artemus Ward will speak":** *The Complete Works of Charles F. Browne, Better Known as "Artemus Ward"* (London: Chatto and Windus, 1871), 192.

147   **"Ladies and gentlemen":** J. E. Preston Muddock, *Pages from an Adventurous Life* (New York: Mitchell Kennerley, 1907), 96.

147   **"And the audience":** *Century,* February 1902.

147   **"I met a man":** *Artemus Ward: His Works, Complete* (New York: G. W. Carleton, 1877), 266.

148   **An example is Ward's penitentiary joke:** For a thoughtful discussion of Ward's precision as a humorist, see John Pullen, *Comic Relief: The Life and Laughter of Artemus Ward* (Hamden, CT: Archon Books, 1983), 50.

149   **"clear as a bell":** Muddock, *Pages from an Adventurous Life,* 95.

150   **"Comic copy is what":** Eli Perkins, *Thirty Years of Wit: And Reminiscences of Witty, Wise, and Eloquent Men* (New York: Werner, 1899), 176.

150   **"Do you believe":** Adah Isaacs Menken to Hattie Tyng, July 21, 1861, printed in *Infelicia, and Other Writings: Adah Isaacs Menken,* edited by Gregory Eiselein (Peterborough, Ontario: Broadview Press, 2002), 231.

CHAPTER 11:
WHITMAN TO THE FRONT

153   **"quicksand":** *CW, Notebooks and Unpublished Prose Manuscripts,* 2:517–518.

153   **"A lady's thimble":** James McPherson, *Battle Cry of Freedom* (New York: Oxford University Press, 1988), 238.

154   **"either insane or drunk":** *CW, Notebooks and Unpublished Prose Manuscripts,* 1:461.

154   **On February 16, O'Brien:** Details of O'Brien getting shot mostly from Francis Wolle, *Fitz-James O'Brien: A Literary Bohemian of the Eighteen-Fifties* (Boulder: University of Colorado Studies, 1944).

155   **"Aldrich, I see":** William Winter, *Old Friends: Being Literary Recollections of Other Days* (New York: Moffat, Yard, 1909), 77.

156   **Velsor Brush:** Jerome Loving, *Walt Whitman: The Song of Himself* (Berkeley: University of California Press, 1999), 10.

156   **"Then let me":** Wolle, *Fitz-James O'Brien,* 236.

156   **"After I'm dead":** Ibid., 246.

157   **"No more electric":** Fred Pattee, *The Development of the American Short Story* (New York: Harper and Bros., 1923), 155.

157   **dizzying succession of major battles:** List of battles that George Whitman fought in from Jerome Loving, ed., *Civil War Letters of George Washington Whitman* (Durham, NC: Duke University Press, 1975).

158   **called a "slough":** WW to Ralph Waldo Emerson, December 29, 1862, *CW, The Correspondence,* 1:61.

158   **"*Thos Gray* good looking":** *CW, Notebooks and Unpublished Prose Manuscripts,* 2:487.

158   **"John McNelly night Oct 7":** Ibid., 494.

159   **"*David Wilson*—night":** Ibid., 496.

160   **"Wounded":** Details about this poem from Ted Genoways, *Walt Whitman and the Civil War* (Berkeley: University of California Press, 2009), 159.

159   **"The vault at Pfaffs":** *CW, Notebooks and Unpublished Prose Manuscripts,* 1:454.

160   **sometime late in the autumn of 1862:** Some accounts date WW's fight with the poet George Arnold as occurring at an earlier point in 1862, or even in 1861. For my account, I place it in late autumn of 1862 based on George Sixbey, "Walt Whitman's Middle Years, 1860–1867" (PhD diss., Yale University, 1941), 124. Sixbey is meticulous about chronology. Further support for the fight with Arnold occurring in the autumn of 1862 comes from the reliable Clara Barrus, *Whitman and Burroughs: Comrades* (Boston: Houghton Mifflin, 1931), 3.

160   **"Success to the Southern Arms!":** William Sloane Kennedy, *Reminiscences of Walt Whitman* (London: Alexander Gardner, 1896), 69.

160   **"Oh! mine gots, mens":** William Shepard Walsh, ed., *Pen Pictures of Modern Authors* (New York: Putnam's, 1882), 166.

161   **"If there is a worse":** James McPherson, *Battle Cry of Freedom,* 574.

161   **"First Lieutenant G. W. Whitmore":** *New York Herald,* December 16, 1862.

162   **"The next two days":** WW to Louisa Van Velsor Whitman, December 29, 1862, *CW, The Correspondence,* 1:58.

162   **"Any pickpocket who failed":** *Atlantic,* June 1907.

162   **"You could stick":** *CW, The Correspondence,* 1:60.

163   **"Remember your galliant":** Ibid., 59.

163   **"healthy beat":** This slang term and subsequent ones such as "dead beat" from *CW, Notebooks and Unpublished Prose Manuscripts,* 2:503.

163   **"Death is nothing here":** Ibid., 508.

163   ***"Sight at daybreak":*** Ibid., 513.

164   **"Both in and out":** *Leaves of Grass* (final edition), 32.

164   **"A beautiful object to me":** *CW, Notebooks and Unpublished Prose Manuscripts,* 2:504.

164   **"I do not see":** *CW, Prose Works, 1892,* 1:33.

165   **"regiments, brigades, and divisions":** *CW, Notebooks and Unpublished Prose Manuscripts,* 2:507.

CHAPTER 12:
BOHEMIA GOES WEST

167   **"held the town":** Joseph Henry Harper, *The House of Harper: A Century of Publishing in Franklin Square* (New York: Harper & Brothers, 1912), 150.

168   **"With his beautiful wife":** Gordon Hendricks, *Albert Bierstadt: Painter of the American West* (New York: Harry Abrams, 1975), 113.

168   **"Fitz did not come back":** Donald Dulchinos, *Pioneer of Inner Space: The Life of Fitz Hugh Ludlow* (New York: Autonomedia, 1998), 143.

168   **"Rose frightened and good cause":** Ibid.

168   **a taste for something far stronger:** Helen Ludlow's knowledge of her brother's drug use from Helen Ludlow to Rev. Leander Hall, June 1, 1876, Special Collections, Union College Schaffer Library.

168   **"to goad wearied nerves":** Ibid.

169   **translation of an Italian poem:** Dulchinos, *Pioneer of Inner Space,* 138.

170   **"the depot of a fur trader":** Nancy Anderson and Linda Ferber, *Albert Bierstadt: Art & Enterprise* (Brooklyn: Brooklyn Museum, 1990), 73.

170   **"golden shower":** *New York Times,* May 17, 1863.

172   **"How I would rejoice":** Otis Skinner, *The Last Tragedian: Booth Tells His Own Story* (New York: Dodd, Mead, 1939), 92.

172   **The eastern half:** Details about this leg of Ludlow and Bierstadt's journey from multiple sources, including Dulchinos, *Pioneer of Inner Space.*

173   **"angry faces, a rolling surf":** Fitz Hugh Ludlow, *The Heart of the Continent* (New York: Hurd and Houghton, 1870), 73.

174   **"wiped out like a grease-spot":** Ibid.

174   **"great oscillating patch":** Ibid., 64.

174   **"I had such a view":** Ibid., 75.

174   **"He rushed forward":** Ibid., 69.

175   **"Overland Mazeppa":** *Golden Era,* February 21, 1864.

175   **"This was a place":** Ibid.

175   **"There are the Rocky Mountains":** Ludlow, *Heart of the Continent,* 130.

176   **"Nature has dipped":** Ibid., 131.

176   **"quite unbreathed before":** Ibid., 178.

176   **"Mount Rosalie":** *Golden Era,* February 28, 1864. In this account, Ludlow says that Bierstadt "by right of first portrayal, baptized" the unnamed mountain as "Monte Rosa." The artist's sketch would become the basis for his painting *A Storm in the Rocky Mountains, Mt. Rosalie.*

177   **"enfilading":** *New York Post,* May 26, 1863.

177   **"rotatory" . . . "our Parrhasius":** *New York Post,* June 5, 1863.

177   **"The conglomerate of the latter":** Ludlow, *Heart of the Continent,* 166.

178   **"To understand the exquisite":** *Atlantic,* April 1864.

178   **148 Mormon pioneers:** This number often appears as "143 men," but there were also three women and two children, hence 148 pioneers.

179   **"Yet I, a cosmopolite":** Ludlow, *Heart of the Continent,* 309.

179   **"Heavens! What strange unsexing":** Ibid., 312.

180   **"Scriptural dignity":** *Atlantic,* April 1864.

180   **"Your Union's gone forever":** Ibid.

180   **"pleasant pungent sense":** Ludlow, *Heart of the Continent,* 401.

181   **"Nazarene":** Ibid., 404.

181   **"mastiff head":** *Golden Era,* March 20, 1864.

181   **"kindest hearted and most obliging murderer":** Ibid.

181   **"out-Bendemered Bendemere":** Ludlow, *Heart of the Continent,* 412.

182   **"a dear absent friend":** *Atlantic,* June 1864.

183   **"that magnificent nonchalance":** *Golden Era,* November 22, 1863.

183   **group of local artists:** Joanna Levin identifies Bret Harte as San Francisco's vanguard Bohemian, indicating that he started using the term in 1860. See Joanna Levin, *Bohemia in America, 1858–1920* (Stanford,

CA: Stanford University Press, 2010), 75. Harte and his artists' circle came after Pfaff's and Clapp's *Saturday Press,* which popularized the term *Bohemian.* Meanwhile, visits by representatives of East Coast Bohemia such as Ludlow "encouraged writers like Bret Harte." See Franklin Walker, *San Francisco's Literary Frontier* (New York: Alfred A. Knopf, 1939), 166, 175.

183 **"inveterate pipe-smoker":** Charles Warren Stoddard, *Exits and Entrances* (Boston: Lothrop, 1903), 243.

183 **"James A. Rogers":** Walker, *San Francisco's Literary Frontier,* 126.

185 **"I am what I was":** Michael Foster and Barbara Foster, *A Dangerous Woman: The Life, Loves, and Scandals of Adah Isaacs Menken* (Guilford, CT: Lyons Press, 2011), 150.

185 **"luscious richness of imagery":** *Golden Era,* November 22, 1863.

185 **"the Hasheesh Infant":** *Westways,* August 1935.

185 **"We purchased their pens":** *Golden Era,* January 17, 1864.

186 **"sham soldiership":** Mark Twain, "The Private History of a Campaign That Failed," *Century,* December 1885.

186 **"I knew more about retreating":** Ibid.

186 **One issue of the *Golden Era*:** Twain's "How to Cure a Cold" and Ludlow's "On Marrying Men" both appeared in the *Golden Era* of September 20, 1863.

186 **"He makes me laugh":** *Golden Era,* November 22, 1863.

186 **"And if Fitz Hugh Ludlow":** Albert Bigelow Paine, *Mark Twain: A Biography* (New York: Harper & Brothers, 1912), 1:244.

187 **he arrived at a hong:** Dulchinos dates Ludlow's visit to a hong in San Francisco to the last week of his western journey. See Dulchinos, *Pioneer of Inner Space,* 192. Ludlow was always furtive about describing his opium use, but he did publish a vague anecdote that may or may not relate to that visit. See Ludlow, *The Opium Habit, with Suggestions as to the Remedy* (New York: Harper & Brothers, 1868), 263.

187 **A typical one:** Description of a typical nineteenth-century hong in San Francisco from multiple sources, including Malcolm Barker, *More San Francisco Memoirs: 1852–1899, the Ripening Years* (San Francisco: Londonborn, 1996).

CHAPTER 13:
THE SOLDIERS' MISSIONARY

189 **"I cannot give up":** WW to Thomas Jefferson Whitman, March 6, 1863, *CW, The Correspondence,* 1:77.

190   **Whitman settled into Washington:** Details of the Civil War–era cap-
ital from multiple sources, including Margaret Leech, *Reveille in Wash-
ington* (New York: New York Review of Books, 1941).

190   **"a sort of German":** WW to Nathaniel Bloom, September 5, 1863,
CW, The Correspondence, 1:142.

190   **Washington had around thirty-five hospitals:** Roy Morris Jr., *The Bet-
ter Angel: Walt Whitman in the Civil War* (New York: Oxford University
Press, 2000), 88.

191   **"That whole damned war":** *WWC,* 3:293.

191   **"the Civil War was fought":** George Worthington Adams, "Confeder-
ate Medicine," *Journal of Southern History* (May 1940).

192   **"Walt Whitman, Soldiers' Missionary":** Justin Kaplan, *Walt Whit-
man: A Life* (New York: Simon & Schuster, 1980), 275.

192   **"Agonies are one":** *Leaves of Grass* (1855), 39, reproduction of an orig-
inal printing, accessed online at the Walt Whitman Archive.

193   **"I supply the patients":** WW to James Redpath, August 6, 1863, *CW,
The Correspondence,* 1:122.

193   **"I fancy the reason":** WW to Louisa Van Velsor Whitman, April 15,
1863, ibid., 89.

193   **"David S. Giles, co. F":** *CW, Notebooks and Unpublished Prose Manu-
scripts,* 2:521.

193   **"Hiram Scholis—bed 3":** Ibid., 605.

194   **"Henry D. Boardman co. B":** Ibid., 521.

194   **"Many of the men":** WW to Louisa Van Velsor Whitman, June 3,
1864, *CW, The Correspondence,* 1:230.

194   **"A wounded soldier don't":** *Cincinnati Commercial,* August 26, 1871.

195   **"Poor young man":** WW to Louisa Van Velsor Whitman, May 13,
1863, *CW, The Correspondence,* 1:100.

195   **"I thought it would":** WW to Mr. and Mrs. S. B. Haskell, August 10,
1863, ibid., 127.

196   **"Open the envelope quickly":** *Leaves of Grass* (final edition), 302.

197   **"To-night took a long":** *CW, Prose Works, 1892,* 1:40–41.

197   **"Redeemer President":** Justin Kaplan, ed., *Walt Whitman: Poetry and
Prose* (New York: Library of America, 1982), 1297.

197   **"I see the President":** WW to James Kirkwood, April 27, 1864, *CW,
The Correspondence,* 1:215.

197   **"He has a face":** WW to Nathaniel Bloom and Fred Gray, March 19,
1863, ibid., 82.

197 **Around 1857, William Herndon:** William Barton, *Abraham Lincoln and Walt Whitman* (Indianapolis: Bobbs-Merrill, 1928), 92. Barton is an authoritative source, since he owned Herndon's book collection. Because Lincoln's law partner usually made his purchases at Blanchard's bookstore in Chicago, the copy that he bought was most likely the 1856 edition, which, while a commercial failure, achieved broader distribution across the United States than the 1855 edition.

198 **It's quite possible that Lincoln:** Henry Rankin, *Personal Recollections of Abraham Lincoln* (New York: G. P. Putnam's Sons, 1916), 126, provides a vivid account of Lincoln reading *Leaves of Grass* out loud to his colleagues in the Springfield law office. But Rankin's account is suspect because there's no evidence that he worked at the firm at the time in question. See Barton, *Abraham Lincoln and Walt Whitman,* 93. All that can be said with certainty is that Lincoln's law partner owned *Leaves of Grass.* Given Lincoln's passion for the arts, it's "quite possible" that he read the work around 1857 in Springfield or even at a later date. The fact that Lincoln never mentioned reading Whitman's book isn't of great significance because *Leaves of Grass* is the kind of controversial fare with which a political candidate, and subsequently a president, would not necessarily want to be associated.

198 **"I had a good view":** WW to Louisa Van Velsor Whitman, June 30, 1863, *CW, The Correspondence,* 1:113.

198 **"I love the President personally":** *CW, Notebooks and Unpublished Prose Manuscripts,* 2:539.

199 **"If you should come safe":** WW to Tom Sawyer, April 21, 1863, *CW, The Correspondence,* 1:93.

199 **"Not a day passes":** WW to Sawyer, April 26, 1863, ibid., 94.

199 **"It would have been":** Ibid.

199 **"I suppose my letters":** WW to Sawyer, May 27, 1863, ibid., 107.

199 **"I do not know":** WW to Sawyer, November 20, 1863, ibid., 186.

199 **"I hardly know what":** Sawyer to WW, ibid., 90–91n86.

200 **"A mighty pain":** *Atlantic,* June 1907.

200 **"stimulating mental society":** Ibid.

200 **"I happened in there":** *WWC,* 1:416.

201 **"our meetings together":** WW to Hugo Fritsch sometime before August 7, 1863, *CW, The Correspondence,* 1:124.

201 **"My darling, dearest boys":** WW to Nathaniel Bloom and Fred Gray, March 19, 1863, ibid., 84.

201 **"I was always between":** *WWC,* 3:581.

202   **"I feel lately":** WW to Louisa Van Velsor Whitman, March 29, 1864, *CW, The Correspondence,* 1:205.

202   **"O mother," he wrote:** WW to Louisa Van Velsor Whitman, March 22, 1864, ibid., 204.

202   **"Mother, I will try":** WW to Louisa Van Velsor Whitman, March 29, 1864, ibid., 205.

CHAPTER 14:

TWAIN THEY SHALL MEET

203   **"My business is still *immense*":** Menken to Ed James, December 1862 (no day), HTC.

203   **painted Confederate gray:** Account of Menken decorating her dressing room from multiple sources, including Allen Lesser, *Enchanting Rebel* (Philadelphia: Ruttle, Shaw & Wetherill), 1947.

204   **"It is really true":** Menken to Ed James, December 1862 (no day), HTC.

204   **sold an incredible forty thousand:** J. C. Derby, *Fifty Years Among Authors, Books, and Publishers* (New York: G. W. Carleton, 1884), 242.

204   **five days after the battle of Antietam:** That Lincoln read to his assembled cabinet from *Artemus Ward, His Book,* on September 22, 1862, confirmed by multiple sources, including Doris Kearns Goodwin, *Team of Rivals* (New York: Simon & Schuster, 2005), 481.

205   **"With the fearful strain":** Don Seitz, *Artemus Ward: A Biography and Bibliography* (New York: Harper and Brothers, 1919), 114.

205   **"Upon somewhat the same":** *New York Herald,* February 3, 1863.

205   **Tom Maguire, a powerful:** Description from multiple sources, including Lois Foster Rodecape, "Tom Maguire, Napoleon of the Stage," *California Historical Society Quarterly* (March 1942).

207   **"They seem crazy":** Menken to Ed James, December 1862 (no day), HTC.

207   **"What will you take":** Albert Parry, *Garrets and Pretenders: A History of Bohemianism in America* (New York: Covici, Friede, 1933), 45.

207   **"dumb and cold":** Michael Foster and Barbara Foster, *A Dangerous Woman: The Life, Loves, and Scandals of Adah Isaacs Menken* (Guilford, CT: Lyons Press, 2011), 135.

208   **August 24, 1863:** Lois Foster, *Annals of the San Francisco Stage, 1850–1880* (San Francisco: Federal Theatre Projects, 1936), 1:322.

208   **a single break, for Yom Kippur:** Lesser, *Enchanting Rebel,* 112.

209   **seventeen men to every woman:** Renée Sentilles, *Performing Menken: Adah Isaacs Menken and the Birth of American Celebrity* (New York: Cambridge University Press, 2003), 191.

209   **"Feminine laundry, hanging":** George Lyman, *The Saga of the Comstock Lode* (New York: Charles Scribner's Sons, 1934), 198.

209   **Virginia City was only:** Description of city from multiple sources, including Roy Morris Jr., *Lighting Out for the Territory: How Samuel Clemens Headed West and Became Mark Twain* (New York: Simon & Schuster, 2010).

209   **"Steam-engines are puffing":** *Harper's New Monthly Magazine,* June 1865.

210   **"feverish":** Ralph Britsch, *Bierstadt and Ludlow: Painter and Writer in the West* (Provo, UT: Brigham Young University, 1980), 42.

211   **Opening night for *Mazeppa*:** It was March 7, 1864, according to Lyman, *Saga of the Comstock Lode,* 270.

211   **"She pitches headforemost":** Virginia City's *Daily Territorial Enterprise,* September 13, 1863, reprinted in *Mark Twain of the "Enterprise,"* edited by Henry Nash Smith (Berkeley: University of California Press, 1957), 78.

212   **"Ada Clare, the beautiful":** *Golden Era,* February 7, 1864.

212   **"The Man's Sphere":** *Golden Era,* April 3, 1864.

213   **"She smoked and rode":** Walter Leman, *Memories of an Old Actor* (San Francisco: A. Roman, 1886), 301.

213   **a small social gathering:** Account of Menken's party with Twain and DeQuille from multiple sources, including Paul Fatout, *Mark Twain in Virginia City* (Bloomington: Indiana University Press, 1964).

214   **"Menken was no nightingale":** *San Francisco Examiner,* March 19, 1893.

215   **"He struck the Comstock":** *San Francisco Chronicle,* January 10, 1892.

215   **a solitary laugh:** Account of Twain as the lone laugher from J. B. Graham, *Handset Reminiscences* (Salt Lake City: Century Printing, 1915), 142–143.

215   **"Has it been watered today?":** Ibid., 143.

216   **"The man who is capable":** Morris, *Lighting Out for the Territory,* 126.

216   **"inimitable way of pausing":** Paul Fatout, ed., *Mark Twain Speaking* (Iowa City: University of Iowa Press, 2006), 45.

217   **"Ah,—speaking of genius":** *Californian Illustrated Magazine,* August 1893.

218   **"sage-brush obscurity":** Albert Bigelow Paine, *Mark Twain: A Biography* (New York: Harper & Brothers, 1912), 1:244.

218 **"I give you Upper Canada":** *San Francisco Chronicle,* January 10, 1892.

218 **"I can't walk":** Ibid.

CHAPTER 15:
"O HEART! HEART! HEART!"

219 **On June 22, 1864:** *CW, The Correspondence,* 1:234.

219 **"The People are wild":** Thurlow Weed to William Seward, August 22, 1864, Abraham Lincoln Papers, LOC, accessed online.

220 **"It is my first":** WW to John Trowbridge, February 6, 1865, *CW, The Correspondence,* 1:254.

220 **"tame & indeed unreal":** WW to William O'Connor, September 11, 1864, ibid., 242.

221 **"I intend to move":** WW to O'Connor, July 5, 1864, ibid., 235.

221 **"unprecedentedly sad":** WW to O'Connor, January 6, 1865, ibid., 247.

221 **"We have seldom seen":** Gene Smith, *American Gothic: The Story of America's Legendary Theatrical Family—Junius, Edwin, and John Wilkes Booth* (New York: Simon & Schuster, 1992), 94.

222 **Albany, Boston, Chicago:** List of cities where John Wilkes Booth played and analysis of why he preferred to perform in the North taken from multiple sources, including Gordon Samples, *Lust for Fame: The Stage Career of John Wilkes Booth* (Jefferson, NC: McFarland, 1982).

222 **"wished the President":** James Cross Giblin, *Good Brother, Bad Brother: The Story of Edwin Booth & John Wilkes Booth* (New York: Clarion Books, 2005), 81.

222 **115 Commonwealth Avenue:** John Rhodehamel and Louise Taper, *"Right or Wrong, God Judge Me": The Writings of John Wilkes Booth* (Urbana: University of Illinois Press, 2000), 87.

222 **"weird and startling elocutionary":** Michael Kauffman, *American Brutus: John Wilkes Booth and the Lincoln Conspiracies* (New York: Random House, 2004), 118.

222 **"In what does he fail?":** Stanley Kimmel, *The Mad Booths of Maryland* (New York: Dover, 1969), 168.

223 **six more performances:** Lincoln attending seven performances of Edwin Booth in *Richelieu* is from Kauffman, *American Brutus,* 127.

223 **"made memorable by":** Samples, *Lust for Fame,* 162.

223 **At the conclusion of act 1:** Details of performance from multiple sources, including Asia Booth Clarke, *John Wilkes Booth: A Sister's Memoir* (Jackson: University Press of Mississippi, 1996).

224   **On the second morning:** The Booth brothers' breakfast occurred on November 27, 1864, according to Nora Titone, *My Thoughts Be Bloody: The Bitter Rivalry That Led to the Assassination of Abraham Lincoln* (New York: Free Press, 2010), 338.

224   **fire that had broken out:** Details of the feeble Confederate plot to burn New York City on November 25, 1864, from multiple sources, including *American Heritage,* October 1971.

224   **The day's news sparked:** Details of Edwin and John Wilkes Booth's argument from multiple sources, including Titone, *My Thoughts Be Bloody.*

225   **"rank secessionist" . . . "treasonable language":** Ibid., 340.

225   **"I take things very easy":** WW to Jeff Whitman, January 30, 1865, *CW, The Correspondence,* 1:250.

225   **"Jeff, you need not":** Ibid.

225   **"The western star, Venus":** *CW, Prose Works, 1892,* 1:94.

225   **His name was Peter Doyle:** First meeting of WW and Peter Doyle in the early months of 1865 from the most authoritative source, Martin Murray, "Peter the Great: A Biography of Peter Doyle," accessed online at the Walt Whitman Archive. While this event is sometimes dated to the autumn of 1865 or even the spring of 1866, Murray draws on such clues as the weather and Doyle's work schedule to conclude that their meeting "likely" happened sometime in the period January to March 1865.

226   **"Walt had his blanket":** Richard Maurice Bucke, ed., *Calamus: A Series of Letters Written During the Years 1868–1880 by Walt Whitman to a Young Friend (Peter Doyle)* (Boston: Laurens Maynard, 1897), 23.

226   **"Love, love, love!":** Charley Shively, ed., *Calamus Lovers: Walt Whitman's Working Class Camerados* (San Francisco: Gay Sunshine Press, 1987), 101.

226   **Doyle had been born in Ireland:** Details of Doyle's early life mostly from Murray, "Peter the Great."

227   **"hearty full-blooded everyday":** *WWC,* 3:543.

227   **"We went plodding along":** Bucke, *Calamus,* 26.

227   **"It was the most taciturn":** *Records of the Columbia Historical Society, Washington, DC* (Washington, DC: Columbia Historical Society, 1918), 21:49.

227   **"They can have the laugh":** Bucke, *Calamus,* 31.

228   **"look'd very much worn":** *CW, Prose Works, 1892,* 1:92.

228   **"country people, some very funny":** Ibid.

228   **"I saw Mr. Lincoln":** Ibid.

228   **Whitman also attended the inaugural:** *New York Times,* March 6, 1865.

228   **"With malice toward none":** Photo of original handwritten Second Inaugural Address of March 4, 1865, endorsed by Lincoln, accessed online at OurDocuments.gov.

228   **"His preservation and return":** *Brooklyn Daily Union,* March 16, 1865, quoted in Charles Glicksberg, *Walt Whitman and the Civil War* (Philadelphia: University of Pennsylvania Press, 1933), 89.

229   **"I am in tip top":** *CW, The Correspondence,* 1:243.

229   **total of eighteen books:** Count of poetry books during the Civil War years from F. DeWolfe Miller, *Walt Whitman's Drum-Taps* (Gainesville, FL: Scholars' Facsimiles & Reprints, 1959), editor's introduction, xxiii.

230   **a "propitious" day:** *CW, Prose Works, 1892,* 2:503.

230   **"woe and failure and disorder":** Ibid.

230   **"no pleasure vehicles":** *CW, Notebooks and Unpublished Prose Manuscripts,* 2:764.

230   **"strange mixture of horror":** Ibid., 762.

230   **"Lincoln's death—black":** Ibid.

230   **Even the morning editions:** See, for example, the *Nashville Union,* April 15, 1865, morning edition, which includes the name of the man (John Wilkes Booth) who was believed, even at that early juncture, to have shot Lincoln.

231   **specific details begin to emerge:** Details of assassination from a number of reliable accounts, including Dorothy Meserve Kunhardt and Philip Kunhardt Jr., *Twenty Days: A Narrative in Text and Pictures of the Assassination of Abraham Lincoln* (New York: HarperCollins, 1965).

232   **"to take a laugh":** Smith, *American Gothic,* 99.

232   *Our American Cousin* **the previous year:** Titone, *My Thoughts Be Bloody,* 352–353.

233   **The second door had a peephole:** I chose not to repeat the common claim that Booth drilled this peephole. Logic suggests he was far too busy that day making other preparations, moving to and fro about Washington. A convincing historical denial of the peephole claim can be found in W. Emerson Reck, *A. Lincoln: His Last 24 Hours* (Jefferson, NC: McFarland, 1987), 73.

233   **"Well, I guess I know":** Tom Taylor, *Our American Cousin* (New York: Samuel French, 1869), 37.

233   **"Sic semper tyrannis":** That these were John Wilkes Booth's words checked with multiple reliable sources, including Doris Kearns Goodwin, *Team of Rivals* (New York: Simon & Schuster, 2005), 739.

233 **"Stop that man!":** That these were Major Rathbone's words checked with multiple reliable sources, including Reck, *A. Lincoln: His Last 24 Hours,* 102.

234 **"Melancholy . . . heavy-hearted":** *CW, Notebooks and Unpublished Prose Manuscripts,* 2:767.

235 **Whitman gave his new love:** Miller, *Walt Whitman's Drum-Taps,* editor's introduction, xliii.

235 **"I heard the pistol":** Bucke, *Calamus,* 26.

CHAPTER 16:
A BRIEF REVIVAL

237 **The funeral train:** Details about the train, its course, and the onlookers from multiple sources, including Victor Searcher, *The Farewell to Lincoln* (New York: Abingdon Press, 1965).

237 **"What did you ever":** *SP,* August 5, 1865.

237 **"How to Write War Lyrics":** Ibid.

238 **"Muck-a-Muck":** *SP,* October 8, 1865.

238 **an "inconceivable number":** *SP,* September 9, 1865.

238 **The saloon was now in a new location:** The very first issue of the revived *Saturday Press* (August 5, 1865) has an ad for Pfaff's, giving the saloon's address as 653 Broadway. As for when Pfaff's moved: it's listed at 647 Broadway in *Trow's New York City Directory* for 1865. The directory is for the year ended May 1, 1865. Thus, Pfaff's must have moved sometime between May and August 1865 (when the ad with the new address appeared in the *SP*).

238 **"The National bird":** *Philadelphia Inquirer,* November 27, 1892.

238 **"Beerdrinkers Song":** *SP,* August 12, 1865.

238 **"Life in a Bar-Room":** *SP,* January 13, 1866.

238 **"Abraham Lincoln was a most":** *SP,* September 16, 1865.

239 **"A teetotal correspondent":** *SP,* August 19, 1865.

239 **"O Captain! My Captain!":** *SP,* November 4, 1865. The version of the poem that appeared in the *SP* is slightly different from the familiar version. For example, here are the last four lines of the first stanza as they appeared in the journal:

> But O heart! heart! heart!
> Leave you not the little spot,
> Where on the deck my Captain lies,
> Fallen cold and dead.

Of course, "spot" and "dead" don't rhyme. Because this is jarring to anyone familiar with the more famous version, I reproduced that one in my account:

> But O heart! heart! heart!
> O the bleeding drops of red,
> Where on the deck my Captain lies,
> Fallen cold and dead.
>   *Source: Leaves of Grass* (final edition), 337–338.

240   **"him I love":** Ibid., 328.
240   **"Ever-returning spring":** Ibid.
241   **"all the slain soldiers":** Ibid., 336.
241   **one did run in the *SP*:** *SP*'s review of *Drum-Taps,* January 27, 1866.
241   **"the most sweet and sonorous":** Daniel Mark Epstein, *Lincoln and Whitman: Parallel Lives in Civil War Washington* (New York: Random House, 2004), 250.
241   **"Jim Smiley and His Jumping Frog":** *SP,* November 18, 1865.
241   **"The papers are copying it":** *Alta California* quoted in Albert Bigelow Paine, *Mark Twain: A Biography* (New York: Harper & Brothers, 1912), 1:279.
241   **Credit is also due Artemus Ward:** Details from multiple sources, including John Pullen, *Comic Relief: The Life and Laughter of Artemus Ward* (Hamden, CT: Archon Books, 1983).
242   **"rat-terriers and chicken cocks":** *SP,* November 18, 1865.
242   **"Mr. A Ward," it begins:** Ibid.
242   **"The 'Jumping Frog' was":** *North American Review,* April 1894.
243   **"I am getting too old":** *SP,* April 28, 1866.
243   **"Of late, however":** *Trenton Gazette* quoted in *SP,* May 19, 1866.
243   **"originally composed of about":** Albert Parry, *Garrets and Pretenders: A History of Bohemianism in America* (New York: Covici, Friede, 1933), 60.
243   **"a peculiar mixture":** Ibid.
243   **"Decimal Currency, Weights, and Measures":** *SP,* March 3, 1866.

CHAPTER 17:
ALL FALL DOWN

245   **"C. Pfaff and die!":** *SP,* August 5, 1865.
246   **On November 21, 1866:** Donald Dulchinos, *Pioneer of Inner Space: The Life of Fitz Hugh Ludlow* (New York: Autonomedia, 1998), 231.

246 **writing over the previous ten years:** Ibid., 231.

246 **Malkasten, as he dubbed it:** Details about Bierstadt's mansion from multiple sources, including Nancy Anderson and Linda Ferber, *Albert Bierstadt: Art & Enterprise* (Brooklyn: Brooklyn Museum, 1990).

246 **"I am the happiest":** Gordon Hendricks, *Albert Bierstadt: Painter of the American West* (New York: Harry Abrams, 1975), 167.

246 **"I pity the strange":** Dulchinos, *Pioneer of Inner Space,* 226.

246 **"Fitz . . . from his long-continued":** Andrew Shores, "Fitz Hugh Ludlow, a Biography" (Union College, June 1980), 41.

247 **"calling it 'Camp Rattlesnake'":** Fitz Hugh Ludlow, *The Heart of the Continent* (New York: Hurd and Houghton, 1870), 433.

248 **"Since Mr. Ludlow":** *Atlantic,* July 1870.

248 **Ludlow died in a little cottage:** Details from Helen Ludlow, sketch about her brother Fitz Hugh, Special Collections, Union College Schaffer Library.

249 **"I have everything":** *Reader,* March 1903.

249 **"would have made St. Anthony":** Victoria & Albert Museum, London, webpage.

249 **"I have the advice":** Allen Lesser, *Enchanting Rebel: The Secret of Adah Isaacs Menken* (Philadelphia: Ruttle, Shaw & Wetherill, 1947), 210.

249 **mind of a young Arthur Conan Doyle:** Michael Foster and Barbara Foster, *A Dangerous Woman: The Life, Loves, and Scandals of Adah Isaacs Menken* (Guilford, CT: Lyons Press, 2011), 262.

249 **"the face of the most beautiful":** Arthur Conan Doyle, *Adventures of Sherlock Holmes* (New York: Harper & Brothers, 1892), 12.

250 **The French, even more than the British:** Details of Menken's run as an actress in Paris from multiple sources, including Foster and Foster, *A Dangerous Woman.*

251 **"a very beautiful woman":** Ibid., 259.

252 **"I am lost to art":** Bernard Falk, *The Naked Lady: Life Story of Adah Menken* (London: Hutchinson, 1934), 224.

252 **"The Menken is dead":** Menken obituary, publication and date unknown, Special Collections, John Hay Library, Brown University.

252 **Various accounts attributed it:** Possible causes of death from various obituaries and reminiscences, including *Chicago Tribune,* April 28, 1878.

253 **Menken had cobbled it together:** Lesser, *Enchanting Rebel,* 212–213.

253 **"Dear Miss Menken":** Adah Isaacs Menken, *Infelicia* (London: J. C. Hotten, 1868), dedication page.

253   **His new act spoofed moving panoramas:** Discussion of these from multiple sources, including John Pullen, *Comic Relief: The Life and Laughter of Artemus Ward* (Hamden, CT: Archon Books, 1983).

254   **"moonist":** T. W. Robertson and E. P. Hingston, *Artemus Ward's Lecture* (New York: G. W. Carleton, 1869), 159.

254   **"she fainted on Reginald's breast":** Ibid., 185.

254   **"that true Transatlantic type":** Don Seitz, *Artemus Ward: A Biography and Bibliography* (New York: Harper and Brothers, 1919), 205.

254   **"The audience fairly laughed":** Ibid., 198.

255   **"He had that unfortunate desire":** Joseph Jefferson, *The Autobiography of Joseph Jefferson* (London: T. Fisher Unwin, 1889), 320.

255   **he arranged for a pharmacist:** Pullen, *Comic Relief,* 167.

255   **"I am so fearfully weak":** Seitz, *Artemus Ward,* 211.

256   **"Death has gathered":** *New York Times,* April 11, 1875.

256   **post he would hold for forty-four years:** Gloria Goldblatt, "Ada Clare: Queen of Bohemia" (unpublished manuscript, 1990, Billy Rose Theatre Collection, New York Public Library for the Performing Arts), 220.

256   **not "genuine Boston":** M. A. DeWolfe Howe, *The "Atlantic Monthly" and Its Makers* (Boston: Atlantic Monthly Press, 1919), 81.

257   **called "the vultures":** James Cross Giblin, *Good Brother, Bad Brother: The Story of Edwin Booth & John Wilkes Booth* (New York: Clarion Books, 2005), 208.

257   **Edwin tossed in his brother's costumes:** Details from Otis Skinner, *The Last Tragedian: Booth Tells His Own Story* (New York: Dodd, Mead, 1939), 144.

257   **"Stale lager-bier":** *Round Table,* May 19, 1866.

258   **"I shall withdraw":** *National Magazine,* September 1905.

258   **"If the name Ada Clare":** Ibid.

258   **Clare dropped by the offices:** Account of visit to agent's office and dog bite from multiple sources, including Goldblatt, "Ada Clare."

259   **"Poor, poor Ada Clare":** WW to Ellen O'Connor, March 8, 1874, *CW, The Correspondence,* 2:285.

259   **Aubrey would grow up to be an actor:** Goldblatt, "Ada Clare," 267.

260   **"Henry Clark":** *Daily Inter Ocean,* August 12, 1888.

260   **seen on the Bowery:** *Brooklyn Eagle,* May 25, 1884.

260   **"shriveled and shabby":** *Detroit Free Press,* April 18, 1875.

260   **"actual want":** *New York Daily Graphic,* April 16, 1875.

260   **"And now, my dear fellow":** Clapp to Edmund Stedman, May 14, 1874, Special Collections, Butler Library, Columbia University.

261 **"He was a witty and pungent":** Frederick Douglass to George Clark, August 11, 1883, Raynors' Historical Collectible Auctions, Burlington, NC, accessed online.

261 **"Henry Clapp stepped out":** *WWC,* 1:236.

261 **checked out was Thackeray's:** Clapp to Stedman, May 31, 1874, Special Collections, Butler Library, Columbia University.

261 **"I have been feasting":** Ibid., May 22, 1874.

261 **"With the death of Henry Clapp":** *Boston Globe,* April 13, 1875.

CHAPTER 18:
"THOSE TIMES, THAT PLACE"

263 **472 M Street:** Gay Wilson Allen, *The Solitary Singer: A Critical Biography of Walt Whitman* (Chicago: University of Chicago Press, 1955), 379.

263 **job for the US attorney general's office:** Details about WW's job from multiple sources, including Dixon Wecter, "Walt Whitman as Civil Servant," *PMLA,* December 1943.

264 **"binding stipulation":** John Binckley to George Corhill, April 16, 1868, collection of scribal documents copied by WW while working in US attorney general's office, accessed online at the Walt Whitman Archive.

264 **"writ of error":** Henry Stanbery to Edwin Stanton, October 4, 1866, ibid.

264 **"*nolle prosequi*":** J. Hubley Ashton to Benjamin Bristow, October 11, 1866, ibid.

264 **"I am Sir":** Henry Stanbery to Schuyler Colfax, December 12, 1867, ibid.

264 **"Often we would go":** *WWC,* 2:511.

265 **"We took great walks":** Richard Maurice Bucke, ed., *Calamus: A Series of Letters Written During the Years 1868–1880 by Walt Whitman to a Young Friend (Peter Doyle)* (Boston: Laurens Maynard, 1897), 26.

265 **"My love for you":** WW to Peter Doyle, August 21, 1869, *CW, The Correspondence,* 2:85.

265 **In 1874, Emerson published:** Details from Ralph Waldo Emerson, ed., *Parnassus* (Boston: Houghton, Osgood, 1880). An 1880 edition was consulted, but the content is the same as the first printing in 1874.

266 **deemed "remarkable":** Ibid., Emerson's introduction to the collection, x.

267   **"the bigots, the dilettanti":** William Douglas O'Connor, *The Good Gray Poet: A Vindication* (New York: Bunce & Huntington, 1866), 38.

267   **"He has been a visitor":** Ibid., 7–8.

267   **On January 23, 1873:** Allen, *Solitary Singer,* 447, meticulously identifies the date of WW's stroke.

268   **"After several hours":** Richard Maurice Bucke, *Walt Whitman* (Glasgow, Scotland: Wilson & McCormick, 1884), 46.

268   **"hospital poison":** WW to Louisa Van Velsor Whitman, June 14, 1864, *CW, The Correspondence,* 1:233.

268   **"whack," as Whitman called it:** David Reynolds, *Walt Whitman's America: A Cultural Biography,* 4.

268   **"Farewell my beloved sons":** Allen, *Solitary Singer,* 452.

269   **"I shall range along":** WW to Eldridge, November 17, 1863, *CW, The Correspondence,* 1:185.

269   **publish seven separate editions:** Because such a variety of printings of *Leaves of Grass* appeared during Whitman's lifetime, it is hard to pin down what truly qualifies as a separate edition. Scholars tend to credit Whitman with anywhere from six to twelve editions. I count seven after consulting a variety of sources, including Amanda Gailey's essay "The Publishing History of *Leaves of Grass,*" published in *A Companion to Walt Whitman,* edited by Donald Kummings (Oxford: Blackwell, 2006). The seven: 1855, 1856, 1860, 1867, 1871–1872, 1881–1882, and 1891–1892.

270   **"that *unkillable* work":** WW to Abby Price, July 30, 1866, *CW, The Correspondence,* 1:282.

270   **"Walt Whitman, poet":** *Brooklyn Eagle,* July 11, 1886.

270   **"the muffled sound":** *Critic,* April 23, 1887.

271   **"He related the death":** William Barton, *Abraham Lincoln and Walt Whitman* (Indianapolis: Bobbs-Merrill, 1928), 211.

271   **"He is a bird":** *WWC,* 8:348.

271   **cut a deal with Mary Davis:** Elizabeth Leavitt Keller, *Walt Whitman in Mickle Street* (New York: Mitchell Kennerley, 1921), 16.

271   **Whitman would repair:** Author's tour of the Walt Whitman House, 330 Mickle Boulevard, Camden, NJ, September 27, 2013.

272   **Vincent Van Gogh painted:** Jean Schwind, "Van Gogh's 'Starry Night' and Whitman: A Study in Source," *Walt Whitman Quarterly Review* (Summer 1985).

272 **"in an upper spiritual":** Richard Maurice Bucke, "Portraits of Walt Whitman," *New England Magazine,* March 1899.

272 **On August 16, 1881:** *CW, Daybooks and Notebooks* (New York: New York University Press, 1978), 1:253.

272 **9 West 24th Street:** As Pfaff's address in 1881, ibid., 252.

272 **"Ah, the friends and names":** *CW, Prose Works, 1892,* 1:277.

FURTHER EXPLORATION

WHILE RESEARCHING America's first Bohemians, one of the great pleasures for me was exploring their remarkable work. This was a talented, eccentric, and passionate group, working during an especially tumultuous era in American history. Sadly, much of their output has been forgotten. But not gone: It's thrilling to be able to hunt down assorted 150-year-old works and bits of realia, often with the aid of the very modern Internet. If you wish to learn more about these fascinating and startlingly forward-thinking artists, here are some recommendations.

EDWIN BOOTH
(NOVEMBER 13, 1833–JUNE 7, 1893)

As the greatest tragedian of the nineteenth century, Edwin Booth's work was necessarily confined to the stage—there were no movie side projects to capture his acting style for future generations. But late in life, Booth made a pair of wax-cylinder sound recordings in which he delivered brief passages from *Hamlet* and *Othello*.

Booth's *Hamlet* has been lost. His *Othello* remains, however, though the sound quality is extremely poor. Still, there's value in simply hearing Booth's deep, sonorous voice and getting a flavor for his famous naturalistic acting style: unembellished, unhurried, almost languid. The recording is widely available. It appears on many CDs such as *Great Historical Shakespeare Recordings and a Miscellany* (Naxos). It is also easy to find the recording on the Internet.

HENRY CLAPP JR.
(NOVEMBER 11, 1814–APRIL 10, 1875)

Clapp's hugely influential *Saturday Press* is filled with the works of the Pfaff's set, providing a vivid record of America's first Bohemia. Whitman's best-known poem—"O Captain! My Captain!"—appeared first in the journal, as did such less familiar poems as "You and Me and To-Day," later retitled "With Antecedents."

The *SP* is also a great way to get to know the King of Bohemia himself in all his jaundiced glory. Each issue contains an editor's note by Clapp, a showcase for his fierce wit. Not to be missed are Clapp's book reviews, most of them scathing. He appears to have gotten a special relish from savaging popular works of the day such as George Eliot's *The Mill on the Floss*. The *SP* is available at a handful of public and university libraries. Fortunately, all 157 issues are available online at the Vault at Pfaff's, a digital archive maintained by Lehigh University.

ADA CLARE
(JULY 1834–MARCH 4, 1874)

"Few women are strong enough," wrote Ada Clare, "to choose between truth and the world's good opinion." She chose truth. In her provocative essays, the Queen of Bohemia was decades ahead of contemporaries, exploring such topics as the element of sadomasochism present in corsets, hoopskirts, and other women's fashions of the day. Clare contributed a regular column, "Thoughts and Things," to the *Saturday Press* and later became a columnist for the *Golden Era*.

Sadly, the *Golden Era*—an important publication and one that was to West Coast Bohemians what the *SP* was to those back East—is difficult to find. Only a handful of libraries have the publication, typically as an incomplete set. A few issues containing essays by Clare can be found online, such as the April 3, 1864, *Golden Era* featuring her satirical "The Man's Sphere of Influence." Clare makes all kinds of mischief in this essay by inverting nineteenth-century gender roles: "We do not want man to be too highly educated; we want him sweet, gentle, and incontestably stupid."

FITZ HUGH LUDLOW
(SEPTEMBER 11, 1836–SEPTEMBER 12, 1870)

Ludlow's mostly forgotten 1857 masterpiece, *The Hasheesh Eater,* remains a fascinating read today. I recommend the *Annotated Hasheesh Eater,* edited by David Gross. Ludlow is outrageously erudite, sprinkling his drug tale with references to Hindu mythology, ancient Chinese folk medicine, and tenth-century Welsh royalty. Gross turns what could be maddening into a pleasure by providing helpful notations that explain the arcana.

Ludlow's *The Heart of the Continent* is also an excellent read as well as a record of a long-lost American West. When the book was published in 1870, a number of accounts of cross-country journeys had recently appeared, and Ludlow was criticized for being late. With the passage of time, that criticism has become irrelevant. Both as a writer and as an observer of natural phenomena, I found Ludlow superior to many of the authors of those rival accounts such as Samuel Bowles and Albert Richardson.

Another Ludlow item worth seeking out: "What Shall They Do to Be Saved?" This is an article from the August 1867 issue of *Harper's New Monthly Magazine* in which Ludlow details his use of novel cures to help *others* break their opium addictions. He neglects to mention his own battles with the drug. It's a harrowing and heart-rending account. "So, coming to me, he told me that his object in trying to leave off opium was to escape from these horrible ghosts of a life's unfulfilled promise," Ludlow writes about one addict. This and other observations by Ludlow about opium users no doubt apply equally to the writer himself.

ADAH ISAACS MENKEN
(JUNE 15, 1835?–AUGUST 10, 1868)

Dickens was no fan of Menken's poetry, and you might not be either. Even so, there are reasons to consult her 1868 collection *Infelicia* such as curiosity (the volume contains experimental work by a Whitman contemporary) and historical relevance (some of her poems address themes and concerns of nineteenth-century Judaism). As for *Mazeppa,* though overlong and convoluted, it's still interesting as the play that made Menken famous.

Where Menken truly shines, however, is photographs. The camera loved her, and she knew it. Like such modern stars as Elizabeth Taylor and Beyoncé, she assembled a vivid photographic record—Menken would no doubt have taken selfies if nineteenth-century cameras were easier to operate. Her most prolific collaboration was with Napoleon Sarony, a pioneering celebrity photographer—the Herb Ritts of his day—who also created iconic images of Mark Twain and Oscar Wilde. An online search will turn up a rich trove of Menken images. Aficionados might want to consult the extensive collection maintained by the Harvard theater library.

FITZ-JAMES O'BRIEN
(DECEMBER 31, 1828–APRIL 6, 1862)

During his brief life, O'Brien was prolific, churning out poems, plays, essays, and fiction. But it's as a writer of macabre short stories that he truly made his mark. His finest works continue to hold up today, including "The Diamond Lens," "The Wondersmith," and "What Was It?" They are available in old collections such as *The Diamond Lens, with Other Stories* (1885), edited by O'Brien's friend and fellow Pfaffian William Winter. You can also find many individual O'Brien stories online.

A note for modern readers: O'Brien's works often hew to a nineteenth-century literary convention that one must ease slowly into the supernatural, first scrupulously grounding a story in real-world detail before introducing a ghost or magic spell. As a consequence, O'Brien's stories tend to drag at the outset. But once he gets going—it's not for nothing that this mostly forgotten master was referred to in his day as the Celtic Poe.

ARTEMUS WARD
(APRIL 26, 1834–MARCH 6, 1867)

Because humor doesn't tend to age well, the 1862 blockbuster *Artemus Ward, His Book*—once so revolutionary—mostly comes across today as quaint and tame. However, it does contain "High-Handed Outrage at Utica," the piece that Lincoln read to his cabinet before introducing the Emancipation Proclamation. It's only a few paragraphs long, and a pleasure to read if only for the fact that Lincoln heartily enjoyed these very same words. An autographed copy of *Artemus Ward, His Book* that the author sent to Lincoln is in the Beinecke Rare Book and Manuscript Library at Yale University.

For anyone interested in Ward's stagecraft as America's first stand-up comedian, *Artemus Ward's Lecture* is a valuable resource. This 1869 book, edited by T. W. Robertson and E. P. Hingston—respectively, a close friend and Ward's agent—contains illuminating details about the comic's style and technique.

WALT WHITMAN
(MAY 31, 1819–MARCH 26, 1892)

Whitman treated *Leaves of Grass* as a living document, continually revising his masterpiece through seven separate editions, each one differing, sometimes in major ways, from the one that came before. As such, the 1860 edition might be called the Pfaff's edition. It was published while he was a regular at the saloon, and many of the poems show the influence of being part of a circle of Bohemian artists. The University of Iowa Press's *Leaves of*

Grass, 1860: The Anniversary Facsimile Edition is highly recommended and includes an excellent introductory essay by Jason Stacy.

If you're curious to see the poet's very first edition, a digitized copy is available online at the Walt Whitman Archive. It's a rare treat given that fewer than two hundred copies of the original printing are still in existence. I enjoyed the opportunity to view the book as it looked in 1855, complete with the quirks of a nineteenth-century printing job done on the cheap.

It's also an opportunity to read some of Whitman's finest works in their earliest published incarnation. (He carried poems such as "I Sing the Body Electric" from the first edition to the last, making changes along the way.)

For Whitman's sublime Civil War poetry, you'll need to consult a later (post-1865) version of *Leaves of Grass*. I suggest the Norton Critical Edition edited by Sculley Bradley and Harold Blodgett. It's comprehensive, featuring everything that appeared in Whitman's 1891–1892 "deathbed" edition of *Leaves* plus additional uncollected poems, even some incomplete fragments.

For a very different flavor of Whitman's Civil War experiences, read his letters from this period. These letters—to his mother, siblings, and friends—have a casual, folksy style that's quite a departure from his poetry. Still, they contain some of Whitman's most beautiful and emotive writing, such as this description of a dying soldier: "At length he opened his eyes quite wide & clear, & looked inquiringly around. I said, What is it, my dear, do you want any thing?—he said quietly with a good natured smile, O nothing, I was only looking around to see who was with me—his mind was somewhat wandering, yet he lay so peaceful, in his dying condition—he seemed to be a real New England country boy, so good natured, with a pleasant homely way, & quite a fine looking boy—without any doubt he died in course of night." Whitman's Civil War letters are available in *The Collected Writings of Walt Whitman,* volume 1, *The Correspondence,* edited by Edwin Haviland Miller.

There are also several Whitman sites well worth a visit. The house where he was born in 1819 still stands, a sliver of history preserved on a busy commercial street in Huntington Station, Long Island. A fascinating tour is available through the home that provided Whitman's earliest formative experiences, as an infant and toddler, before he moved to Brooklyn. Whitman's last home, in Camden, New Jersey, is also open to the public for tours. Its clutter has been meticulously and lovingly re-created so that it looks and feels as it did in Whitman's day. Here, you can see Whitman's favorite rocking chair, cane, bed, the paintings on his walls, the books he owned, and the medications he took (some items are originals, some simply from the period).

Nearby in Camden is the Harleigh Cemetery where Whitman is buried in a mausoleum. On an autumn day, I sat beside Whitman's grave and read my favorite poem, "Crossing Brooklyn Ferry." At first I felt a bit self-conscious. In such a serene setting, however, Whitman's words soon took over, and across the span of a century and a half, his poetry worked its magic.

INDEX

Abolitionism, 7, 64, 112, 120, 200, 222
Adams, George Worthington, 191
Adams, John, 47
"Adhesiveness," as phrenology term 75, 104
Admiral Sir Isaac Coffin Lancasterian School, 6
Agesilaus, 60
Alboni, Marietta, 35
Alcoholics Anonymous, 8
Aldrich, Thomas, 45, 90, 155
   Atlantic Monthly and, 256
   Civil War military post and, 139, 155
   Customs House job, 169
   on darkness among Pfaff's Bohemians, 47
   Edwin Booth and, 56
   hashish and, 55
   Saturday Press and, 79, 87
Alexander the Great, 83
Algonquin Round Table, 86
Alta California (newspaper), 241
"Amativeness," as phrenology term 75
American (magazine), 28
American Revolution, 154
American Temperance Society, 8
American Whig Review (journal), 21
Amputation, Civil War soldiers and, 191, 195
Anderson, Robert, 135, 137
Anicet-Bourgeois, Auguste, 250
Antietam, 157, 226
Apple-Blossoms (Tyng), 150
Appomattox Courthouse, 230
Arnold, George, 29, 139
   death of, 256

New York Leader and, 155
at Pfaff's, 22, 62, 160
poetry of, 22, 83
toast to Confederacy, fight with Whitman, 160
Artemus Ward, His Book (Ward), 204, 205
Artemus Ward, His Travels (Ward), 242
"As a Strong Bird on Pinions Free" (Whitman), 266
Ashtabula (OH) Sentinel (newspaper), 89
Asphodel (Clare), 109, 120–121, 258
Astor Hotel (New York), 122
"At the Café" (Aldrich), 47
Atlantic Monthly (journal), 80–81, 86, 89, 185, 248, 256
Aurora (newspaper), 34
A.W. Faber, 86

The Babes in the Wood (Ward), 146–149, 203, 204
   in Virginia City, 215–216
Baker, Frank, 200
Baltimore, Menken in, 203–204
Barkley, James Paul, 249–250
Barkley, Louis Dudevant Victor, 250
Barksdale, William, 48
Barrière, Théodore, 13
Barton, Clara, 191–192
Baudelaire, 27
Beats, the, 2
Beecher, Henry Ward, 112
"Beer" (Arnold), 83
Beer-making in nineteenth century, 18–19
Benchley, Robert, 86

ABOUT THE AUTHOR

Justin Martin is the author of three previous books, most recently *Genius of Place: The Life of Frederick Law Olmsted*. This biography of the pioneering landscape architect behind Central Park and dozens of green space masterpieces earned glowing reviews nationally. As one of the few journalists to gain access to a famously secretive Fed chairman, Martin also wrote *Greenspan: The Man Behind Money*, a best-selling biography selected by the *New York Times Book Review* as a notable book. *Nader: Crusader, Spoiler, Icon*, Martin's biography of the controversial consumer advocate and presidential candidate, served as a primary source for *An Unreasonable Man*, an Academy Award–nominated documentary. Martin's articles have appeared in a variety of publications including the *New York Times*, *Newsweek*, and *San Francisco Chronicle*, and he is frequently called upon to give speeches. A 1987 graduate of Rice University in Houston, Texas, Martin lives with his wife and twin sons in Forest Hills Gardens, New York.

Additional information can be found at the author's website
(www.justinmartin1.com) and this book's Facebook page
(www.facebook.com/BohoBook)